A HANDBOOK FOR DEVELOPING MULTICULTURAL AWARENESS

Paul Pedersen

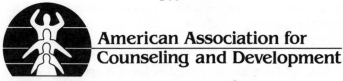

American Association for
Counseling and Development

Serving the counseling,
guidance and human
development professions
since 1952.

American Association for Counseling and Development
5999 Stevenson Avenue
Alexandria, Virginia 22304

Library of Congress Cataloging-in-Publication Data

Pedersen, Paul, 1936–
    Handbook for developing multicultural awareness.

    Bibliography: p.
    Includes index.
    1. Cross-cultural counseling.
    2. Minorities—Counseling of.
    3. Ethnopsychology.
I. American Association for Counseling and Development.   II. Title.
BF637.C6P336   1988   158'.3   88-1720
ISBN 1-55620-042-0

(Second Printing) Printed in the United States of America

NWST
ALB 7916

*Dedicated to Anne Bennett Pedersen,
the source of the motivation as well as
many of the ideas for developing a multicultural
awareness in this book*

CONTENTS

PREFACE

This book is based on the assumption that all counseling is to some extent multicultural. On the one hand, each counselor/client, presenting problem, counseling environment, and significant other brings cultural influences into the counseling relationship. On the other hand, culture is within each person, combining an individual's many different social roles to construct his or her basic internal identity. Understanding group differences, as well as individual differences, is important to the accurate interpretation of behaviors. Counseling strategies that disregard the influence of a client's cultural context are unlikely to interpret a client's behavior accurately. The same behavior across cultures might have a very different interpretation, just as different behaviors might have the same interpretation. Therefore, developing multicultural awareness is essential for all counselors in order to learn the range of cultural similarities and differences.

The counselor has only two choices: to ignore the influence of culture or to attend to it. In either case, however, culture will continue to influence a client's behavior with or without the counselor's awareness. It seems likely, therefore, that the current trend toward multicultural awareness among counselors will have as great an impact on the helping professions in the next decade as Rogers's "third force" of humanism had on the prevailing psychodynamic and behavioral systems.

Multicultural awareness provides a safe and accurate approach to differences across groups in a multicultural population. Multicultural awareness is safe because it provides a third alternative to judgments of right or wrong between two culturally different persons in conflict. Multicultural awareness is accurate because it interprets behaviors in the context of the culturally different client's intended meaning. Culture is not a vague or exotic label attached to faraway persons and places, but a personal orientation to each decision, behavior, and action in our lives.

The power and importance of culture have been most evident in minority groups' political struggle for equity. Culture has provided a rationale and "roots" for unifying and defining populations of Blacks, Asian-Americans, Hispanics,

Native Americans, and—more recently—White ethnics. The same model also has coalesced support among the elderly, groups of men or women, physically handicapped, and homosexuals, among many others. The importance of culture is broader than indicated by any of these special interest groups, however. Culture provides a metaphor better to understand differences between groups of people as they relate to one another. Perhaps more importantly, culture provides a metaphor for understanding different perspectives within each of us as our different social roles compete, complement, and cooperate with one another in our decisions.

Some terms used in this book may be unfamiliar to the reader. In most cases the term can be understood from the context in which it appears, but it may be useful to review some of the more basic definitions at the beginning of this book.

Culture itself is difficult to define. Kroeber and Kluckhohn (1952) found over 150 different definitions of culture. Culture is described as the things a stranger needs to know to behave appropriately in a specific setting. Geertz (1973) likewise takes a broad definition when he speaks of culture as "thick description" in the tradition of Max Weber and, more recently, systems theories. We spin webs of significance that we call culture. The analysis of culture is both an experimental science in search of rules and an interpretative study in search of meaning.

Multicultural counseling is a situation in which two or more persons with different ways of perceiving their social environment are brought together in a helping relationship. The term *multicultural* tends to be preferred over *crosscultural*, *intercultural*, or *transcultural* because it describes a variety of co-equal status without comparing one group to another. By implying comparison, the terms *crosscultural*, *intercultural*, and *transcultural* sometimes implicitly suggest that one culture is better than the other.

Race refers to a pseudobiological system of classifying persons by a shared genetic history or physical characteristics such as skin color. Many emotional and political implications in the term *race* have led to its frequent misuse (Casas, 1984). The term *race* too often has promoted myths of superiority of one group over another.

Ethnicity includes a shared sociocultural heritage that includes similarities of religion, history, and common ancestry. Ethnicity is important to individual and family identity as a subset of culture. In the past *ethnicity* more frequently has referred to non-White groups, but more recently White ethnic groups also have emerged as separate groups (McGoldrick, Pearce, & Giordano, 1982).

Minority generally refers to a group receiving differential and unequal treatment because of collective discrimination. Minority is frequently defined by the condition of oppression rather than by numerical criteria. In this sense women are sometimes classified as a minority.

Transcultural goes beyond culture to include the more universal constructs of before birth, after death, and religious philosophical concepts.

Counseling, as mentioned in chapter 7, is defined broadly to include the full range of formal and informal means of helping others. In a multicultural setting the functions of counseling are frequently present even though the traditional counseling relationship may be absent.

This volume is organized into three parts. The first part emphasizes the awareness of our culturally learned opinions, attitudes, and assumptions. In chapter 1, the awareness, knowledge, and skill sequence is applied to assessing needs, developing objectives, designing training, implementing training, and evaluating outcomes.

Chapter 2 presents a dozen different exercises or strategies to help trainees identify their own culturally learned assumptions, opinions, and attitudes. The primary emphasis of this chapter is on increasing multicultural awareness of one's self or in others. After identifying assumptions, the chapter discusses barriers to changing assumptions toward more intentional decision-making strategies.

Chapter 3 discusses a series of 10 culturally biased assumptions from a White, middle-class, urban, male, dominant culture perspective. A test of reasonable opposites is provided to challenge unexamined assumptions. This strategy is followed by two examples of reasonable opposites: that *complexity* is our friend, not our enemy, and that a two-directional balance of pain and pleasure is preferred to the simple search for pleasure as an outcome of counseling.

Chapter 4 begins the second part of the book by emphasizing knowledge about multicultural counseling. The research literature on development is applied to the task of developing a multicultural identity. Cultural labels are important means of classifying groups and individuals; they also can be used to control them. At the international level the process of culture shock provides an example of developing a multicultural identity. At the intranational level, the Minority Identity Development Model and other researched strategies are described. A multicultural synthesis is presented to suggest other approaches for developing a multicultural identity. The Kluckhohn and Strodtbeck model is the most frequently cited model from an anthropological viewpoint. An alternative Cultural Grid is also presented that assumes culture to be both dynamic and complex. The Cultural Grid combines social system variables with cognitive variables of behavior, expectation, and value in personal-cultural orientation toward specific decisions. The Cultural Grid applies both to intrapersonal understanding of culture within the person and interpersonal understanding of how two culturally different persons relate to one another.

Chapter 5 emphasizes research on multicultural counseling generally. The research studies result in data-based conclusions on the minority perspective, where ethnic groups compete for power. International research from around the world allows us to take a global perspective. The research on theoretical perspectives provides the structure for discussing the therapist's perspective and the client's perspective of multicultural counseling.

Chapter 6 reviews data and information, describing why we need a multicultural awareness in the counseling profession. The data describing inequities in the presentation of cultural programs in publications and national meetings contradict rhetorical support for multicultural awareness in professional documentations. The representation of culturally different faculty and students in educational programs to prepare counselors likewise highlights this discrepancy. The political dynamics of complex social systems and the cultural encapsulation of counselors are discussed both in terms of classic arguments for and against multicultural awareness.

Chapter 7 begins the third part of this book by discussing skills used in multicultural counseling. This chapter expands the definition of counseling to include formal and informal methods as well as formal and informal contexts. This somewhat more complicated definition of counseling accommodates clients from a wide range of cultural backgrounds, in which talk therapy in a formal office setting is less preferred. Benjamin Bloom's taxonomy leads off a discussion of the competencies of multicultural counseling. Critical incidents illustrating multicultural situations where these competencies apply are presented as examples.

Chapter 8 describes one of the many different models in the literature for developing multicultural skills in counseling—the Triad Model. Each counseling interview combines three simultaneous dialogues: that between the client and the counselor, the counselor's internal dialogue, and the client's internal dialogue. Resource persons form the client's culture simulate the role of anticounselor and procounselor in role-played interviews to help counselor trainees understand the internal dialogue of culturally different clients.

Chapter 9 describes four dimensions of skill development that apply to developing multicultural awareness. Accurately perceiving a problem from a client's viewpoint provides the foundation for good counseling. Identifying resistance among culturally different clients in specific rather than general, vague terms facilitates progress in multicultural interviews. Reducing the counselor's own need to be defensive allows counselors to be more effective in their focus on culturally different clients. Finally, recovering effectively by saying or doing "the right thing" prevents the multicultural interview from going off track when "uncomfortable moments" are encountered.

The conclusion summarizes basic elements of awareness, knowledge, and skill as they contribute to developing a multicultural awareness. The multicultural elements of counseling are discussed, and one of the unanswered questions is identified for future research. The counseling profession is still unclear whether multicultural development should become a special focus in counseling with its own courses, experts, and professional associations, or whether it should become an essential aspect of all quality counseling. Given the importance of multicultural awareness for accurate interpretation of culturally learned behaviors, the trend seems to be toward including multicultural awareness as a generic aspect of counseling.

The approach described in this book, and more particularly in the Triad Model, is theoretically eclectic. The author's own theoretical position has been influenced by a range of theories. Considering the four categories of trait, psychodynamic, behavioral, and phenomenological theories, it is possible to identify contributions from each perspective.

Culture, like a network of traits, is located within the person. Like traits, culture provides a flexible disposition toward one or another perspective that changes from time to time, situation to situation, and person to person. Although a person's culture can be known in part, there are core elements of our culture that are not known even to ourselves. Like traits, some elements of a person's culture can be measured, however imprecisely, and labeled, although sometimes inaccurately. Counselors need to identify a client's cultural disposition to communicate accurately and appropriately, even though our measures of culture are at best approximate.

The psychodynamic perspective has contributed a personal historical perspective of cultural dynamics. Concepts such as defensiveness and resistance in chapter 9 are used to identify these internal states. The search for hidden meanings, symbols, metaphors, and personal histories in chapter 2 is an important part of explaining the meaning of culture for and to a client. Whether unconscious or not, there certainly are patterns and habits of culturally learned assumptions that are unquestioned within culturally similar groups, and which provide an identity to members of those groups.

The behavioral perspective is emphasized in linking behavior change to the environment and matching each behavior with culturally learned expectations behind that behavior. According to the Cultural Grid of chapter 4, it is not possible for counselors to accurately interpret a behavior without first understanding the client's expectation for presenting that behavior in the first place. In the Triad Model introduced in chapter 8, the anticounselor and procounselor attempt to shape a counselor's behavior through modeling, positive reinforcement, and a variety of other reinforcing stimuli.

The phenomenological or existential-humanistic emphasis on meaning comes through in chapter 3, where assumptions are analyzed as the basis of awareness. The holistic systems perspective in developing a multicultural identity is likewise emphasized in chapter 4. In the Triad Model of chapter 8 and 9, the emphasis is less on techniques than on the relationship between a counselor and a culturally different client. The techniques of an anticounselor and procounselor are useful only to the extent that they enhance the counseling relationship as a means toward the desired end.

Many of the persons doing good counseling in other cultures are not aware that they are counseling, and some might even be offended if they were labeled counselors. They have developed what Ivey (1988, p. 2) calls their "natural style," independent of formal counseling theories. When approached to "explain" their success in counseling, they frequently have difficulty articulating their own theory of counseling. However, when matched with a client, counselor, anticounselor, or procounselor, they easily are able to demonstrate their own successful approach. This book is an attempt to identify culturally different natural styles of counseling.

PART ONE

Awareness of Multicultural Assumptions

Awareness is the beginning of change, and the first three chapters in this handbook begin by emphasizing awareness. After explaining how the three-step approach to multicultural development proceeds *from* an awareness of culturally learned assumptions *to* increased knowledge about relevant information *to* informed ability in taking the right action, the first chapter of part 1 provides the rationale for the rest of the book.

Practical methods and structured experiences for changing a person's assumptions to overcome culturally learned barriers to understanding are then discussed and explained. Some of these exercises resemble a "cookbook" approach, and, to be effective, the exercises must be seen in the necessary context of *relevant* knowledge and *informed* ability or skill.

Examining 10 of the most frequent assumptions that lead to multicultural misunderstandings further illustrates the importance of developing multicultural awareness in all aspects of personal relationships. When we make a mistake while working with someone from another culture, it is frequently one of these 10 assumptions that has betrayed us.

The three chapters on awareness are designed to audit the reader's own culturally learned assumptions. A thorough examination of your assumptions is a necessary preparation for looking at multicultural knowledge and skill.

CHAPTER 1

The Three Stages of Multicultural Development: Awareness, Knowledge, and Skill

Developing multicultural awareness is not an end in itself, but rather a means toward increasing a person's power, energy, and freedom of choice in a multicultural world. Multicultural awareness increases a person's intentional and purposive decision-making ability by accounting for the many ways that culture influences different perceptions of the same situation.

Culture is not external but is "within the person," and it is not separate from other learned competencies. Developing multicultural awareness is therefore a professional obligation as well as an opportunity for the adequately trained counselor. Millions of people today live and work in a culture other than their own. People who live in another culture are likely to become multicultural in their awareness of alternative values, habits, customs, and life styles that were initially strange and unfamiliar. Sometimes they have learned to adjust even more profoundly and effectively than they themselves realize. They have learned to respond in unique ways to previously unfamiliar situations and come up with the right answers without always being aware of their own adjustment process.

This handbook is an attempt to review the development of multicultural awareness. Readers should benefit from this awareness in two ways. *First*, reviewing the influence of their own multicultural contact will help readers already living in another culture to better understand the constant changing of their own viewpoint, and, *second*, they will be able to anticipate the right questions to ask as they adapt their life style to multicultural alternatives. Increased awareness will provide more freedom of choice to persons as they become more aware of their own multiculturalism.

1. Basic Questions

Before we even begin discussing the process of multicultural development, it is important to consider some of the more controversial questions in the literature about the concept called "culture" and the culture-learning process. It is also important to identify the assumptions behind this book's approach to describing multicultural development for each of the more controversial questions.

1. How is "objective" culture different from "subjective" culture?

Objective culture refers to the visible "point-at-able" (Hines & Pedersen, 1980) artifacts or behaviors that are culturally learned or derived, and that can be objectively identified or pointed at by both persons within and outside a given culture. Subjective culture refers to the internalized feelings, attitudes, opinions, and assumptions members of a culture hold that, although profoundly important to the culture, are difficult to verify. In order to work with a culture, it is important to go beyond its more obvious objective and verifiable symbols toward the more subjective perspective its members hold (Triandis, 1980).

2. Is the concept "culture" broadly or narrowly defined?

The narrow definition of culture is limited to ethnographic variables such as nationality and ethnicity, although it may include language and religion. A broader "social system" definition of culture includes: demographic variables such as age, sex, and place of residence; status variables such as social, educational, and economic levels; and affiliation variables that may be formal memberships or informal affiliations (Hines & Pedersen, 1980). Each element within the full range of demographic, status, and affiliation factors functions in ways similar to ethnographic categories to define a person's cultural identity. On occasion, any of these factors may be more salient to the person's personal cultural orientation than the ethnographic features. It therefore seems reasonable to include the full range of social system variables within the broad definition of culture.

3. Is culture learning best pursued through the "university model" or through more "experiential" learning?

The university model of didactic, lecture-based classroom teaching is certainly one of the valuable ways a person can learn about another culture. For persons unfamiliar with the culture, however, the experiential methods seem to have worked more efficiently (Harrison & Hopkins, 1967). Experiential methods place emphasis on less formal, field-based experiences and a two-way interaction between teachers and learners. Because both methods have their place, this book will seek to identify those conditions when formal training may be better than informal experience as well as those conditions where experience is indeed the best teacher.

> *4. Can culture learning take place as a general process independent of any specific cultural context?*

Culture-general approaches teach about principles that apply to all multicultural contact whenever and wherever it may occur. Culture-general approaches emphasize self, flexibility, and increased tolerance of cultural differences (Brislin, Cushner, Cherrie, & Young, 1986). Culture-specific approaches teach about a particular nationality, ethnicity, or cultural group in terms of its special perspective (Triandis, 1975). Culture-specific and culture-general training approaches complement one another in providing a full range of multicultural development for the person being trained.

2. Multicultural Development Designs

Multicultural development is basically a training process and should be understood from the perspective of multicultural training methods. The various types of multicultural training methods have been classified elsewhere (Brislin, Landis, & Brandt, 1983; Brislin & Pedersen, 1976; Gudykunst & Hammer, 1983).

The developmental approach in this book follows the "educational" model rather than the medical model by assuming that the target audience is healthy and normal, with an interest in learning about developing a multicultural awareness. As you read this book think of yourself as a teacher or trainer. The chapters will frequently refer to you, the reader, as a teacher or trainer. You may be training other trainers or other students; you may even be training yourself, where you become both teacher and student at the same time. There is no more exciting a way to learn a subject than to teach it to someone else, even if that someone is yourself.

Some of those seeking increased multicultural development will be *trainers of providers*. These trainers are twice removed from the ultimate recipients of the training. Persons in this "train-the-trainers" role will emphasize training *methods* as well as content to enable other trainers to do a better job in a variety of multicultural situations.

A second group will be *providers*. These participants will themselves be providing multicultural training to a variety of recipient populations; thus they are likely to have a sharper focus on the particular cultures and on methods of teaching others that most interest them.

A third group will be the *recipients* of multicultural training themselves who will move directly into a multicultural activity with little additional training from anyone else. Their task is to train themselves. The recipients are likely to be concerned about multicultural development only insofar as it will help them do their assigned task more efficiently and effectively.

Because the agenda at each level of training is somewhat different, it is important to keep all three levels of the training process in mind. Figure 1 shows the relationship of these three levels as a pyramid extending from the relatively few trainers of providers to the relatively many recipients of multicultural orientation.

The structure of multicultural development discussed in this book will proceed through a sequence of three stages. The focus of multicultural development will proceed from increased awareness of a person's culturally learned opinions, attitudes, and assumptions to increased knowledge about relevant facts and information about the culture in question, and finally to increased skill for making effective change and taking appropriate action.

Teaching multicultural development is an attempt to increase a person's alternatives for understanding and being accurately understood in a wide variety of cultures. Good teaching must relate to a wide variety of multicultural situations and also accurately describe how the conditions of specific, real life situations are more easily understood from a multicultural perspective. The more alternatives in a person's cultural repertoire of potential responses, the more likely the person will be to match the right response to each culturally different situation.

To determine a correct teaching method for increasing multicultural communication skills, the teacher must proceed through each of three stages in the analysis of *both* the culture being taught and the student's level of understanding. The teacher must examine the level of:

1. *Awareness* to make sure that the student has accurate and appropriate attitudes, opinions, and assumptions about the culture. In many cases, a student will develop a false awareness of the culture in question (i.e., biases, stereotypes), which must be changed and corrected before multicultural development can continue.
2. *Knowledge* or comprehension a student has of the culture. Does the student have all the facts and information accurately under control? In many cases students will have serious gaps in their knowledge and information base about a culture that will require filling in or correcting before multicultural development can continue.

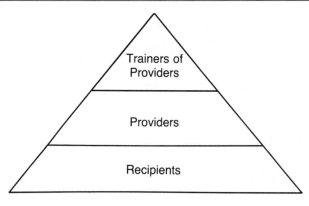

FIGURE 1
Levels of Multicultural Orientation

3. *Skill* a student has for interacting with persons from the culture. Is the student able to identify an appropriate way to bring about changes in the culture or to be accepted by persons from that culture? In many cases a student will have the skill to change a culture but lack the awareness or knowledge to make things better rather than worse.

Each of these three stages must be assessed as adequate before multicultural development can proceed.

The first stage of training is a needs assessment of strengths and weaknesses. Trainers need to be sure that there is indeed an unmet need in the people they plan to train. Even if the trainees recognize that a change is necessary, they may not see training as the most appropriate way to bring that change about. Here again the trainers need to consider all the possibilities for change before they proceed to design a training program.

It is assumed in this book that the trainer has a certain amount of background awareness of the trainee's needs, knowledge about how to meet those needs, and skills to convey the knowledge accurately and appropriately. Trainers will need to assess their own capabilities thoroughly to make sure that they are ready. In each particular group they meet, trainers will need to develop additional specialized knowledge to be precisely on target.

In one training program to teach prisoners to work with new social workers in a federal penitentiary, the entire training staff were required to be locked up with the prisoners for 48 hours so that they could better learn the prisoners' viewpoint before they tried to teach them anything.

Reciprocity is important in good teaching or training. A good trainer welcomes the possibility of reciprocal exchange in the training context. That is particularly important for multicultural training, where so much of the learning is subjective to a particular group's point of view.

3. Three Stages of Multicultural Development

Most multicultural training programs fail in three ways. Teaching programs that overemphasize "awareness" through the exclusive use of values clarification or the presumption of simplistic "good" or "bad" value judgments toward a particular culture fail unless the student is guided toward the knowledge that documents proper awareness and the skills to apply that awareness. Some of the programs emphasize awareness objectives almost exclusively. As a result, the participants become painfully aware of their own inadequacies or the inadequacies of their environment and the hopelessly overwhelming problems the group faces in bringing about equitable change. Trainees who overdose on awareness are frustrated because they don't know what to do with the awareness they have gained in terms of increasing their knowledge or information and learning appropriate action.

A second way programs fail is by overemphasizing "knowledge" objectives. Teaching programs that overemphasize knowledge about a culture through lectures, readings, and excessive accumulation of information fail unless the student already is aware of the importance of this knowledge as the basis for developing skills in applying the accumulated knowledge. These programs provide large amounts of information through readings, lectures, and factual data regarding a particular group or topic. The participants are frustrated first because they don't see the need for this information, and, second, because they are not sure how to use the information once it has been gathered.

A third way programs fail is by overemphasizing "skill" objectives. Teaching that overemphasizes skill without providing appropriate awareness and documented knowledge about the culture may be implementing change in the wrong or culturally inappropriate directions. Participants in these programs emerge with the capability of changing other people's lives, but they are never sure that they are making changes for the better. Without the benefit of awareness and knowledge, misapplied skills may make things worse. Each of the three stages builds on the former toward a comprehensive and balanced perspective that fits both the culture studied and the student's own development.

Multicultural development, as presented in this handbook, is a continuous learning process based on three stages of development. The AWARENESS stage emphasizes assumptions of differences and similarities of behavior, attitudes, and values. The KNOWLEDGE stage expands the amount of information about culturally learned assumptions. The SKILLS stage adapts effective and efficient action with people of different cultures to participants' clarified assumptions and accurate knowledge.

4. Needs Assessment

The first step in structuring an orientation or training program is a needs assessment of the group's level of: (a) awareness, (b) knowledge, and (c) skill. Assessing the level of a student's awareness is an important first step. Awareness is the ability to accurately judge a cultural situation from both one's own and the other's cultural viewpoint. The student should be able to describe a situation in a culture so that a member of that culture will agree with the student's perception. Such an awareness would require an individual to have:

- ability to recognize direct and indirect communication styles;
- sensitivity to nonverbal cues;
- awareness of cultural and linguistic differences;
- interest in the culture;
- sensitivity to the myths and stereotypes of the culture;
- concern for the welfare of persons from another culture;
- ability to articulate elements of his or her own culture;
- appreciation of the importance of multicultural teaching;
- awareness of the relationships between cultural groups; and
- accurate criteria for objectively judging "goodness" and "badness" in the other culture.

Assessing the level of a student's knowledge becomes important once the student's awareness has been corrected and judged to be adequate. If awareness helps the student to ask the "right questions," then knowledge provides access to the "right answers." The increased knowledge and information should clarify the alternatives and reduce the ambiguity in a student's understanding about a culture. Learning the language of another culture is an effective way to increase one's information. Anticipating preconceptions and stereotypes from another culture's viewpoint requires knowledge about the myths and widely "understood" perceptions from that culture's viewpoint. It is also important to know the right way to get more information about the culture in question so that the teaching/learning resources will be appropriate.

In a needs assessment to determine the student's level of knowledge about a culture, the following questions provide guidelines for measuring knowledge awareness.

- Does the student have specific knowledge about the culturally defined group members' diverse historical experiences, adjustment styles, roles of education, socioeconomic backgrounds, preferred values, typical attitudes, honored behaviors, inherited customs, slang, learning styles, and ways of thinking?
- Does the student have information about the resources for teaching and learning available to persons in the other culture?
- Does the student know about his or her own culture in relation to the other culture?
- Does the student have professional expertise in an area valued by persons in the other culture?
- Does the student have information about teaching/learning resources about the other culture and know where those resources are available?

A great deal of information is necessary before the student can be expected to know about another culture. Some assessment of the student's level of knowledge prior to training is essential so that the teacher can fill in any gaps with accurate factual information that will allow the student to proceed with an accurate and comprehensive understanding of the other culture.

Assessing the level of a student's skill becomes important once the student's informed awareness is supplemented with factual data about the other culture. Skill becomes the most important stage of all and therefore requires a great deal of preparation in teaching about awareness and knowledge. By teaching a skill, the teacher is enabling the student to ''do'' something that he or she could not do before. It is possible to measure the things a student now can do effectively that he or she could not do before. Skill requires the student to do the right thing at the right time in the right way and provides the final test of whether the teaching has after all been effective.

Skills are difficult to evaluate. Sometimes the suggested solution is not credible to all persons in the other culture. Skill requires the ability to present a solution in the other culture's language and cultural framework. Skill requires the student to test stereotypes against real and present situations and to modify them accordingly. Skill requires the student to seek agreement on evaluation criteria and to implement change that will effect an improvement.

In a needs assessment to determine the student's level of skill development, a teacher might examine several aspects.

- Does the student have appropriate teaching/learning techniques for work in the other culture?
- Does the student have a teaching/learning style that will be appropriate in the other culture?
- Does the student have the ability to establish empathic rapport with persons from the other culture?

- Is the student able to receive and accurately analyze feedback from persons of the other culture?
- Does the student have the creative ability to develop new methods for work in the other culture that will go beyond what the student has already learned?

5. Objectives

Once the needs of participants of training have been analyzed, the next step is to design appropriate objectives for a training plan. The relative emphasis on awareness, knowledge, or skills will depend on the results of the needs assessment. An awareness objective will change the person's attitudes, opinions, and personal perspectives about a topic. The primary need may be to help a group discover their own stereotypical attitudes and opinions. Usually the awareness objectives focus on a person's unstated assumptions about another culture or about themselves in relation to the other culture.

Once clearly stated training objectives are identified, it is useful to look at the awareness aspect, the knowledge aspect, and the skill aspect of each objective. We may, therefore, look at the matrix vertically (in terms of different objectives about awareness, knowledge, and skill) or horizontally (in terms of the same objective with an awareness aspect, knowledge aspect, and skill aspect). Figure 2 indicates these two ways of viewing training objectives.

The awareness objective for multicultural teaching focuses on changing the students' attitudes, opinions, and personal perspectives about themselves and the other culture so that these elements will be in harmony with one another. Specific objectives for multicultural teaching might be based on several important elements of awareness.

- Is the student aware of differences in cultural institutions and systems?
- Is the student aware of the stress resulting from functioning in a multicultural situation?
- Does the student know how rights or responsibilities are defined differently in different cultures?
- Is the student aware of differences in verbal and nonverbal communication styles?
- Is the student aware of significant differences and similarities of practices across different cultures?

In identifying the needs of a particular group of students, it is useful to proceed from an analysis of their awareness needs to their knowledge or information needs and finally to their skill needs. It is important to identify the needs from the group's viewpoint rather than that of outsiders.

	COMPONENT		
	Awareness	Knowledge	Skill
OBJECTIVE			
1			
2			
3			

FIGURE 2
Three Components of Multicultural Training Objectives

The knowledge objective for multicultural teaching focuses on increasing the amount of accurate information available to the student. Having developed a correct and accurate awareness of the other culture, students enrich that awareness by testing attitudes, opinions, and assumptions against the body of factual information they now control. The students' level of awareness is certain to increase in direct proportion to the extent of their knowledge about the other culture. Specific objectives for multicultural teaching might be based on several elements of knowledge.

- Does the student know about social services and how they are delivered to needy and deserving members of the culture?
- Does the student know about the theory of culture shock and stages of cultural adaptation as they relate to the other culture?
- Does the student know how the other culture interprets its own rules, customs, and laws?
- Does the student know patterns of nonverbal communication and language usage within the other culture?
- Does the student know how differences and similarities are patterned in the other culture and how priorities are set in different critical situations?

The skill objective for multicultural teaching focuses on what the students now can do. If any of the previous teaching about awareness and knowledge is missing or inadequate, the students will have difficulty making right decisions in multicultural communication. If awareness has been neglected, they will build their plan on wrong assumptions. If knowledge has been neglected, they will describe the cultural situation inaccurately. If skill has been neglected, they may well change a situation in counterproductive directions. Specific objectives for multicultural teaching of skills might be based on several important elements.

- Is the student able to gain access to social services and resources that will satisfy his or her basic needs?
- Is the student able to cope with stress and manage difficulties in the new culture?
- Is the student able to understand consequences of behavior and choose wisely among several options that the other culture presents?
- Is the student able to use the culture's language to react appropriately to others from that culture?
- Is the student able to function comfortably in the new environment without losing his or her own cultural identity in the home culture?

These are a few examples of skills that must be assessed to make sure that the student has been taught to communicate in the other culture. Many additional skills will be developed for each specific situation.

6. Design

The next step in developing a training program is to design a plan that shows how the identified objectives will be carried out in such a way that the identified needs will be met. There are many different ways to match techniques with awareness, knowledge, or skill objectives. Some examples follow:

TECHNIQUES TO STIMULATE AWARENESS

Experiential exercises such as:
- Role plays
- Role reversals
- Simulations

Field trips
Critical incidents
Bicultural observation and experiences
Questions/answers/discussion
Case studies and critical incidents

Teaching increased awareness frequently relies on experiential exercises such as role plays, role reversals, or simulations of a multicultural interaction. Other approaches include field trips to areas where the culture exists normally on a day-to-day basis. Sometimes critical incidents or brief case studies from the culture can be analyzed to increase a student's awareness of the culture. A resource person or informant from the culture enables effective bicultural observation whereby both individuals and groups may exchange questions and answers in a thorough discussion. Almost any approach that involves the student's basic assumptions, tests the student's prevailing attitudes, and elicits the student's implicit opinions about the culture will serve to increase the student's awareness.

TECHNIQUES TO IMPART KNOWLEDGE

Guided self-study with reading list
Lecture and discussion
Panel discussion
Audiovisual presentations
Interviews with consultants and experts
Observations

Teaching increased knowledge frequently relies on books, lectures, and classroom techniques. Guided self-study with a reading list also is an effective way to help students increase their knowledge. Panel discussions about the other culture help students absorb more information relevant to their particular situation. Audiovisual presentations, when available, provide valuable knowledge. Interviews with consultants or resource persons and experts knowledgeable about the other culture help students fill in gaps where accurate information might otherwise be impossible to secure. Simply observing persons from the other culture in their daily activities is an important means for learning about the culture, providing the student knows what to look for.

Teaching for increased multicultural skill takes many forms. Modeling and demonstrating a skill is an effective means of developing the skill in students. When available, audiovisual resources provide important feedback to students both about how the skill is performed in the other culture and how they are doing in modeling that skill. Supervising students' work in the other culture provides a valuable ongoing means of assessing developing levels of skill. The opportunity to practice new skills and behaviors enables students to improve their skills in a variety of different situations.

TECHNIQUES TO DEVELOP SKILLS

Modeling and demonstration
Using video and media resources for feedback
Supervising;
Practicing a new behavior pattern
Practicing writing skills

7. Training

The fourth stage in developing a training package is the actual implementation of a training design. After determining the date, time, place, and cost of the training, the trainer needs to draft an agenda, check supplies, and locate physical facilities for training. Trainers need to select resource participants or guest speakers and gather relevant resource materials. Preparation should include assembling packets or workbooks so that all the information conveyed to trainees verbally is also available in writing for later clarification. Finally, the trainer needs to develop evaluations of the workshops.

Most workshops begin in more or less the same way. There is an introduction with some attempt to break the ice. This might include a formal welcome from an official host or an informal welcome by the workshop leader. A discussion of the group's objectives and expectations as well as a sharing of the trainer's objectives and expectations ensues. Then the agenda is reviewed so that all participants know what is likely to happen in sequence; this helps them to review the materials in their workshop packet for any necessary clarification. The better trainees are prepared to work with one another, the more positively they are likely to view the training experience.

Once these general group-building tasks have been completed, the workshop may begin by emphasizing a balance of appropriate objectives focused on awareness and planning data. Each of these three alternative components (awareness, knowledge, and skill) would suggest a different training format. Figure 3 presents an example of how each stream would differ in training cultural orientation (CO) providers to work with refugees.

8. Evaluation

The last stage of a training sequence is evaluating whether the persons you trained have met your objectives in awareness, knowledge, and skill. This is called "formative" evaluation. Another kind of evaluation is a long-term and much more complicated evaluation to verify whether or not your objectives were accurate and met the needs of your group. This second type of evaluation is called "summative" evaluation.

Evaluation methods range from informal discussions over wine and cheese to formal written evaluations of long-term changes in productivity determined by random work samples. However you proceed, you should allow room for evaluation in your training activities. These data will be valuable to your trainees in giving them feedback on their accomplishment, valuable to you in demonstrating the strength or weakness of your design, and valuable to those sponsoring the

FIGURE 3

Three Alternative Training Sequences

I. Introduction/ice breaker
  A. Formal welcome by official, or
  B. Informal welcome by workshop leader

II. Discussion of group expectations
  A. Group objectives
  B. Leader/trainer objectives

III. Review of agenda

IV. Review of materials or packet

Awareness Focus	Knowledge Focus	Skills Focus
OBJECTIVE: In training, you should help the CO providers to become aware of the contrast and conflict between their background and that of the refugees.	OBJECTIVE: In training, you should help the CO provider to have knowledge of the refugee resettlement process including institutions at national, regional, and local levels.	OBJECTIVE: In training, you should help the CO provider to be skilled in working with interpreters and cultural informants.
V. Introduction to the experiential exercise *Bafa Bafa* A. Processing *Bafa Bafa*	V. An overview of the refugee resettlement process to be given by the trainer or a knowledgeable resource person.	V. Introduction to the need of working with interpreters/cultural informants and qualities of a good interpreter/cultural informant
VI. Reactions to *Bafa Bafa* as a training method and how the group experience relates to meeting the above objective.	VI. Panel discussion of the resettlement process. Resource persons might include: local Volag director, local welfare agency, local social service agency contracted by federal or state government, and representation of MAA's	VI. Team demonstration—CO provider and interpreter role-play with a CO recipient
VII. Divide into groups of twos or threes to write their own critical incidents relating to their professional and personal interaction with the recipients of CO.	VII. Question and answer period	VII. Discussion of the role-play and qualities of an effective interaction between CO provider and interpreter
VIII. Presentation and discussion of the critical incidents.	VIII. The panel member representing the local welfare agency presents and distributes a directory of social services in the area.	VIII. Videotaped triads composed of CO provider, coached interpreter/cultural informant and coached CO recipient.
IX. Application of awareness gained during the workshop to professional activities.	IX. Application of knowledge gained during the workshop to professional activities.	IX. Discussion of the videotapes.
X. Evaluation	X. Evaluation	X. Application of skills learned during the workshop to professional activities. Individual practice with interpreter/cultural informant.
XI. Adjournment	XI. Adjournment	XI. Evaluation
		XII. Adjournment

Note: From *Providing Effective Orientation: A Training Guide* (p. 12) by P. Pedersen with staff from Center for Applied Linguistics, Refugee Services. Unpublished monograph. Copyright 1982 by the Center for Applied Linguistics, Washington, D.C. Adapted by permission.

training activity as a basis for making decisions. Some criteria for evaluating follow.

Students are trained to increase their *awareness* so they will:

- appropriately recognize the valued priority they give to basic attitudes, opinions, and assumptions;
- accurately compare their own cultural perspective with that of a person from the other culture;
- sensitively articulate their own professional role in relation to the other culture;
- appropriately estimate constraints of time, setting, and resources in the other culture; and
- realistically estimate the limit of their own resources in the other culture.

Students are trained to increase their *knowledge* so they will:

- understand the process of institutional change in the other culture at local, national, and regional levels;
- cite the relevant literature of the other culture;
- identify similarities and differences of their own home culture and the other culture;
- identify referral resources in the other culture; and
- select key resource persons from the other culture for more information.

Students are educated to increase their *skill* so they will:

- efficiently plan, conduct, and evaluate training about the other culture;
- accurately assess the needs of persons from the other culture;
- utilize the talents of interpreters and cultural informants from the other culture;
- observe, understand, and accurately report about culturally learned behaviors in the other culture; and
- interact, advise, and appropriately manage their assigned task in the setting of the other culture.

Multicultural development is presumed to proceed from an awareness of attitudes, opinions, and assumptions to a knowledge of facts and information to skill in taking the appropriate action. Most persons being trained, however, are at different stages of development. Some trainees will require more emphasis on awareness, some on knowledge, and others can proceed directly to skill development.

9. Conclusion

Multicultural training should be guided by a sequence of learning objectives that reflects the needs of both the student and the culture being studied. Teaching multicultural communication needs to include all methods relevant to the culturally defined population, and be comprehensive enough to include both culture-specific and culture-general perspectives. The multicultural three-step process of awareness, knowledge, and skill provides an eclectic teaching strategy with a rationale for educational development.

CHAPTER 2

Asking the Right Questions: The First Stage of Awareness

Our basic assumptions determine how we see the world, and each of us sees the world more or less differently. Patterns of assumptions constitute ''culture'' within the person and are not external to the person. The first stage of training, awareness, identifies the trainee's assumptions or cultural patterns. With this awareness, the trainee should be able to begin asking the right questions, as envisioned by the training objectives.

Several guidelines are important to consider in organizing the awareness stage of a training program. Each trainee will come in with a separate agenda. It is important to help trainees identify their own agenda and then build on that agenda or revise it to fit the needs of the unit. A frequent mistake in training is a trainer's presuming assumptions or questions on the part of the trainees while ignoring the trainees' perceived needs. One way of building on the trainees' implicit or explicit agenda is to draw data and examples from the participants themselves. In that way the training is based less on abstractions and is more immediately relevant to the persons present. If the awareness component can teach participants something about themselves that they did not already know—in relation to their own needs, values, or assumptions—then the participants will be more receptive to the knowledge and skill training components. It is also important to allow every opportunity for trainees to demonstrate their own pretraining skills for teaching one another. Once they have had an opportunity to teach, they will be more receptive to being taught.

Awareness training needs to balance lectures or information with experiential exercises that apply information in practical ways. The exercises need to be kept short (5 to 10 minutes), with clearly defined objectives to hold the trainees' attention. Preview the training plan at each stage to indicate where you are going next. Each group will have several "gatekeepers" who will shape the group's reaction to the training. Identify gatekeepers early and attend to their advice so they become invested in the program's success and legitimacy. It is important not to move on to the next training agenda without debriefing participants to make sure none are confused about the exercise objectives or unintentionally offended. Finally, keep a back-up plan in mind for unexpected opportunities or problems that emerge.

1. Changing Assumptions

We do not give up our prevailing assumptions easily. We have a tendency to see evidence that supports our assumptions more clearly than evidence that challenges those assumptions. For that reason it is important to develop training approaches that guide multicultural learning and development in a structured way. The various approaches to training need to provide enough "safety" so that trainees are willing and able to consider changing their prevailing assumptions about other cultures, but also enough "challenge" so that trainees accept the necessity to learn new assumptions.

The intellectual approach, teaching about another culture's style of living and social patterns in a formal lecture classroom setting, is perhaps the most traditional training approach. Adaptations of the intellectual or "university" approach have focused on cognitive skills and factual information needed to adjust to an unfamiliar culture.

Knowing the right response to a situation, however, doesn't guarantee the facility or the inclination to use it. The advantage of an intellectual approach is its inclusion of factual background in describing another culture accurately in its similarity and dissimilarity to more familiar cultures. The disadvantages arise when the cognitive or intellectual aspects of adjustment are emphasized to the exclusion of other approaches.

The self-awareness approach emphasizes learning about your own cultural bias before you enter into another culture. You have to understand your own values before you can adjust to the value systems of another culture. Persons understand their appropriate role in another culture through contrasts between familiar and unfamiliar assumptions. To some extent self-awareness may be a necessary preliminary to any intercultural training approach, even though self-awareness doesn't deal directly with the other culture. In learning about other cultures we learn a great deal about ourselves. Self-awareness provides a secure understanding of our own priorities and value assumptions, but self-awareness is only the beginning of the training process.

The culture assimilator is a technique presenting a paragraph-length situation requiring a decision and several responses, one being more culturally appropriate than the others. The participant is trained to identify the best of several alternative responses to the situation. Examples are situation- or context-specific, and participants have to select from alternative explanations. Thus participants learn to "assimilate" into the unfamiliar culture by learning to anticipate both the alternative responses and the characteristics of a favored response. The advantage of a culture assimilator is its combining several elements of culture learning in a measure of intercultural competency. The disadvantages lie in its oversimplification of both the limited alternatives and the uniform appropriateness of one alternative response in a complex cultural setting.

Behavior modification also combines elements of other training approaches. The emphasis is on specific behaviors appropriate to a specific situation in a specific foreign culture in order to increase the positive effects and reduce the negative effects of desired outcomes. If trainees learn the skills necessary to increase comfort and foster positive experiences, they also will be able to decrease stress, anxiety, or negative experiences. In a simulation of a series of potentially stressful situations, the trainee can rehearse an attitude and behavioral response that will help to perceive the situation in a positive perspective. The advantage of behavior modification is in bridging the differences between familiar back-home and unfamiliar foreign situations, which helps the trainee to develop specific adaptive attitudes and behaviors. The disadvantage is a narrow focus and the difficulty of anticipating complex stressful situations in a foreign culture in advance.

Experiential training approaches depend on direct contact between the trainees and persons from the foreign culture. Such an approach might take place at a simulated Southeast Asian village in Hawaii, such as the one that was designed for Peace Corps training, or in an "intercultural communication workshop" where foreign students and local residents compare their impressions, attitudes, and insights. Experiential approaches depend on the simulated or real multicultural experiences themselves, within a structured environment, to produce culture learning. The emphasis is more on emotional rather than rational aspects of multicultural adjustment. Experiential training distinguishes the direct "experience" of another culture from indirect "discussions" about the other culture. The advantages of experiential training are in providing an authentic and realistic setting to learn culture-specific multicultural skills. The disadvantages relate to the need for a skilled facilitator to interpret the experience and the need for access to persons from the foreign culture.

Multicultural training is far from a precise science, but it continues to build on the hope that past mistakes need not be repeated and the knowledge that failure of multicultural contact is always enormously expensive and often tragic. Although existing methods are vulnerable to criticism, continuing attempts to identify alternatives for intercultural awareness are becoming more critically important than ever in our global village.

Improving one's effectiveness in multicultural communications involves much more than learning a new language of terms and concepts. There is as yet no objective measure of cultural differences. Students must first recognize their own style of behavior, attitudes, and underlying assumptions. Unless students become participants in the multicultural communications process they will not be able to benefit from the experience. In training for increased multicultural understanding it is necessary to generate experience-based learning about oneself in an active rather than a passive role.

Trainees are placed in situations similar or analogous to those they might encounter in the host culture to rehearse their own response to the problems they might expect to encounter in the host culture. Trainees then can explore alternative solutions to those problems and discover the consequences of each alternative. The unfamiliar situation also forces trainees to examine not only their own feelings and reactions to the problem situations but also their personal values, beliefs, attitudes, assumptions, and expectations related to multicultural experience. After becoming more thoroughly acquainted with the other culture, trainees can begin to integrate and conceptualize learning, generalizing from the training experience to the anticipated living and working situation in the host culture. Each person begins to recognize the kinds of information needed to solve new problems, or skills that must be acquired to be effective. In the host country trainees are better able to utilize available resources to meet those needs and continue their multicultural education. Also, by taking advantage of spontaneous learning opportunities as they arise, trainees gain practice in applying skills and knowledge.

Earlier research has pointed out the weakness of a university-based classroom for training persons in multicultural communications. In the experience-based learning model the trainee learns the skills of empathetic understanding of others' feelings through decisions of communication. The participant learns how to make independent decisions based on incomplete, unreliable, and often conflicting information. The participant learns to become involved and committed by staying in emotional contact with the target culture. The participant learns to accept and understand the value systems of others, allowing participants to shape and influence their own personal behavior. Finally each participant learns to follow the problem-solving process through to a specific and appropriate action. The experience-based model entails learning directly from one's social environment through observation and questioning, turning every situation into an opportunity for learning. The participant learns to define as well as to solve problems in a context where the facts are less relevant than the perceptions of those facts. The criteria of success are not external or even measurable but more frequently evidenced in the intangible relationship established with the target audience.

2. Barriers to Changing Assumptions

Once counselors are trained and begin to apply their training, they confront barriers that must be crossed skillfully. Training does not *eliminate* barriers. Some of our communications, particularly those across cultures, are accidental and not intended to be sent. Other messages that are directed toward others are deliberate and are communicated with a specific intention on the part of the sender. Ideally, the amount of communication we send will be more *intentional* and less *accidental*. Messages sent accidentally are beyond our control and thus will not present the picture we intend. Training, however, can improve and increase our intentional communication across cultures.

There are several obvious barriers to accurate communication across cultures (Barna, 1982). First, there is the obvious barrier of language differences. Language is much more than learning new sound symbols. Knowing a little of the foreign language only may allow visitors to make fluent fools of themselves if they are unaware of the implicit meanings behind the sound symbols.

Listed below are some ways that may help you decrease multicultural communication barriers.

DECREASING THE LANGUAGE BARRIER

Learn the language.

Find someone who can speak the language.

Ask for clarification if you are not sure what was said.

Second, nonverbal communications such as gestures, posture, tone of voice, and timing often change what we say. There is some difficulty in recognizing unspoken codes that come so automatically that they may not even be deliberate in our own more familiar culture but communicate a definite feeling or attitude nonetheless.

DECREASING THE NONVERBAL COMMUNICATION BARRIER

Do not assume you understand any nonverbal communication unless you are familiar with the culture.

If the nonverbal communication is insulting in your culture, do not take it personally.

Develop an awareness of your own nonverbal communication that might be insulting in certain cultures.

The third barrier—preconceptions and stereotypes—consists of overgeneralized beliefs that provide structure in any ambiguous contact. We see or hear pretty much what we want to or expect to see or hear, screening out many contradictory impressions. When you first become slightly aware of another culture, these half-formed stereotypes are most likely to betray communications. The stereotype has a tendency to become realized through a "self-fulfilling prophecy" of the communicator.

DECREASING THE PRECONCEPTIONS AND STEREOTYPES BARRIER

Make every effort to increase awareness of your own preconceptions and stereotypes of cultures you encounter.

With this awareness, reinterpret the behavior of people from another culture from their cultural perspective.

Be willing to test, adapt, and change your perceptions to fit your new experiences.

A fourth barrier is the tendency to evaluate by an approving or disapproving judgment the content of communication received from others. "Everyone seems to speak with an accent except those people who talk like myself." Premature evaluation frequently interferes with our accepting and understanding other persons from their point of view.

DECREASING THE EVALUATION BARRIER

Maintain objectivity.

Recognize that you cannot change a person's culture overnight.

Do not judge someone from another culture by your own cultural values until you have come to know the people and their cultural values.

A fifth barrier is the typically high level of anxiety that goes along with the multicultural contact where the visitor is dealing with unfamiliar experiences.

DECREASING THE STRESS BARRIER

Multicultural situations are often ambiguous and result in stress because you are not sure what others expect of you or what you can expect of them. As multicultural barriers are reduced, you can expect the level of stress to diminish.

A sixth barrier relates to the "organizational constraints" that may control what we do even when we know they are inequitable. Organizations shape our communications in ways that primarily protect their own interests.

DECREASING THE ORGANIZATIONAL CONSTRAINTS BARRIER

Identify the authority/responsibility/reporting relationships reflected in the formal organization chart.

Look for patterns of personal interaction that seem to deviate from the formal organization. These are your informal communication channels.

Recognize that an organization does not exist apart from people; check and confirm the limits of formal and informal personal influence.

Clarify your role, knowledge, and experience with the other person to the extent that you maintain the integrity and loyalties demanded by your position.

Changing assumptions and crossing barriers to multicultural understanding can best be accomplished through distinct structured training approaches. The rest of this chapter will describe and explain a dozen such approaches that you may find useful in changing assumptions or crossing barriers.

Several brief exercises that have been helpful for multicultural awareness training are described below. Each exercise needs to be matched carefully with the specific needs of a training situation. The awareness exercises serve both to identify the questions participants are already asking and to teach them some of the alternative questions they should be asking to complement what they know.

The Truth Statement

We often focus on the process of training without looking at the basic assumptions that are implicit in our training content. Generate a "truth statement" related to the training content that most or all of the group are likely to accept, and modify it through discussion until everyone agrees to its truthfulness.

When everyone has written a statement, ask them all to write a second statement explaining why their first statement is true.

When everyone has completed a second statement, ask them to write a third statement explaining why the second statement is true.

When everyone has completed a third statement, ask them to write a fourth statement explaining why the third statement is true.

You may choose to go on to a fifth and sixth statement, but probably by this time most participants have reached the point where they're saying "I don't know or even care why it is true. It's just true!" Most in the group are probably frustrated and irritated and some may be even hostile toward the trainer. Discuss:

(a) how hard it is to follow the chain of implicit assumptions underlying statements we accept as truthful; (b) how we get angry when pushed back to those assumptions in an argument or discussion; and (c) how frequently the implicit underlying assumptions go unexamined. You may want to discuss how group members believed in the same beginning statement for entirely different reasons.

THE TRUTH STATEMENT AWARENESS EXERCISE ·

Participant Objectives:
1. To identify a statement believed to be true;
2. To identify the chain of evidence proving the statement true; and
3. To identify the basic assumption behind the evidence.

Learning Objective:
Truth is based on culturally learned assumptions.

The Label Exercise

How do you discover when another person's perception of you may differ from your own perception of yourself? Organize participants into small groups of five to eight persons. Attach a gummed label of adjectives or nouns to the forehead of each group member (on the back if putting labels on foreheads is offensive) and ask the group to discuss a topic relevant to the program. Interact with each participant *as though* the adjectives or nouns on their forehead label were true for each of the other participants, with all considering each other's label simultaneously.

Each participant will know which labels are on the foreheads of the *others* in the group but *will not* know his or her *own* label. The labels may be typed up beforehand, or you may ask each participant to write an appropriate label, making sure that no participant gets his or her own label for the discussion. When the participants successfully have identified the label on their foreheads they can remove the label. The objective is to provide clues to others about the label on their forehead through behavior toward that person without directly giving away his or her identity.

Can participants successfully guess their labels or accurately interpret cues from others in the group? When all participants have guessed their labels, discuss the *actual* function of labels by which others perceive us. If some participants have not guessed their labels within 8 to 10 minutes, ask them to remove their labels anyway and begin the discussion. The emphasis is on the wide diversity of perceived identity labels we present to others.

THE LABEL AWARENESS EXERCISE

Participant Objectives:
  1. To provide feedback to others appropriate to their assigned label;
  2. To analyze feedback from others appropriate to one's own label; and
  3. To identify one's own label accurately based on feedback.

Learning Objective:
  Each of us wears a culturally assigned label on the forehead.

Stereotypes Awareness

Distribute one or more note cards to each participant. Write an incomplete sentence stem on the blackboard relevant to the training program such as, "Most refugees will say that Americans are . . . ." Ask participants to complete the sentence with one or two words on their note card. An associate will gather the note cards and code the responses while the trainer discusses stereotypes and generalizations.

When the note cards are tabulated they probably will illustrate how most participants responded in approximately the same way, demonstrating the opinions that are "known" to be true even prior to discussion. The stereotypes discussed after this exercise are not abstractions but concrete examples from the participants themselves.

STEREOTYPES AWARENESS EXERCISE

Participant Objectives:
  1. To display a consistent and uniform stereotype to others;
  2. To analyze stereotypes displayed by others; and
  3. To examine the basis of stereotypes.

Learning Objective:
  Culturally learned perceptions may be more important than reality.

Outside Experts

Sometimes it is difficult for outside experts to understand information provided by a host culture. Patterns of response that are obvious and consistent from the host culture's point of view may seem frustrating, inconsistent, uncooperative, and even hostile to the outside expert who does not know the host culture's rules.

Request a male and female volunteer from the group to leave the room briefly and return as an "outside expert team" invited into the host culture to identify the group's *problem* and suggest *solutions*. In a large group you may select a separate team for every 8 or 10 participants to work simultaneously.

While the volunteers are outside the room, instruct the *remaining* participants in the three "rules" of their "host culture."

(1) They may respond only by a "yes" or "no" to any question.

(2) Men may respond only to men and women only to women. Female participants will ignore all questions by male experts and male participants will ignore all questions by female experts.

(3) If the expert is "smiling" when asking a question, the same-sex participant will say "yes," but if the expert is not smiling when asking a question, the same-sex participant will say "no."

The experts return and are instructed about the first rule, that all their questions must be answered "yes" or "no," to give them a clue about the host culture's rules and to reduce frustration. The experts are free to roam the room asking as many participants yes/no questions as possible, speaking loudly enough so that all participants can hear as data are gathered. After about 10 minutes the experts report back to the group on the nature of the host culture's problem with suggestions for solutions.

Typically the experts have generated an elegant interpretation of their data based on the yes/no responses. When the experts have shared their observations, thank them, lead a round of applause for their contribution, and *then reveal the other two cultural rules*. The discussion may emphasize the importance of understanding a culture's rules before collecting data. Participants learn to recognize that inconsistency may be in the outside expert as well as in the host culture, and that what one person says may differ from what the other person hears. Discussion should emphasize the *process* of entering the host culture as an outside expert.

OUTSIDE EXPERT AWARENESS EXERCISE

Participant Objectives:
1. To identify communication cues in an unfamiliar culture;
2. To gather information systematically from an unfamiliar culture; and
3. To report ambiguities and stress factors from the interaction.

Learning Objective:
Misunderstandings occur between the expert and the host culture.

Drawing a House

We are culturally conditioned to respond in predetermined ways to different situations. Ask participants to select a partner as culturally different from themselves as possible. Distribute one page of paper and one pen to every team of two persons. Ask each two-person team to hold on to the same pen or pencil and, with both persons holding the same pen at the same time, to draw a house on the paper. Instruct the teams *not to talk* with one another while doing the task.

After 2 or 3 minutes ask them to stop and collect the house drawings. Show each drawing in turn to the group and encourage participants to talk about or present their "house" to the group, discussing any special problems or surprises that came up during the task. Then lead a discussion on how we are culturally conditioned to respond by emphasizing relationship (e.g., the agenda of our partners) or task (e.g., the drawing of a "good" house). Likewise we may be culturally conditioned to favor the role of leader (who controlled the pencil) or follower (who facilitated the drawing).

The cultural patterns of real-life responses are of course situationally specific for each cultural group, and in real life no single extreme will apply uniformly to any one cultural group. The discussion should focus on examples of how two cultures might not share the same culturally conditioned expectations in the same situation. In some cases cultural differences will be preferred, as in a work team where one member favors the leader role and the other favors the follower role. In other cases cultural differences will present problems, as in a work team where one member favors relationships and the other favors task accomplishment.

DRAW A HOUSE AWARENESS EXERCISE

Participant Objectives:
  1. To demonstrate situational leader-follower patterns;
  2. To demonstrate situational relationship-task patterns; and
  3. To report patterns of personal culture.

Learning Objective:
  Cultural differences are displayed in situational patterns of behavior.

Nested Emotions

Sometimes it is difficult to interpret what someone from another culture is feeling. Our emotional response to a situation is usually mixed, emphasizing conflicting feelings. Role play with and interview a particularly articulate participant on an emotionally loaded simulated situation for about 3 minutes. After the interview, distribute a rating sheet listing 10 or more emotions such as love, happiness, fear, anger, contempt, mirth, surprise, suffering, determination, or disgust. Beside each emotion provide a semantic differential from the number "1" (least) to the number "10" (most), asking participants to describe the degree of emotional feeling *they thought* the interviewee was feeling *while in the role* of the person being interviewed. Ask the interviewee also to complete the semantic differential indicating how he or she was *actually* feeling.

When everyone has completed their semantic differentials, ask the interviewee to read the degree of feeling he or she checked for each item while the participants check the accuracy of their *perceptions* about what the interviewee was feeling. The discussion that follows might emphasize clues to identifying nested emotions for the interviewee's culture and highlight emotions that are particularly difficult for an outsider to detect.

THE NESTED EMOTIONS AWARENESS EXERCISE

Participant Objectives:
1. To estimate the degree of each emotion displayed by the resource person;
2. To determine the degree of each emotion reported by the resource person; and
3. To identify cues to emotional expression in different cultures.

Learning Objective:
Emotions are always complicated and interrelated with one another.

Public and Private Self

Professor Dean Barnlund from San Francisco State University developed a list of topics based on the work by Sidney Jourard. These topics may be public to some persons and private to others. Frequently we assume that topics we consider public also will be considered public by others, and unintentionally violate the other person's privacy. The list of items, available from Professor Barnlund, includes five items from each of the areas of attitudes and opinions, tastes and interests, work or studies, money, personality, and body. The trainer may wish to generate a new list appropriate to the specific training program. The more extensive original list of public and private items can be found in Sidney Jourard's book *The Transparent Self* (1964). Figure 4 shows Barnlund's modified list.

FIGURE 4

Categories of Public and Private Self-Disclosure

Objective

To compare different rules for public disclosure of private information appropriate to visitor and host culture residents.

Instructions

Please mark each of the following topics as:

Private: if it is comfortable to discuss only with self and intimates;

Public: if it is comfortable to discuss with casual friends, acquaintances, or strangers.

	PUBLIC	PRIVATE
ATTITUDES AND OPINIONS:		
1. What I think and feel about my religion: my personal religious views	_____	_____
2. My views on Communism	_____	_____
3. My views on racial integration	_____	_____
4. My views on sexual morality	_____	_____
5. The things I regard as desirable for a person to be	_____	_____
TASTES AND INTERESTS:		
1. My favorite foods; my food dislikes	_____	_____
2. My likes and dislikes in music	_____	_____
3. My favorite reading matter	_____	_____
4. The kinds of movies and T.V. programs I like best	_____	_____
5. The kind of party or social gathering I like best; the kind that bores me	_____	_____
WORK OR STUDIES:		
1. What I feel are my shortcomings that prevent me from getting ahead	_____	_____
2. What I feel are my special strong points for work	_____	_____
3. My goals and ambitions in my work	_____	_____
4. How I feel about my career; whether I'm satisfied with it	_____	_____
5. How I really feel about the people I work for or with	_____	_____

continued

FIGURE 4 *continued*
Categories of Public and Private Self-Disclosure

	PUBLIC	PRIVATE
MONEY:		
1. How much money I make at work	_____	_____
2. Whether or not I owe money; if so, how much	_____	_____
3. My total financial worth	_____	_____
4. My most pressing need for money right now	_____	_____
5. How I budget my money	_____	_____
PERSONALITY:		
1. Aspects of my personality I dislike	_____	_____
2. Feelings I have trouble expressing or controlling	_____	_____
3. Facts of my present sex life	_____	_____
4. Things I feel ashamed or guilty about	_____	_____
5. Things that make me feel proud	_____	_____
BODY:		
1. My feelings about my face	_____	_____
2. How I wish I looked	_____	_____
3. My feelings about parts of my body	_____	_____
4. My past illnesses and treatment	_____	_____
5. Feelings about my sexual adequacy	_____	_____
TOTAL PRIVATE TOPICS		_____

Note: From personal communication with Dr. Dean Barnlund, San Francisco State University. Cited with his permission.

Ask each participant to review the list (in written or verbal form) and indicate whether the topic is *private* (e.g., comfortable to discuss only with self and intimate friends) or *public* (e.g., comfortable to discuss with casual friends, acquaintances, or strangers).

When everyone has identified the number of public items, tabulate the number of participants who had public items (30–25; 24–20; 19–15; 14–10; 9–5; 4–0) in six or more categories. You will probably discover a bell-shaped distribution of public and private levels among group members. You may then discuss the effect of respecting one another's privacy in working together.

> ## PUBLIC AND PRIVATE SELF-AWARENESS EXERCISE
>
> Participant Objectives:
> 1. To demonstrate culturally learned and differentiated levels of privacy in a group;
> 2. To assess one's personal level of privacy relative to the group; and
> 3. To examine the basis of public and private information in different cultures.
>
> Learning Objective:
> What is public for one person may be private for another.

Critical Incidents

The effectiveness of a training program usually is determined by its relevance to solving specific practical problems of a participant. Problem situations can become valuable training tools. Collect examples of problem situations that have no easy answers, project serious consequences, and occur with some frequency. You might divide participants into problem-solving groups to discuss the *cultural element* and perceived *conflict* within each situation, along with an *intervention* plan for dealing with the situation. You also might ask individuals to respond to a situation (a) as they would *like* to respond, (b) as they think they *should* or are *expected* to respond, and (c) as they actually *would* respond in real life. By distinguishing between these three levels of response choices, the situation might open up a discussion on response alternatives participants face in real life.

> ## CRITICAL INCIDENTS AWARENESS EXERCISE
>
> Participant Objectives:
> 1. To identify culturally appropriate responses to a situation;
> 2. To identify personally preferred responses to a situation; and
> 3. To examine the influence of cultural norms in responding to a situation.
>
> Learning Objective:
> Situations are defined by both personal and cultural considerations.

What You Said, Felt, and Meant in a Tape Recorder Exercise

We tend to confuse messages about what others actually said, what they felt while they were saying it, and what they meant or intended by a statement. Cultural differences tend to confuse communication messages even further. By

---

separating these three functions, we may be able better to analyze the messages we receive and be more articulate about the messages we send.

Organize participants into three-person groups with one person designated as a "speaker," the second person as a "tape recorder," and the third person as an "interpreter." Instruct the speaker to talk for *one minute* about him- or herself. The tape recorder will listen without taking notes and then repeat the introduction back as accurately as possible, without *adding* any new information or *omitting* any actual information. The interpreter will then draw conclusions about what the speaker said and why. No member is allowed to take notes during the interaction.

When each person has had a turn, the triad may discuss how accurately the speaker's message had been repeated and interpreted. After a brief discussion, the triad members rotate roles until each member has experienced each of the three roles. This exercise emphasizes the process of communication between culturally different persons.

TAPE RECORDER AWARENESS EXERCISE

Participant Objectives:
1. To attend accurately to the factual information being conveyed;
2. To articulate clearly the facts and inferences being conveyed; and
3. To interpret the meaning and feelings being conveyed.

Learning Objective:
Accurate articulation and attending rely on recognizing patterns in the information.

Implicit and Explicit Cultural Messages

There are explicit and implicit levels of communication across cultures. Participants are matched into culturally similar two-person teams where both members are likely to understand one another's point of view. Each team will contain one speaker and one "alter ego." The alter ego is instructed to say out loud what the speaker is thinking but not saying.

Two teams will work together to plan a script that contains two levels of the conversation between culturally different persons, one explicit and one implicit.

The four-person group will then present a role play to the larger group where two persons from culturally different backgrounds carry on a discussion while, after each statement, the alter ego for the speaker says out loud what the speaker is probably thinking but not saying directly. The exercise is useful for learning to interpret the mixed messages we send and receive in multicultural communication.

IMPLICIT AND EXPLICIT CULTURAL MESSAGES

Participant Objectives:
1. To express accurately what someone from a similar culture is thinking but not saying;
2. To interpret the implicit messages accurately; and
3. To incorporate both explicit and implicit messages in an appropriate response.

Learning Objective:
What someone says may be different from what he or she means.

Decision Making

Sometimes the decisions persons from another culture make do not seem logical to those outside that cultural context. Bring an articulate and authentic "resource person" into the training session from a particular culture. Ask the resource person to describe to the group one difficult decision he or she has had to make where the person's cultural values were an important factor. Ask the resource person *not* to disclose the *actual* decision that was made but to provide background material leading up to a final decision. When each participant has had a chance to ask questions and learn the appropriate background information, ask each group member to *predict* the resource person's actual decision and to provide the reason for making such a decision.

When all participants have completed their prediction and rationale, ask the resource person to disclose the actual decision and the *reason* for making it. The resource person's presentation could be prerecorded on videotape and used for many sessions. The objective of this exercise is to understand the decision alternatives from the resource person's cultural perspective rather than from each participant's own outside point of view.

DECISION-MAKING AWARENESS EXERCISE

Participant Objectives:
1. To articulate the logic leading up to decision making in another culture;
2. To identify the decision outcome by a culturally different person; and
3. To match culturally appropriate outcomes with logical decision-making processes.

Learning Objective:
What seems logical in one culture may not seem logical in other cultures.

Drawing Your Culture

Sometimes our verbal facility in describing our culture betrays us by abstracting the less rational and more emotional aspects of our cultural influences. By drawing the symbols that describe what our culture means, it is possible to escape from the preconceived format we usually use to describe our identity.

Divide the group into units of about three to five persons sitting in a circle. If possible, arrange for the group to sit around a table. Provide each individual with a sheet of paper that may be ordinary typing paper or newsprint, depending on the space available. Provide each individual also with a pen or pencil. If possible, provide participants with pens or pencils of different colors or felt tip markers if the paper is large enough.

Ask each individual to spend about 5 to 10 minutes drawing his or her culture. Participants may draw pictures of events in their lives that have influenced them in their culture. They may also draw symbols that are particularly meaningful in their culture. They may draw any combination of designs, doodles, or lines that have meaning to them in terms of their culture. They may *not*, however, draw or write any *words* on their paper.

At the end of the predetermined time limit, ask the participants to stop drawing. Then ask them to present their drawing, with explanations of what the symbols or drawings mean, to the other members of their small unit. Each member of the unit should be instructed to spend about the same amount of time, about 5 minutes, describing and explaining the drawing to their unit members so that each person has the same opportunity, and all units will complete their explanations at about the same time.

When all members of all units have completed their explanations to the other members of their unit, you may ask each unit to report back to the larger group on any particularly useful insights they discovered during the exercise. This exercise is useful for articulating some of the nonverbal, symbolic, or less rational aspects of our culture that are often difficult to describe in words.

DRAWING YOUR CULTURE

Participant Objectives:
1. To draw the figures or symbols important to their cultural identity;
2. To explain or express the figures or symbols they have drawn to other members of a small group; and
3. To listen and understand the figures or symbols other members of a small group have identified as important to their cultural identity.

Learning Objective:
   Our cultural identity contains nonverbal, nonrational, and symbolic elements that are difficult to express using language.

These brief examples have been used in a variety of multicultural training programs to motivate participants toward knowledge and skill development. The exercises each depend on an appropriate training context where the purpose of the exercise is followed up by the trainer. By creating an appropriate context, the trainer may facilitate learning indirectly as the participants exchange ideas with one another. Sometimes the unintended outcomes of meaningful interactions may be more important than anticipated, and frequently the "surprises" that come up during training provide the most exciting opportunities to a skilled trainer. Exercises are not a substitute for skill in training, and these suggestions are offered in the hope that they may supplement the trainer's own detailed planning of a carefully prepared program.

3. Conclusion

We might assume that we direct more accidental or unintended communication toward people from other cultures than toward persons from our own culture. Persons who share the same cultural background are in a better position to interpret what is said and what is not said in the terms intended by the sender, whereas persons from another culture may grossly misinterpret a simple gesture, expression, or implied attitude owing to a different cultural viewpoint. Hints, clues, understatements, and appropriate omissions are some of the more subtle tools of communication that present barriers to multicultural communication.

Although we are not able to eliminate all accidental communication without seriously reducing the spontaneity of normal communication, accidental messages are likely to complicate and frustrate communication when they become excessive. As a measure of multicultural awareness we might establish the goal that accidental communication be no more frequently directed to culturally different persons than to culturally similar persons. Through training, we are likely to become more aware of accidental communications among persons from *our own* culture as well and learn to communicate more accurately, meaningfully, and intentionally.

Unfortunately, there is seldom any opportunity to confirm whether the message sent and message received fit with one another. More often two persons assume they know what the other is saying without feeling any need to check their interpretation. As the sender and receiver become more familiar with one another's culture, they are more likely to be in control of their communication. The goal is to facilitate feedback skills that minimize accidental and maximize intentional communication among persons from different cultures, thereby reducing barriers of communication.

CHAPTER 3

Culturally Biased Assumptions and Their Reasonable Opposites

It is high time that we recognize Western cultural biases in our conventional thinking as having little to do with geography and a great deal to do with social, economic, and political perceptions. Just as there are many "Western" thinkers in non-Western parts of the world, there are also many "non-Western" thinkers in the Western hemisphere. In strictly numerical terms, it is increasingly true that the 'Western" viewpoint is the more "exotic." Despite that numerical reality, the social scientists—including psychologists—depend on textbooks, research findings, and implicit psychological theory based almost entirely on Euro-American, culture-specific assumptions. These assumptions are usually so implicit and taken for granted that they are not challenged even by fair-thinking, right-minded colleagues. The consequences of these unexamined assumptions are institutionalized racism, ageism, sexism, and other examples of cultural bias.

1. Culturally Biased Assumptions

This chapter is an attempt to identify 10 of the most frequently encountered examples of cultural bias that keep coming up in the literature on multicultural counseling and development. The examination of culturally learned assumptions must become a more important part of the curriculum in the development of counselors for a multicultural world.

The *first* such assumption is that we all share a single measure of "normal" behavior. There is a frequent assumption that describing a person's behavior as "normal" reflects a judgment both meaningful and representative of a particular pattern of behaviors. There is an implicit assumption that the definition of normal is more or less universal across social, cultural, and economic or political backgrounds.

Behavior considered normal will change according to the situation, the cultural background of a person or persons judged, and the time period during which a behavior is displayed or observed. Many psychological research projects are based on backgrounds that may have influenced the definition of normality. Our own personal complex but not chaotic patterns describe our own personal cultural orientation.

A *second* assumption is that "individuals" are the basic building blocks of society. The presumption is that counseling is primarily directed toward the development of individuals rather than units of individuals or groups such as the family, the organization, or society. If we examine the jargon used in counseling, our preference for the welfare of individuals becomes quickly evident. The criteria of self-awareness, self-fulfillment, and self-discovery are important measures of success in most counseling. The constructs of person in personality, of individuality in measuring achievement and aptitude, and of separation from the group in developing abilities all presume that a counselor's task is to change the individual in a positive direction even, perhaps, at the expense of the group in which that individual has a role. In some cases, the welfare of an individual counselor is seen to be frustrated by the conflicting agenda of a group in which the counselor is a member.

While teaching English as a second language in Indonesia, I was asked why English speakers always capitalize the first person singular ("I") in writing English. I confessed that, because I was no expert in ESL (English as a second language), I really had no idea why the letter "I" was capitalized when referring to the first person singular. The students smiled at me and said knowingly that they already knew why. It was, they assumed, because English speakers are so thoroughly individualistic that the capitalization of first person singular comes naturally.

In Chinese culture it would be normal and natural to put the welfare of the family before the welfare of any individual member of that family. To speak of an individual's health and welfare independently of the health and welfare of the family unit would not make sense in that context. Individual counseling has even been described as destructive of society in promoting the individualistic benefits of individuals at the expense of the social fabric. It is important for counselors to work comfortably and skillfully in both those cultures where the primary emphasis is on the welfare of the individual and in those cultures that emphasize the value of the unit.

A *third* assumption is that problems are defined by a framework limited by academic discipline boundaries. There is a tendency to separate the identity of counselor from that of psychologist, sociologist, anthropologist, theologian, or medical doctor. Unfortunately, the problems a client faces are not inhibited by any of our artificial boundaries. The research literature in our various disciplines frequently overlaps with questions in one area unmatched by answers suggested by a complementary discipline. Wrenn (1985; 1962) spoke of cultural encapsulation owing to the substitution of symbiotic stereotypes for the real world that disregard cultural variations among clients and dogmatize a technique-oriented job definition of the counseling process.

In many cultures, for example, the really important questions related to mental health relate to questions of life (or before life) and death (or after death). If a client believes in reincarnation then which person are we considering? The person(s) they were, are, or will become may each be a legitimate focus of a conversation if, indeed, it is possible to separate these identities at all! Once again, it is important for counselors to become skilled in going beyond the boundaries of their own "self-reference criteria" to examine the problem or issue from the client's cultural perspective. Kleinman (1978, 1980) described how frequently a medical doctor may take the limited "disease" perspective in dealing with a patient as a "malfunctioning unit" whereas the patient is more likely to take the broadly defined "illness" perspective where a particular problem has a systems-wide impact on the patient's family, friends, and total surrounding context. The self-imposed boundaries we place on our description of counseling are themselves culturally learned and must be relearned as we move from one culture to another.

A *fourth* assumption, based on our dependence on abstract words, is that others will understand our abstractions in the same way as we intend. Concepts such as "good" or "bad" have little meaning without putting the concept in a contextual setting for many, if not most, of the world's population. Because the dominant culture in our century has tended to be a low-context culture, there is a dependence on abstract concepts such as "fairness" or "humane" that, outside of a particular context, are difficult to understand.

Although low-context abstractions are useful shortcuts in conveying an idea, they may foster misunderstandings and inaccuracies in high-context cultures.

A *fifth* assumption is that independence is desirable and dependence is undesirable. As part of our emphasis on individualism there is a belief that an individual should not be dependent on others nor should the individual allow others to be dependent on them. If we encounter "excessive" dependence in a counselee, a counselor is likely to see the elimination of that dependence as a desirable outcome of counseling. Yet there are many cultures where dependence is described as not only healthy but absolutely necessary. One example would be the Japanese concept of "*amae*." Doi (1974) described the Japanese concept of *amae* as technically referring to the relationship between a mother and her eldest son. While the son is young and dependent he is being prepared for the time when his mother will be old and dependent. Significantly, this concept of *amae* is widely used as the criterion for evaluating relationships between employer and employee, teacher and student, or many other relationships in society where dependence is considered a healthy and normal aspect of relationships.

The counselor needs to consider a client's cultural perspective in determining the extent to which dependence might or might not be excessive. Because most counselors have been trained in a cultural context where dependence is devalued, it is even more important to consider the function dependence might have in the client's cultural context.

A *sixth* assumption is that clients are helped more by formal counseling than by their natural support systems. Counselors need to endorse the potential effectiveness of family and peer support to a client. What happens more frequently is that counselors erode the natural support systems by substituting the "purchase of friendship" through professional counseling services in formal contexts. In many cultures the notion of formal counseling is less preferred than nonformal or informal alternatives available to a client. The idea of telling intimate family secrets to a stranger is not allowed in many if not most of the world's cultures. These problems are dealt with inside the family or group context with little or no outside involvement. Wherever possible the natural support systems surrounding a client should be mobilized as a valuable ally rather than as an assumed rival for the client's attention. If a client has to choose between the support system and the counselor, there is a strong likelihood that the client will choose the support system. Those natural support systems can be identified and mobilized in a counseling context.

The health of the individual is tied in many ways to the health of the support unit surrounding that individual. The counselor needs to include consideration of a client's natural support system in an effective treatment plan for counseling.

A *seventh* assumption is that everyone depends on linear thinking to understand the world around them, where each cause has an effect and each effect is tied to a cause. This sort of linear thinking is most evident in the dependence on measures. The use of measures for describing the goodness, badness, appropriateness, or inappropriateness of a construct is an almost unquestioned necessity for good counseling. Tests in counseling require these measures, and any evaluation of counseling tends to be stated in measured degrees. How then can we adapt counseling to a culture context where the cause and the effect are seen as two aspects of the same undifferentiated reality (as in Yin and Yang) with neither cause nor effect being separate from the other?

Counseling has frequently erred in assuming that if a test, book, or concept is accurately translated in terms of its content, the translated tool will be effective and appropriate for most cultures. Not all persons from all cultures are socialized to think in the same way. Consequently, it is important to change not just the content of a message for counseling but also the way of thinking underlying the message. Whereas we spend a lot of time making sure that the content of our message is culturally appropriate, we spend less time adapting the underlying way of thinking behind the translated message.

The *eighth* assumption is that counselors need to change individuals to fit the system and not the system to fit the individual. We need to recognize when counseling should change the system to fit the individual in a more activistic mode rather than always try to change the individual to fit the system. In many minority groups, counseling as a source of help has a bad reputation for taking the side of the *status quo* in forcing individuals to adjust or adapt to the institutions of society.

It is important for counselors to differentiate between the best interests of the client and those of the surrounding social institutions. Frequently the counselor assumes that it is much more difficult to change the social institutions than to help the individual adapt to conditions "as they are." Counselors who do not at least ask the question about whether the best interests of the client are being served by existing social institutions—and whether those institutions can be changed at least in small ways—are failing in professional obligations.

A *ninth* assumption is that history is not too relevant for a proper understanding of contemporary events. Counselors are more likely to focus on the immediate events that created a crisis. If clients begin talking about their own history or the history of their "people," the counselor is likely to "turn off" and wait for the client to "catch up" to current events, which are held to have greater salience than past history. The client's perspective might require historical background knowledge a client feels is relevant to the complete description of the client's problem from the client's point of view. In many cultures, a clear understanding of the historical context to understand present behavior is necessary.

We are a young profession in a young country in comparison to other nations and professions of the world. We lack a sufficient awareness of the ways in which people solved their psychological problems in the last thousands of years. We lack the patience for a longer perspective in which the current situation may be transitional. We are perceived to lack a respect for traditional time-tested ways in which a particular culture has dealt with personal problems in preference for the latest trend or fad in counseling.

The *tenth* and last assumption to consider is that we already know all of our assumptions. In an era of diminishing resources we need to recognize the dangers of a closed, biased, and culturally encapsulated system that promotes domination by an elitist group representing a special point of view. If we are unwilling or unable to challenge our assumptions, we will be less likely to communicate effectively with persons from other cultures.

Multicultural counseling is an attempt to integrate and coordinate our assumptions with contrasting assumptions of other persons from different cultures. In this way, culture complicates our lives as counselors, but it brings us closer to culturally defined reality.

All counseling is to a greater or lesser extent multicultural. As we increase our contact with other countries and other cultures we can expect to learn a great deal about ourselves. We can expect to challenge more of our unexamined assumptions about ourselves and the world about us. We can expect to move beyond the parochial concerns of our culturally limited perspective to look at the world around us in a new, more comprehensive perspective. The primary argument for multicultural awareness in counseling has less to do with the ethical imperative of how we should relate to others and more to do with the accuracy and effectiveness of counseling as an international professional activity.

2. Test of Reasonable Opposites

We are moving toward a culture of the future that promises to be so different from our present lives that we hardly can imagine what it will be like. Furthermore, those who cannot adapt to that future culture will not survive. We are left with the alternative of learning adaptive skills through contact with cultures whose assumptions are different from our own. The means for learning those adaptive skills are contact with different cultures, developing new ways of thinking, and challenging our unexamined assumptions.

Rothenberg's (1983) creativity research on the "janusian process" type of cognition involves actively conceiving two or more opposites or antitheses at the same time. In the janusian process, ideas or images are clarified and defined by opposite or antithetical concepts coexisting simultaneously. Janusian thinking is not illogical but a conscious and adaptive cognitive process. Carl Jung emphasized the reconciliation of opposites in self much in the same mode as Asian followers of Zen or the Tao tried to capture truth in a dialectical process. In science, the janusian process has been documented as important to the creative achievements of Einstein, Bohr, Watson, Darwin, Pasteur, and Fermi (Rothenberg, 1983, p. 938). Albert Einstein, for example, described the following as his "happiest thought," the key idea leading to his general theory of relativity: that a man falling from the roof of a house is both in motion and at rest simultaneously (Rothenberg, 1979).

Most of our educational emphasis is spent examining the rational and reasonable process of a viewpoint. I suggest we reexamine the starting point assumptions that determine the trajectory of those viewpoints. Many viewpoints, however similar, disagree because they have different starting points and make divergent assumptions. Looking at reasonable opposites will enlarge our repertoire of adaptive skills. A "test of reasonable opposites" provides a means of testing those basic assumptions that frequently escape examination in our educational system.

The application of this test begins by identifying a basic but unexamined truth, such as the 10 assumptions discussed earlier, and the assumption(s) behind that truth statement. Second, it asks what the alternative policy positions are that would reverse those assumptions and provide a policy based on opposite or contrary assumptions. Finally, it compares the two statements and their assumptions to determine which alternative is more reasonable. In a surprisingly large number of instances the opposite assumption seems at least as reasonable and sometimes even more so than the original assumption. In applying the test of reasonable opposites I have found (a) that our thinking is usually so ambiguous that it is difficult to identify the opposite of what we say is true, (b) that once an opposite truth statement has been generated, it is often as reasonable as what you originally accepted, and (c) that the generation of reasonable opposites results in new and creative alternatives that otherwise might not have been discovered.

The reasonable opposite provides a stimulating alternative to unexamined assumptions. Two people can disagree without one being right and the other being wrong, providing they begin with different assumptions. There is an urgency for us to distinguish between multicultural disagreements (e.g., where the assumptions are different) and interpersonal conflict (e.g., where the assumptions are similar). By challenging our assumptions we can develop adaptive skills for working with a wider range of different persons, and we can learn more about our own environment from other viewpoints. In the course of our social and professional evolution these adaptive skills are likely to be very important.

As an example, let us consider the assumption that a more complete "understanding" between two individuals will contribute to their communication whereas "misunderstanding" is likely to damage the relationship. The reasonable opposite would be that a more complete understanding will be damaging whereas misunderstanding might contribute to a more healthy relationship.

Pearce (1983) contended that a complete understanding is not only irrelevant and unexciting in a relationship but may even be dangerous. The alternative is a kind of creative ambiguity that can deepen friendships, save marriages, improve businesses, and prevent wars; this alternative has 35 supporting studies to its credit. The theory of "coordinated management of meaning," or C.M.M., boils down to this: How a listener interprets a speaker's remarks and acts upon the interpretation is more important than whether the two understand each other. In short, good things *can* happen when there is misunderstanding among people, businesses, or nations.

The originator of C.M.M., Dr. W. Barnett Pearce, offered one example of the theory's potential. "Just a few weeks before he died Brezhnev made a speech in which he said he was increasing the military budget. The United States responded by saying this represented increased Soviet threats to the West. What the U.S. could have said was this was a speech given by an ailing leader for domestic consumption as a way of consolidating his power. Wouldn't that have initiated a somewhat different sequence of actions?'' (Pearce, 1983, p. 2).

Pearce favors interpretation over understanding. People are getting along well despite and sometimes because of misunderstandings. If nations really understood one another accurately, there might be more war and turmoil than there is now! Relationships can *sometimes* thrive on misunderstandings. More understanding will not *necessarily* result in more harmony.

3. Alternative Constructs of Complexity and Balance

Perhaps one reason that research on human behavior has not made more progress with regard to the special needs of culturally different populations is that the constructs underlying our research assumptions are inadequate or influenced by cultural bias. This section explores the appropriateness of two constructs, complexity and balance, as alternatives to, if not opposites of, the 10 culturally biased assumptions discussed previously.

Complexity

Complexity is our friend and not our enemy because it protects us from our own reductionistic assumptions. This process is most apparent in our use of scientific theories.

In attempting to understand complexity we develop simplified models that can be explained and understood but that reflect only selected aspects of reality. Our imbedded rationality requires that we construct simplified models of complex reality in order to deal with it. If we behave rationally with regard to the model, we assume the behavior is appropriately generalized to the real world. The danger is that we confuse labels with reality. We have little tolerance for the confusion of aggregate, mixed-up, unsorted, undifferentiated, unpredictable, and random data. We move quickly to sort, order, and predict emerging patterns from the chaos.

Rather than resort to the "digital model" where alternatives are sorted in either/or categories with discrete criteria, the more complex analog or family resemblance alternative is preferred. The analog approach describes natural categories through prototypes of the same "family" within a continuum of increasing or decreasing similarity of membership (Rosch, 1975). The clearest metaphor to this phenomenon is color membership where each color represents a prototype surrounded by colors of decreasing similarity. The analogy makes boundary judgments difficult because of a "fuzzy" characteristic in family membership, but it allows variation both within and between categories without rigidly imposing judgments of correct or incorrect evaluation.

By perceiving the world from a narrow frame of reference we ignore the complex reality around us in the illusion of simplicity. Alternatively, the principle of complementarity (Bohr, 1950) suggests that many phenomena can be understood only from a variety of different perspectives. Theories of cognitive complexity suggest that people who are more cognitively complex are more capable than others of seeing these multiple perspectives. Research in adult development likewise suggests that cognitive complexity is related to broader and more advanced levels of development.

Bohr used the principle of complementarity to prove that sometimes light may be regarded as a particle and sometimes as a wave, so that both quantum and wave theories are necessary to explain the "real" nature of light. The principle has likewise proved itself useful in gastroenterology, exclesiology, literary criticism, the philosophy of science, organizational behavior, economics, and political science. Some persons are able to use complexity better than others: These people are either better at differentiation—perceiving several dimensions in a range of alternatives—or integration—seing complex connections between different sources.

People who are more complex are able to see many different dimensions, classifications, theories, or alternatives to explain a situation. Because reality tends to be complex, those who are able to identify more alternatives are more likely to see correctly and make more appropriate decisions, although this process requires a high tolerance for ambiguity. In *The Crack Up*, Scott Fitzgerald's essay about his own midlife crisis, he suggests that the test of a first-rate intelligence is the ability to hold two opposed ideas in the mind at the same time and still retain the ability to function.

Balance

We need to change not just the content of what we are thinking, but also the way and process by which we handle that content if we are to account for complexity in education and human behavior.

In many non-Westernized systems there is less emphasis on separating the person from the presenting problem than in Western cultures. There is less tendency to locate the problem inside the isolated individual but rather to relate that individual's difficulty to other persons or even to the cosmos. Balance describes a condition of order and dynamic design in a context where all elements, pain *as well as* pleasure, serve a useful and necessary function. The non-Western emphasis is typically more holistic in acknowledging the interaction of persons and environments in both their positive and negative aspects.

Success is achieved indirectly as a by-product of harmonious two-directional balance rather than a more simplistic one-directional alternative. In a one-directional approach my goal is to make people feel more pleasure, less pain; more happiness and less sadness; more positive and less negative. In the two-directional alternative my goal is to help people find meaning in *both* pleasure and pain; *both* happiness and sadness; *both* negative and positive experience. In the Judeo-Christian tradition God not only tolerates the devil's presence but actually created demonic as well as angelic forces in a balance of alternatives.

The restoration of value balance provides an alternative goal to the more individualized goal of *solving* social problems. In the context of value balance, social change is perceived as a continuous and not episodic process, taking place independently both because of and despite our attempts to control that change. Value balance is a process rather than a conclusive event or events. In a similar mode, the problems, pain, and other negative aspects of education provide necessary resources for creating a dynamic value balance.

4. Conclusion

There are numerous implications for counseling and education in the accommodation of complexity in our analysis of information. First of all, simple explanations of reductionism are temptingly convenient but dangerous approaches to understanding the real world around us. The educator is guilty of reductionism when assuming that all persons from a particular group or culture have *exactly* the same needs and behaviors, substituting symbiotic stereotypes for the real world of the unique individual before them. Reductionism ignores cultural variations among clients from the same culture. The measure of educational competence is not merely identifying the many cultures, groups, or identities to which we each belong, but being able to track which of those identities is salient at any given point in time from the client's viewpoint. The competent educator will avoid reductionism in counseling.

Second, complexity is our friend and not our enemy in the search for the fuzzy, approximate, and indeterminate truths of reality. Every student is looking for easy answers and the "magic bullet" to cure all problems. Teachers usually help students simplify their understanding of problems and solutions. Sometimes that simplification results in distorting reality. If a teacher can accept the necessity and even the potential usefulness of helping a student accept and even understand problems in more complicated—but perhaps more culturally authentic—terms, then the positive value of complicated thinking may become apparent.

Third, only those who are able to escape being caught up in the web of their own assumptions and maintain a balanced perspective will be able to communicate with other cultures. The dangers of cultural encapsulation and the dogma of increasingly technique-oriented definitions of the educational process have frequently been mentioned in the rhetoric of professional associations for counselors and criteria for accreditation of educational programs. In order to escape from encapsulation, counselor educators need to challenge the cultural bias of their own untested assumptions. This may be done by looking at the reasonable opposite conclusions where dependence may (under some conditions) be good and individualism bad, for example. To leave our assumptions untested or, worse yet, to be unaware of our culturally learned assumptions is not consistent with the standards of good professional counseling.

Until we learn to ask the right questions, we will never discover the right answers, and until we have the right answers, we will never know the right actions required of us.

PART TWO

Knowledge of Multicultural Information

Knowledge, based on awareness of underlying assumptions, is the beginning of understanding. The three chapters in part 2 are intended to provide information and facts about developing a multicultural awareness.

In chapter 4 it is shown that in studying the development of a person's multicultural identity, it is important to consider the range of cultural labels and terms used to describe alternative identities. Culture shock occurs when your familiar system of identities is disrupted and unfamiliar identities are imposed on you. The imposition of labels by outsiders is a familiar experience to minority group members and affects the development of identity in predictable ways. The synthesis of several different models to describe the range of cultural identities underlines the importance of culture as a complex and dynamic phenomenon.

Although some of the major research on multicultural counseling is included in chapter 5, other research sources are needed for a more comprehensive treatment of the many issues raised. It is useful to organize the research literature into different perspectives beginning with the minority perspective, where most of the research has been done. The international perspective provides a global context for issues that are less clear but no less important within each country's setting. The theoretical perspective identifies focal issues for understanding past research and guiding future research on multicultural development. The therapist perspective, together with the client perspective, provides a context of contrasting viewpoints on multicultural counseling. This is especially true when the counselor is typically from the dominant culture and the client typically from a minority group.

The need for multicultural counseling is explained from a historical perspective in chapter 6. First of all it is important to document the extent of inequity in the representation of culturally different groups within the counseling profession. In order to understand how this disparity came about, it is important to review the range of social events that have given rise to cultural differences during the last several decades. It is also necessary to review the demographic and social explanations of cultural differences that have been used to justify inequity. A dependence on simplistic explanations has led to cultural encapsulation, justified by a long series of popular but unproven arguments favoring inequity. A more complicated explanation is needed if counselor education and training are to develop a multicultural awareness.

CHAPTER 4

Developing a Multicultural Identity

Multicultural training is a developmental process that we already have described as moving from awareness through knowledge to skill. Multicultural training is not limited to exotic populations but applies to the rich variety of cultures that have contributed to each of our individual identities. Tapp (1980) provides the most comprehensive description of personality development in a multicultural context. As we become more aware of how ethnographic, demographic, status, and affiliation variables have systematically influenced us, we become aware more intentionally of our own multicultural identity. Models have been invented for developing an intentional awareness of multicultural identity through cultural labels, in the "culture shock" literature for contact with other countries, in the "ethnic minority awareness" literature, and in the "social systems" literature that looks at a synthesis of the categories defining culture. Findings at all four levels apply to developing a multicultural identity.

1. Cultural Labels

The alternative to developing a multicultural identity is what White (1984) described as "Euro-American ethnocentricity." This is a dualistic perspective that polarizes good and bad or superior and inferior, idealizes the role of individuals rather than families or collectives, and defines power in terms of special interest groups in socio-political-economic terms. Liberation movements for women, minorities, the handicapped, the aged, and other special populations in the 1960s and 1970s began to establish the importance of a multicultural identity. In addition each special population also has begun to develop its own separate identity criteria as a separate cultural group. White (1984) developed a seven-dimension psychology of Blackness. Jones and Korchin (1982) described research about how psychology is understood in the third world, with Khatib and Nobles (1977) describing African peoples, Tong (1971) describing the Chinese, and Martinez (1977) describing the LaRaza psychology of Hispanics and others. McGoldrick, Pearce, and Giordano (1982) have led the field of mental health to include White ethnics as a culturally defined group also. Terry Soo-Hoo (1979) classifies the development of culturally relevant psychologies into a psychology for all third-world minorities, a psychology for each major ethnocultural group, and specific ethnic psychologies.

The differentiation of culturally defined groups in terms of their own separate identity (Black, Asian-American, Hispanic, Native American) and the increased awareness of each person's multicultural identity are further reflected in the range of psychological professional organizations with overlapping memberships. The importance of developing a multicultural identity is clearly documented in these socioeconomic and political trends of our times.

As a first step in developing a multicultural identity, it is therefore important to clarify how some of the most frequently used cultural terms might be used (Atkinson, Morton, & Sue, 1983).

The term *race* or *racial* has been used to differentiate groups even though it more accurately refers to biological differences of physical characteristics or genetic origin that might differentiate one group of people from another. We have generally recognized differences between Caucasoid, Mongoloid, and Negroid races, which satisfies the biological requirements of differentiation and genetic relationships but does not justify or explain differences in social behavior where similar patterns cut randomly across racial lines.

The term *ethnic* is derived from the social or cultural heritage a group shares that relates to customs, language, religion, and habits passed on from one generation to the next. Jews, for example, are not appropriately described as a race but would more appropriately be an ethnic group.

The term *culture* is again different, where members of the same racial or the same ethnic group might still be culturally different from one another. There are perhaps thousands of definitions of *culture* in the literature, but generally they agree that it is a shared pattern of learned behavior that is transmitted to others in the group. Not only may different ethnic groups in a single racial group have different cultures, but within a single ethnic group there may also be different cultures.

A fairly recent controversy is whether age, life style, socioeconomic status, sex role, and other such affiliations should be referred to as "culturally" different from one another. On the one hand these groups fit many if not most of the definitions of culture, but on the other hand they detract from the precision of culture as a concept. The development of value typologies where culturally different groups can be identified according to their "subjective culture" suggests patterns of values that are or are not shared with one another. The concept of subjective culture has given an appropriately flexible measure for the degree of cultural similarity in contrast to a polarized "us or them" division of insiders from outsiders.

Within each individual there is still another level of analysis that differentiates members of the same culture. Each individual has to cope with culturally different roles, particularly when visiting a foreign culture. We can cope with our conflicting cultural roles (a) because we rank them in terms of the importance of each role for our own identity, (b) because most identities apply only in certain contexts and are constantly changing, and (c) because these rankings and identities themselves are constantly changing. The roles we value most highly define our "primary" identities, which we have either learned since childhood or been converted to as adults. All interpersonal role relationships are therefore, to some extent, multicultural (Brislin & Pedersen, 1976).

In the relationships between cultures, one group will often tend to dominate the other. A variety of terms such as *culturally deprived* or *culturally disadvantaged* have emerged to identify the less dominant culture, or *minority* group. In usage at least, these terms have tended to take on a pejorative meaning that is frequently offensive to the less powerful or more exploited group. More neutral terms such as *culturally different* or *culturally separate* have been used to avoid the offensive connotations, but these terms also have been less than totally satisfactory. The political implications of the unequal distribution of power among groups of people have tended to confuse our descriptions of how culturally different groups relate to one another. In our contact with cultural groups other than our own, it is important to be aware of the political as well as the social implications of our presence.

On a global scale the phenomenon of nationalism and the rediscovery of indigenous values present a full range of possibilities in defining identity through social relationships. Within each social group we see differentiation into clusters of shared identity whose members become increasingly dependent on one another while asserting their independence from other clusters. As we get more complex in defining the many people of different cultures, we encounter a variety of ways that cultural diversity is accommodated in different social systems. The visitor to a foreign culture will need to recognize the various ways a host culture accommodates culturally different persons—both to understand multicultural differences in the host culture and to understand his or her role as a stranger in that culture.

Alternative cultures are often described in patronizing stereotypes as irrelevant or dangerous. Culturally encapsulated individuals are able to evade alternative realities through creating an artificial world around themselves. *Isolation* requires cultivation of insensitivity to cultural variations among individuals and loyalty to a singular unchanging notion of truth. Different cultural values are excluded, and the world is typically divided into polarized categories of political confrontation.

Those who are brought up to depend on one authority, one theory, and one truth become trapped in their way of thinking, believing that theirs is the universal and the only way. They become trapped in an inflexible structure that resists adaptation to alternatives. They are unable to see the world as others see it, trapped by the boundaries of their own parochial belief system.

Pluralism refers to groups that share a similar cultural identity across groups, with each group having its own rich and poor, powerful and weak, old and young. Pluralism is the preferred mode for developing a multicultural identity. We may best look at pluralism by contrast with the other alternatives. *Assimilation* would be less desirable in a culture that tolerates a wide range of differences among its peoples. *Integration* in a pluralistic society occurs through a series of shifting alliances on a more equal rather than an unequal basis. *Isolation* in a pluralistic society would be dangerous and likely to result in conflict between cultural groups for limited resources through a series of internal conflicts.

Research on the "contact hypothesis" suggests how different cultural groups can relate to one another successfully in a pluralistic society by creating "favorable" conditions for multicultural contact and avoiding "unfavorable" conditions (Amir, 1969; Miller & Brewer, 1984). Favorable conditions that tend to reduce intergroup conflict exist when: (a) there is equal-status contact between members, (b) the contact is between members of a majority group and the higher-status members of a minority, (c) the social climate promotes favorable contact, (d) the contact is intimate rather than casual, (e) the contact is pleasant or rewarding, and (f) the members of both groups interact in functionally important activities developing shared goals.

Unfavorable conditions that increase the likelihood of intergroup conflict occur when: (a) contact produces competition, (b) contact is unpleasant and involuntary, (c) one's group's prestige is lowered as a result of the contact, (d) frustrations lead to scapegoating, and (e) moral or ethical standards are violated.

Intergroup contact typically doesn't occur under favorable conditions but is much more likely to occur under unfavorable conditions, resulting in conflict between cultural groups. It is important to examine the conditions of intergroup contact and to provide favorable conditions to promote a multicultural identity. Pluralism provides the most promising context for equitable multicultural development. It is considered in this book as the preferred mode that presents fewer barriers than do other alternatives.

2. Culture Shock

We have discussed the barriers to multicultural identity as abstractions, but they also are evident in individual cases. The multicultural barrier most familiar to someone entering a new culture is called "culture shock." Kalvero Oberg described culture shock as the anxiety resulting from losing one's sense of when to do what and how. When familiar cues are removed and strange or unfamiliar cues are substituted, as might happen to a visitor in a foreign culture, our response is likely to range from a vague sense of discomfort, until we have learned the new expectations, to a profound disorientation that requires a complete reorganization of our lives. Any new situation such as a new job, new friends, new ideas, and new neighborhood will involve some adjustment of role and change of identity. Consequently each of us already has experienced an adjustment similar to culture shock. Culture shock generally refers to those adjustments related to entering a new social system where the cultural values are "foreign" to the person's previous background and experience.

There are many positive aspects in learning to adjust to other cultures through culture shock. All learning involves change and movement from one frame of reference to another. Culture shock is that learning opportunity related to exploring a new cultural landscape. The individual goes through a highly personal experience of special significance that results in learning new, previously unfamiliar self-identities. Change is provocative. The individual is forced into sometimes painful self-examination and introspection, with the consequence of frustration, anxiety, and personal pain. The individual is confronted with new relationships as an outsider looking in. The individual learns to try out new tentative attitudes through trial and error until the right responses are discovered. As a result, however, the individual has learned about self, about the home culture, and also about new identities in the host culture. By comparing the familiar and the unfamiliar the individual learns to grow toward multicultural perspectives and develop alternative futures from which to choose. The very frustrations lead to self-understanding and personal development. The related phenomena of role shock, culture fatigue, and future shock likewise present the same opportunities and difficulties to each individual experimenting with new ideas.

The process of culture shock goes through a series of stages. Peter Adler (1975) summarized the descriptions of these stages into: (a) initial contact; (b) disintegration of the old familiar cues; (c) reintegration of new cues; (d) gradual autonomy; and finally (e) independence. Each stage is described in terms of its perceptions, emotional ranges, behaviors, and interpretations. It is important to recognize that culture shock does not progress neatly and in an orderly manner from one stage to another. Sometimes the experience of culture shock is delayed far beyond the actual multicultural contact itself, whereas in other situations the process may be compressed into a very short period.

Thomas Coffman (Coffman & Harris, 1978) described culture shock as having six identifying features: cue problems, value discrepancies, an emotional core, a set of typical symptoms, adjustment mechanisms, and a pattern of emergence over time.

When the cues or messages we receive in another culture are confusing, it is usually because familiar cues we've learned to depend on are missing, important cues are there but not recognized as important, or the same cue has a different meaning in the new culture. Much of the problem in culture shock involves learning to deal with new cues.

Familiar values define the meaning of good, desirable, beautiful, and valuable. Each culture values its own behaviors, attitudes, and ideas. Although the visitor does not need to discard familiar values, it is necessary to recognize alternative value systems in order to adapt to a new cutlural system.

Culture shock has an emotional core and produces a heightened emotional awareness of the new and unfamiliar surroundings whether as a sudden "shock" or as a gradual "fatigue" that occurs over a period of time. The emotional effect of this experience may include anxiety, depression, or even hostility ranging from mild uneasiness to the "white furies" of unreasonable and uncontrolled rage.

The specific symptoms of culture shock focus either on dissatisfaction with the host country or idealization of the home country. The host culture is criticized as being peculiar, irrational, inefficient, and unfriendly. The visitor is likely to fear being taken advantage of, being laughed at or talked about, and not being accepted, and wants to spend more time around people from his or her home culture. The visitor might develop a glazed, vacant, or absentminded look nicknamed the "tropical stare," or withdraw for long periods by sleeping or being otherwise inactive. Minor annoyances in the host culture become exaggerated, and the few remaining links with the home culture, such as mail from home, become extraordinarily important.

Strategies for adjustment that worked in the home culture might not work for the visitor in a new host culture, so that the visitor needs to spend a greater amount of energy in making adjustments and learning new strategies. Direct confrontation and openness might facilitate adjustment in the home culture, but may further complicate the problems in the host culture. Defensive strategies might range from hostile stereotyping and scapegoating of the host culture to "going native" and rejecting the visitor's own home culture.

Culture shock is likely to last—to a greater or lesser extent—over the visitor's entire stay in foreign cultures, reappear in a variety of forms, and not be limited to an initial adjustment. As familiar cues are replaced by unfamiliar cues the visitor experiences a genuine identity crisis, requiring either that the former identity be disowned or that multiple identities for each of the several cultures encountered be created and maintained. In either case, the visitor is required to reintegrate, confront, and challenge the basic underlying assumptions of his or her personality.

Coffman goes on to make suggestions for visitors experiencing or anticipating culture shock. *First*, the visitor needs to recognize that transition problems are usual and normal in the stress of adjusting to a strange new setting. The visitor can be helped to recognize, understand, and accept the effects of adjustments in the context of a host culture support system.

Second, the maintenance of personal integrity and self-esteem becomes a primary goal. The visitor often experiences a loss of status in the new culture where the language, customs, and procedures are strange or unfamiliar. The visitor will need reassurance and support to maintain a healthy self-image.

Third, time must be allowed for the adjustment to take place without pressure or urgency. Persons adjust at their own rate, and recognize that their reconciliation with the host culture, although painful, will enhance their future effectiveness.

Fourth, recognizing the patterns of adjustment will help the visitor make progress in developing new skills and insights. Depression and a sense of failure will be recognized as a stage of the adjustment process and not as a permanent feature of the new experience.

Fifth, labeling the symptoms of culture shock will help the visitor interpret emotional responses to stress in adjustment.

Sixth, being well adjusted at home does not ensure an easy adjustment in a foreign culture. In some cases visitors may find it easy to adjust to a foreign culture. In extreme cases of maladjustment visitors are more likely to carry their ''back home'' problems with them into the new culture. With existing methods it is difficult to predict a hard or easy adjustment for most individuals.

Seventh, although culture shock cannot be prevented, preparation for transition can ease the stress of adjustment. Preparation might include language study, learning about the host culture, simulating situations to be encountered, and spending time with nationals from the host culture. In all instances the development of a support system is essential to helping the visitor reconstruct an appropriate identity or role in the new culture.

In reviewing the literature about culture shock, the recurring theme in the opportunities for learning its presence, the process or stages of adjustment, the identifying features, and suggestions for minimizing its negative effects is a subjective reevaluation of individual identity. The key to understanding and controlling the effect of culture shock lies within the visitor rather than in the manipulation of the environment.

Ruben and Kealey (1970) found that in at least some cases sojourners from the Canadian International Development Agency who had undergone intensive culture shock during transition abroad were utltimately more productive than those who had experienced little or no culture shock. Perhaps those who are most aware of their own subjective perception experience more shock. For whatever reason, culture shock teaches lessons that perhaps cannot be learned in any other way, and in that respect culture shock contributes to developing a multicultural identity. Considerable research has been done on international adjustment, but thus far there are few widely accepted guidelines.

3. Minority Identity Models

Traditional development theories apply less accurately to minority groups than to the dominant culture. On the other hand we do not yet have enough data to measure development accurately in the great variety of minority group populations. The early development of typologies for describing categories of adaptation of Black Americans (Vontress, 1981), Asian-Americans (Sue & Sue, 1972), and Hispanics (Szapocznik & Kurtines, 1980) and of other stage development models (Cross, 1971) emphasizes a range of alternative developmental theories.

Helms (1985) characterized stage development models as putting the responsibility for adaptation on the minority individual rather than society, which thereby tends to blame the victim. Also, these models all emphasize an ideal of bicultural identity. Most models incorporate a lower stage where minority group members dislike their own cultural group. As Helms points out, the classification systems do not account for the adaptation process of change, and the stage models assume that identity will develop in a linear and continuous process. Helms's (1985) five assumptions about minority development models summarized the extensive literature on development of an identity by minority peoples. These five assumptions seem to pervade the literature on developing a minority identity.

1. Minority groups develop modal personality patterns in response to White racism.
2. Some styles of identity resolution are healthier than others.
3. Cultural identity development involves shifts in attitudes involving cognitive, affective, and conative components.
4. Styles of identity resolution are distinguishable and can be assessed.
5. Intracultural and intercultural interactions are influenced by the manner of cultural identification of the participants. (p.241)

Most stage development models suggest that individuals experience three to five phases or stages of cultural identification. First, there is an identification with the dominant culture in a pre-encounter, conformity, or traditional stage; second, an awakening to the impact of racism in a transitional encounter or dissonant stage; third, an identification with one's own ethnic group; and fourth, an internalization and integration of both cultures.

Helms (1984) has been a leader in researching the various minority identity models. In her own cognitive development model, she traces the development of racial consciousness from historical and sociocultural information, through skill building and cognitive and affective self-awareness, and finally to cultural emersion. Helms's model is both complex and interactive. It applies both to within-group and across-group development.

Of all models related to minorities, the Minority Identity Development Model (MIDA) is the most widely cited. This model, presented by Atkinson, Morten, and Sue (1983) describes development in five stages.

1. Conformity stage: preference for values of the dominant culture to those of their own culture group;
2. Dissonance stage: confusion and conflict toward dominant cultural system and their own group's cultural system;
3. Resistance and immersion stage: active rejection of dominant society and acceptance of their own cultural group's traditions and customs;
4. Introspection stage: questioning the value of both minority culture and dominant culture;
5. Synergetic articulation and awareness stage: developing a cultural identity that selects elements from both the dominant and minority cultural group values.

The Minority Identity Development Model (see Table 1) provides additional detail on the stages and the changing attitudes during development. Sue (1981) adapted the MIDA to the study of internal/external locus of control and locus of responsibility. Helms (1984) and Parham and Helms (1981) suggested that counselors must be particularly aware of their own stage of multicultural development and respect their clients' stages as well. Parham and Helms (1981) found that Black students in the pre-encounter stage preferred White counselors whereas those in the other three stages of their paradigm had varying degrees of preference for a Black counselor.

4. Multicultural Syntheses

Contrasting cultural dimensions separate groups of individuals from one another. We can look at those differences on three levels:

- the international level;

TABLE 1
Summary of Minority Identity Development Model

Stages of minority development model	Attitude toward self	Attitude toward others of the same minority	Attitude toward others of a different minority	Attitude toward dominant group
Stage 1: Conformity	self-depreciating	group depreciating	discriminatory	group appreciating
Stage 2: Dissonance	conflict between self-depreciating and appreciating	conflict between group depreciating and group appreciating	conflict between dominant-held views of minority hierarchy and feelings of shared experience	conflict between group appreciating and group depreciating
Stage 3: Resistance and immersion	self-appreciating	group appreciating	conflict between feelings of empathy for other minority experiences and feelings of culture centrism	group depreciating
Stage 4: Introspection	concern with basis of self-appreciation	concern with nature of unequivocal appreciation	concern with ethnocentric basis for judging others	concern with the basis of group depreciation
Stage 5: Synergetic articulation and awareness	self-appreciating	group appreciating	group appreciating	selective appreciation

Note: From *Counseling American Minorities: A Cross-Cultural Perspective* (2nd ed., p. 198) by D.R. Atkinson, G. Morten, and D.W. Sue, 1983, Dubuque, IA: Brown. Copyright by Wm. Brown Publishers. Adapted by permission.

- the ethnic level; and
- the social role level.

At the *international level*, cultural factors such as country and its role in world affairs, national allegiance, language, and upbringing serve to separate people from one another. At the *ethnic level*, ethnic background separates groups often within the same country. Groups labeled as Blacks, Chicanos, Native Americans, Asian-Americans, and "White ethnics" are distinct from one another as well as from a loosely defined dominant American culture. At the third level of *social role*, groups or individuals such as administrators, housewives, hardhats, or club members may define themselves as sharing the same culturally subjective viewpoint.

Several contrasting approaches synthesize cultural value systems across the three levels. The two approaches described in this chapter are the Kluckhohn-Strodtbeck model and the Cultural Grid model. Both attempt to describe a balance of cultural values in relationship to one another. Each approach begins with different assumptions, thus providing a different approach to increased awareness and knowledge.

The Kluckhohn-Strodtbeck value orientations approach builds on a more traditional perspective of culture than does the Cultural Grid. Many of the more traditional applications of culture in social science research are based on this perspective. The difficulty with the traditional perspective is that cultures are often more complicated than the traditional perspective seems to imply. Cultural variables are like traits or dispositions that are characterized by constancy even though they may seem to vary from time to time, place to place, and person to person. For example, an individual with a generally kind disposition may act unkindly. The same variability holds true for people who share the same cultural values and priorities. Rather than mirroring one another, they may behave differently while maintaining the same general cultural disposition. The clearly defined cultural categories found in more traditional perspectives tend to bend the data to fit a more or less rigid framework of standard typologies for a convenient definition of culture.

The second approach, the Cultural Grid, defines culture as comparatively more complicated and dynamic. Culture is broadly defined by boundaries that include the social system variables introduced in chapter 1: demographic (age, sex, place of residence), status (social, educational, economic), and affiliation (formal and informal), in addition to the more typical ethnographic categories (nationality, ethnicity, language, and religion). In the Cultural Grid approach, culture is also dynamic in that the emphasis or salience of each cultural variable relative to other variables continuously will shift from one situation to another, becoming more or less important in terms of the person's cultural identity. In the framework of the Cultural Grid, culture is described more as an interaction of personal and cultural variables that are constantly changing. This approach will be explained in greater detail later in this chapter (Pedersen & Pedersen, 1985).

The Kluckhohn-Strodtbeck Model

In order to understand a pluralistic society, it is necessary to recognize value orientations that describe each different system of cultural affiliation. The system of value orientations described by Kluckhohn and Strodtbeck (1961) is perhaps the most frequently studied attempt to organize diverse values into a comprehensive structure. In terms of the values these orientations represent, Kohls (1979) interpreted the Kluckhohn-Strodtbeck Model as shown in Figure 5.

As illustrated in Figure 5, it is possible to see a horizontal dimension where the characterizations disclose contrasting value orientations and alternatives. The differentiated value orientations demonstrate the complexity of cultural differences. Values influence or determine behaviors, and the potential for conflict between these different value orientations as they compete with one another is significant.

The Kluckhohn-Strodtbeck Model, and Kohls's interpretation of it, suppose that each person makes assumptions about human nature with a predisposition in a positive or negative direction. A cultural system may socialize its members to be trusting or suspicious, and this predisposition is probably reflected in the attitudes, opinions, and assumptions of people from that culture. Although this stereotype would not be true for all members of that culture in all situations, there would be a disposition toward one direction or another for each individual.

Similarly, the model takes for granted that each person makes assumptions about the relationship of people and nature from the extreme of internal to the alternative external locus of control. Aggregate research data suggest that some groups or cultures tend to score higher or lower than others on locus of control measures. Each group is likely to reward different behaviors among its members, with some groups rewarding a more fatalistic or accepting viewpoint, others a more activistic and proactive perspective, and still others a harmony between people and nature in which neither is clearly in control of the other.

Cultures frequently emphasize time in varying degrees. Some cultures emphasize their history and tradition, others emphasize the immediate present, and still others focus on the distant future. In some cultures, it is appropriate to be casual about time scheduling, and being late for an appointment is accepted. In other cultures, an exact time schedule is required and being late for an appointment is not accepted.

Attitudes toward activity will also differ from one group to another. In some cultures a person's worth is described by task accomplishment whereas is others

FIGURE 5

Kohls's Interpretation of the Kluckhohn-Strodtbeck Model

ORIENTATION		RANGE	
HUMAN NATURE	Most people can't be trusted	There are both evil people and good people, and you have to check people out to find out which they are.	Most people are basically pretty good at heart.
PERSON-NATURE RELATIONSHIP	Life is largely determined by external forces, such as God, fate, or genetics. A person can't surpass the conditions life has set.	People should, in every way, live in complete harmony with nature.	Our challenge is to conquer and control nature. Everything from air conditioning to cloning new cells has resulted from having met this challenge.
TIME SENSE	People should learn from history and attempt to emulate the glorious ages of the past.	The present moment is everything. Let's make the most of it. Don't worry about tomorrow; enjoy today.	Planning and goal-setting make it possible for people to accomplish miracles. A little sacrifice today will bring a better tomorrow.

continued

FIGURE 5 continued
Kohls's Interpretation of the Kluckholm-Strodtbeck Model

ACTIVITY	It's enough to just "be." It's not necessary to accomplish great things in life to feel your life has been worthwhile.	The main purpose for having been placed on this earth is for our own inner development.	If people work hard and apply themselves fully, their efforts will be rewarded.
SOCIAL RELATIONS	Some people are born to lead others. There are "leaders" and there are "followers" in this world.	Whenever I have a serious problem, I like to get the advice of my family or close friends in how best to solve it.	All people should have equal rights. And all should have complete control over their own destiny.

Note: From *Survival Kit for Overseas Living* (pp. 84–85), by L.R. Kohls, 1979, Chicago: Intercultural Network, SYSTRAN. Copyright 1979 by Intercultural Press. Adapted by permission.

people are not evaluated in terms of what they do. A frequently quoted English language expression is: "If you don't know what to do, at least *do* something." An equivalent common Chinese expression is: "If you don't know what to do, at least *don't do* anything." A task-oriented person is likely to be uncomfortable in a culture that values relationship building before task accomplishment.

Finally, under the Kluckhohn-Strodtbeck Model, attitudes toward social relations likewise are assumed to be different from one group to another. The power structure in hierarchical cultures is authoritarian—from the role of the father in a family to the role of a ruler in the state. In other cultures, equality is emphasized and each individual group member is allotted equal power. In a third alternative, the group as a unit is expected to manage power and control its own members.

The Cultural Grid

The second approach to describing cultural systems introduced in this chapter, the Cultural Grid, is quite different from the Kluckhohn and Strodtbeck Model in that it combines individual or personal features with social system or collective variables in describing a *personal-cultural orientation.* This approach is based on the premise that culture is within the person and not within the group. Pedersen and Pedersen (1985) developed the Cultural Grid to help identify and describe the cultural aspects of a situation, to help form hypotheses about cultural differences, and to explain how to train people for culturally appropriate interactions. The Cultural Grid is an open-ended model that matches social system variables with patterns of behavior, expectation, and value in a personal-cultural orientation to each event (Pedersen & Pedersen).

The Cultural Grid provides a means of describing and understanding a person's behavior in the light of learned expectations and values. This more complicated approach to culture takes a broad and comprehensive perspective of culture beyond the traditional limits of fixed categories or dimensions. Although complicated, the Cultural Grid actually makes it easier to separate cultural from personal variables by identifying patterns of similarities and differences in the attributions or expectations attached to an action or behavior.

The three by four categories of the Cultural Grid, as shown in Figure 6, assume that culture is so dynamic and complex that it changes even for each individual from one situation to another. Rather than describe a person's "culture" in the abstract, it seeks to identify an individual's personal-cultural orientation in a particular situation through attention to his or her behavior and its meaning.

A multicultural identity is *complex* (incorporating a great many cultures at the same time) and *dynamic* (in that only a few cultures are salient at any one point in time). The Cultural Grid presents a synthesis of the personal and social system variables that contribute to a multicultural identity. The Cultural Grid also pro-

FIGURE 6
The Cultural Grid

SOCIAL SYSTEM VARIABLES	BEHAVIOR	EXPECTATION	VALUE
ETHNOGRAPHIC nationality ethnicity religion language other _____			
DEMOGRAPHIC sex age residence other _____			
STATUS socioeconomic educational political other _____			
AFFILIATION formal informal			

vides guidelines for integrating your own multicultural identity with the identity of others through managing culturally learned behaviors and expectations.

The Cultural Grid is based on the notion that culture is "within the person." The Grid provides a framework for integrating the cognitive variables of behavior, expectations, and value with the social system variables that have shaped the cultural identity for a single individual. The elements of the Cultural Grid are also useful for understanding the relationship between two or more individuals. The following examples will demonstrate applications of the Cultural Grid to the relationship of two or more persons.

A person's behavior by itself does not communicate a clear message or intention. Only when that behavior is analyzed within a context of the person's salient social system variables will the person's intended message become clear. The context is best described by what is called "expectation." Expectation is a cognitive variable that includes behavior-outcome and stimulus-outcome expectancies and guides an individual's choices. The social system variables are essential to both persons in a relationship for understanding one another's anticipated outcome. The skill of extrapolating expectations from social system variables improves with practice.

After having examined your own and the other person's most salient social system variables, it should be possible for you to identify both your own and the other person's expectations or anticipated outcome such as "friendliness," "trust," or "harmony." By applying the Cultural Grid to relationships, it is possible to understand and modify each person's behavior so that an appropriate step is taken toward a mutually valuable anticipated outcome.

Every counseling relationship contains a multicultural perspective to a greater or lesser extent. The Cultural Grid serves to:

- classify cultural perspectives in a complex yet dynamic framework without reducing culture to static and fixed dimensions;
- differentiate between personal and cultural perspectives in an event;
- link culturally learned behaviors with the culturally learned expectations and values behind those behaviors; and
- link culturally learned behaviors, expectations, and values with the appropriate social system contexts in which those responses were learned.

Behaviors do not reveal the learned expectation, or consequence, or meaning that is intended through that behavior. Similar behaviors may have different meanings and different behaviors may have the same meaning. It is important to interpret behaviors accurately in terms of the intended expectations, consequences, and meanings attached to those behaviors. If two people are accurate in their interpretation of one another's behavior, they do not always need to agree. The two people may agree to disagree and work together in harmony nonetheless. The pressing question is: "How can you tell if your interpretation or attribution is correct?" The Cultural Grid attempts to answer that question by examining relationships with the same or different behaviors and the same or different expectations. These four types of relationships provide a framework for analysis.

Type I relationships: Two people have similar behaviors and similar expectations. There is a high level of accuracy in both people's interpretations of one another's behavior. Communication theory describes this as an example of an ideal relationship.

Type II relationships: Two people have different behaviors but share the same expectations. There is a high level of agreement that the two people both intend and expect to be trusting and friendly, but there is a low level of accuracy because each person perceives and interprets the other person's behavior incorrectly and inaccurately. This type illustrates the most common example of multicultural conflict. If there were a high level of accuracy, the relationship might change to a Type I relationship.

Type III relationships: Two people have the same behaviors but differ greatly in their expectations. There is actually a low level of agreement between the two people. One person is trusting and friendly whereas the other is distrusting and unfriendly. Both people are presenting the same smiling, glad-handling behaviors, however. If both eventually can assess accurately the other's real expectation, the relationship may change to a Type II relationship as each person adjusts expectations. If there is a low level of accuracy in assessing the other's expectation, however, the relationship is likely to result in personal conflict.

Type IV relationships: Two people have different behaviors and different expectations. The two people do not agree in their interpretation or expectation of each other. If there also is a low level of accuracy in their interpretations of one another's action, this relationship will result in hostile disengagement. If both people eventually become more accurate in their assessment of one another, they may modify their expectations or behaviors accordingly and move to a different type of relationship.

Smiling is an ambiguous behavior. It may imply trust and friendliness or it may not. The smile may be interpreted accurately or it may not. Outside of its learned context the smile has no fixed meaning. The example of smiling provides a means to apply the four types of interaction to distinguish among ideal, multicultural, personal, and hostile alternatives.

Now, let us consider how the Cultural Grid describes two alternative sequences of events between an employer and employee over a 5-week period. In the first example, the importance of expectation behind each behavior is *not* considered. You can see the relationship disintegrate as the participants move toward increasingly hostile perspectives. In the second example, the importance of expectation behind each behavior *is* considered. You can see that the participants have maintained the relationship between the more workable Type I and Type II perspectives.

EXAMPLE 1:

A young employee is having difficulty working with his older employer from a different country, but neither is skilled in attending to the other's cultural identity.

First week

- The employer and employee behave quite differently, with the employee being friendly and informal whereas the employer is formal and professionally cool toward others. The different behaviors suggest at face value that the employer and employee have different expectations for what constitutes "appropriate" behavior. However, in this case both intend friendliness. (Type II)

Second Week

- The differences between this employer and employee have continued to persist and have now become a source of irritation and conflict between them. As the different behavior patterns persist, both people may well conclude that they do not share the same expectations for efficiency or effectiveness in the work place or perhaps even for liking one another as persons. (Type III or Type IV)

Third Week

- The employee considered modifying his behavior to become more formal because he needed the job, but he felt like he was being dishonest in compromising his own ideals. The employer considered modifying his behavior to become less formal because he needed the employee, but he felt like that would not be fair to his other employees nor to his concept of how the office should be run. One or the other partner may compromise his beliefs and change his behavior to fit the other's, but even if their behaviors become similar, their expectations for *why* they are behaving as they are will become even more divergent. Compromise by either person would be likely to result in personal as well as professional dislike and animosity. (Type III)

Fourth Week

- Both the employer and employee finally give up, saying they have tried everything humanly possible to make the situation work. As a result, the employee either leaves or is fired. This total conflict situation occurs when both behaviors and expectations are now so totally different that there is little motivation to work toward harmony. (Type IV)

Fifth Week

- Both employer and employee conclude that there is a low level of agreement between them. Neither person is aware that there is also a low level of *accuracy* in his communication with the other. (Type IV)

EXAMPLE 2:

In an alternative scenario, the young employee is having difficulty working with his older employer from a different country but both are skilled in attending to cultural variables of interaction.

First Week

- Although the employer and employee behave quite differently, they examine the reason or expectation for each other's behavior from the other person's viewpoint. The different behaviors are understood as different expressions of the same shared expectation for excellence. (Type II)

Second Week

- Because both the employer and employee share the same expectation, they are able to interpret one another's behavior accurately and focus on the expectation they both share rather than on their differences. (Type II)

Third Week

- Because they have the same expectations, the employer and employee may modify their behaviors toward the other without feeling they are compromising their principles. They may also agree to disagree and maintain their contrasting behavior style, now that they know what the other's behavior means. (Type II or Type I)

Fourth Week

- Both partners are likely to move toward a more harmonious situation where the similarity of expectations results in more similar behaviors, with both employer and employee modifying their behaviors somewhat to fit the other. Ultimately, both expectations and behaviors are likely to become more similar and harmonious. (Type II or Type I)

Fifth Week

- By examining the cultural expectations and values behind each other's behavior, both employer and employee are now able accurately to assess the other's intention. At this point, it will be easier to decide if the two people are similar enough in their behaviors and expectations to work together or to tolerate the other's different behavior. (Type II or Type I)

The open-ended range of personal and social system categories indicated by the Cultural Grid provides a conceptual road map for the counselor or interviewer to interpret a person's behavior accurately in the context of learned expectations. For example, a counselor might be interviewing a Black, teen-aged, wealthy, highly educated student on a personal problem. The student refers back to each of these indicated social system variables as salient to the problem during the half-hour interview. The counselor, however, is so fixated on the fact that the student is in a wheelchair and is paraplegic that the counselor treats the student's handicap as the single most salient aspect of the student's culture during the whole interview. The actual problem had little or nothing to do with the student's handicap and the counselor's assessment was inaccurate.

The introduction of a personal-cultural orientation construct provides the means to resolve a dilemma in multicultural counseling. On the one hand, data suggest that patterns of both group and individual similarities and differences must be accounted for in multicultural contact. On the other hand, attempts to describe patterns of similarities and differences through fixed dimensions or categories result in stereotyping. Although data about cultures may be predictive in the form of aggregate data about large groups that are more or less homogeneous, they are less predictive for individuals within those cultures (Atkinson, Staso, & Hosford, 1978). Evidently an accurate assessment of another person's personal-cultural orientation is complex and dynamic, and is important to counselors and interviewers.

The Cultural Grid is a useful tool for analyzing multicultural situations. It provides practical assistance in managing the complexity of culture. The Grid is also useful for analyzing case studies:

- The Cultural Grid provides a framework to portray a perspective that confirms the personal and cultural orientation for each situation.
- Personal-cultural orientations can be compared across time or people to demonstrate how the same behavior can be explained by different expectations or values in different cultural settings.
- The dynamic and changing priorities of social system variables are matched with personal-cognitive variables for each time and place.
- A comprehensive description of culture includes demographic, status, and affiliation as well as ethnographic cultural variables in the range of analysis.
- The close relationship between culturally learned behaviors and culturally different expectations or values behind similar behaviors is clearly distinguished.

We have introduced two different approaches for interpreting cultural systems. The Kluckhohn-Strodtbeck approach is the more conventional and traditional basis for defining culture. In an attempt to build on this conceptual and fixed-dimension perspective of culture, we considered an alternative approach in the Cultural Grid, which describes culture as complex and dynamic. When multicultural conflict is not appropriately understood and accounted for, it may quickly evolve into interpersonal conflict where differences in behavior produce differences in expectation and value also. The Cultural Grid suggests one framework for assessing the range of complex variables that determine behavior and reflect expectations or values in each event for each individual. By combining both the personal and systems aspects of a person's cultural identity in the Cultural Grid, it is possible to take "snapshots" of how a person's culture influences each behavior in specific rather than general ways.

The practical advantage of the Cultural Grid is that it increases a person's accurate assessment of another person's behavior in the context of that person's culture. Without reference to these expectations and values, we are unable to interpret accurately any behavior outside its cultural context.

The matching of cultural with personal data provides a framework for understanding how culture works both in the aggregate and in the individual instance. This understanding of culture will be an important foundation for developing basic multicultural skills in subsequent chapters.

The Cultural Grid may have a practical use in managing cultural differences. In each application the same series of steps for applying the Cultural Grid are followed:

Step 1: Identify the relevant social system variables (about 10 or 12) in the person or persons being considered;

Step 2: Identify the behaviors displayed or presented by the person or persons being considered;

Step 3: Identify the expectations that probably would be attached to the behavior for *each* of the social systems if that system were salient;

Step 4: Identify the social system variable that is most likely to be salient for the person or persons being considered at the time the behavior was displayed; and

Step 5: Explore the possibility that the expectation for the most likely salient social system variable is the interpretation intended by the person or persons.

Usually there are many different expectations attached to each behavior. If you begin by emphasizing those expectations that are shared by two persons, you are more likely to move toward a Type I (ideal) or Type II (multicultural) relationship with a higher potential for harmony and positive outcomes.

5. Conclusion

If culture is indeed within the person, then developing a multicultural identity becomes as essential part of personal development. We need to go beyond the obvious labels used to describe individual and collective cultural identities. We need to recognize the principles of culture shock in all processes of adapting our identity to each new context. We need to understand the process of developing an identity as a minority group member as a complex but not chaotic series of stages or categories. Finally, we need to see our multicultural identity as a synthesis of the many cultures in our lives. This synthesis is both complex and dynamic, shaping both our expectations and our behaviors.

As we continue to develop our multicultural awareness, knowledge, and skill, a clear and accurate perception of our own multicultural identity becomes an essential element. Our ability to shape and influence our environment, bring about desired changes, and find harmony with others depends on knowing ourselves and our cultures. The next few chapters will present knowledge and information toward building a growing awareness of our own multicultural identity.

CHAPTER 5

Research on Multicultural Counseling

By viewing counseling and therapy in their multicultural context, several points will become apparent: (a) These functions have spread rapidly to a complex social industry on a worldwide basis; (b) Counseling and therapy as we know them are labels for one of the many alternatives for intervention to influence a person's mental health; (c) Counseling and therapy as the *preferred* alternatives are based on assumptions generic to a very small portion of the world's people; and (d) A multiculturally appropriate application in counseling and therapy is necessarily responsive to the social context (Pedersen, 1985; Lefley & Pedersen, 1986).

The historical spread of counseling and therapy has been documented in a wide range of cultures. Although mental health problems and solutions are continuous, the labels have changed from one culture to another over time. Support services and problems have been around for a long time. What has changed has been the complex classification of the environments where counseling and therapy are being applied, and the categories of problems, illness, difficulty, or crisis. A specialized therapeutic industry has developed to meet this need. The number of consumers as well as the number of providers is rising in proportion to the increasingly liberal definition of "appropriate" criteria for entering counseling and therapy (Triandis, 1985; Favazza & Oman, 1977). Although the labels of counseling might be new, the functions of how help is provided are probably not new. Torrey (1986) makes a strong case that therapy provided by witch doctors and psychiatrists uses the same techniques.

Multicultural counseling and therapy in the domestic context have been characterized by the political and economic interaction of special interest and minority groups throughout the country. The domestic context of multicultural relations has been characterized by political influence and socioeconomic impact. The basis of dissatisfaction, ironically, was written into the practically unfulfilled idealistic promises of the Declaration of Independence. As a nation we have experienced a social revolution that has idealized a state of equality among races, sexes, generations, and peoples. We have been taught that only those who make use of their opportunities and develop special skills can be assured of their fair share. The concept of equality is thereby diluted to a doctrine of equal opportunity, granting us the equal right to become unequal—as perceived by the minorities—through competing with one another (Dreikurs, 1972). Bryne (1977) pointed out how the perception of equality has politicized the delivery of mental health services in our domestic social context. Aubrey (1977) likewise pointed out the trend in mental health to emphasize normal developmental concerns of individuals to the exclusion of a special group's concerns in the name of "equality."

With the civil rights movement of the 1950s, the militancy of minorities for change gained momentum. With the growth of the community mental health movement of the 1960s, mental health care became the right of all citizens and not just the wealthy or middle-class dominant majority (LeVine & Padilla, 1980; Atkinson et al., 1983). The issues of feminism and popular dissent nurtured by the anti-Vietnam War movement fostered a climate of discontent where protest was accepted and in some cases even demanded. The stigma of discrimination became synonymous with any attempt to treat groups differently. Sue (1981) suggested that minority groups may not be asking for equal treatment as much as for equal access and opportunity. Differential treatment is not necessarily discriminatory or preferential. Multiculturally skilled counseling is almost necessarily and inevitably differential across cultures in providing an appropriate mental health service. In response to the same problem, a therapist may help one client be more dependent and another be less dependent, depending on the context.

1. The Minority Perspective

The "contact hypothesis" tests the assumption that just bringing people from different groups together will result in more positive intergroup relations. Amir (1969), Miller and Brewer (1984), and others reviewed the literature from social psychology on the contract hypothesis and drew three basic conclusions. First, when groups come together under favorable conditions, the intergroup contact does indeed result in more positive relationships. Second, when groups come together under unfavorable conditions, the intergroup contact results in an increase of negative relationships and disharmony. Third, spontaneous intergroup contact is more likely to occur under unfavorable conditions than under favorable conditions. These unfavorable conditions are most easily illustrated in the relationships between dominant and minority groups. Atkinson et al. (1983) included the *condition of being oppressed* as an important defining characteristic of any minority group. This might be the case even when the group is not a numerical "minority" as in the literature about women as a minority group. The literature on minority relations therefore relects the struggle of each minority against a dominant majority group and also of some minority groups against other minority groups competing for limited resources.

More recently, Ibrahim and Kahn (1985) reported data on five values orientations to measure counselors' awareness of culturally different client value orientations. Sue (1977; 1978) likewise developed a world view paradigm based on locus of control and locus of responsibility. Helms's (1984) cognitive development model proposes that trainees develop a multicultural awareness by starting with historical and sociocultural information, then proceeding to skill-building, cognitive, and affective self-awareness, and finally to emersion in a contrasting culture. Carney and Kahn (1984) presented a developmental training model that suggests five stages of development. Other models include those of Arredondo-Dowd and Gonslaves (1980), Copeland (1983), McDavis and Parker (1977), and Sue (1973).

With increased publications on minority group counseling in the late 1960s and 1970s, a great deal of confusion has occurred in the use of terms like *race, ethnicity, culture*, and *minority* (Atkinson et al., 1983). The term *race* technically refers to biological differences, whereas *ethnicity* rightly refers to group classifications as was discussed earlier in chapter 2. People of the same ethnic group within the same race might still be culturally different. Other terms such as *culturally deprived* or *culturally disadvantaged*, and even the more modern *culturally different* and *culturally distinct*, were created to explain why a minority group is out of step with the majority population. Minorities, then, are groups of people singled out for unequal and different treatment and who regard themselves as objects of discrimination (Atkinson et al., 1983).

Abundant evidence came to light in the 1970s about how mental health services were being underutilized by minority groups and that behavior described as pathological in a minority culture such as individualistic assertiveness may be viewed as adaptive in a majority culture client (Wilson & Calhoon, 1974; Grier & Cobbs, 1968). Asian-Americans, Blacks, Chicanos, Native Americans, and members of other minority groups terminate counseling significantly earlier than do Anglo clients (Sue, 1977; Atkinson et al., 1983). In most of the literature, these examples of differentiation are credited to cultural barriers such as language barriers, class-bound values, and culture-bound attitudes that hinder the formation of good counseling relationships. To some extent these conditions certainly do exist and do result in a minority group's disillusionment with the professional field of mental health as a solution for social and individual coping. Casas (1984) suggested that minority clients have been ignored in the past because of (a) a blatant and irresponsible lack of interest in these groups by the dominant culture, (b) continued racism, bias, and prejudice against minorities, (c) an ethnocentric perspective by the dominant culture, and (d) counselors' preference to work with clients more like themselves.

There have been numerous efforts to compensate for inequitable practices in providing mental health services to minorities in culturally sensitive ways (Lonner & Sundberg, 1985). One example of such an effort is in the area of testing. There have been extensive studies of problems in the use of psychological tests with American minority clients, particularly mental intelligence tests across cultures. The development of *culture-free* and more recently *culture-fair* intelligence tests is included in the several attempts to measure intelligence across cultures (Brislin, Lonner, & Thorndike, 1973). Frijda and Jahoda (1966) pointed out that a culture-fair test would need to be either equally familiar or equally unfamiliar to persons from responding cultures—an impossible precondition. Tests are more widely accepted as inevitably biased, and in more recent multicultural research, the emphasis has been placed on accounting for cultural differences in the *interpretation* of test results that are sensitive to these inherent biases.

Another area where the reality of cultural bias is recognized is public policy statements that acknowledge the importance of mental health consumers' cultural environment. The National Institute of Mental Health (Fields, 1979), The American Psychological Association (Korman, 1974), the American Psychological Association Council of Representatives (APA, 1979), the American Psychiatric Association's Task Force on Ethnocentricity among Psychiatrists (Wintrob & Harvey, 1981), and the recent President's Commission on Mental Health (Fields) all have emphasized the ethical responsibility of counselors and therapists to know their clients' cultural values, and the public responsibility of professional organizations to meet the culturally different mental health needs within a pluralistic society.

This has resulted in *culturally sensitive* guidelines for accreditation of mental health training programs, special funding for research on cultural differences in mental health services, and the development of resources for collective pressure to make mental health services more responsive to cultural differences. The adjustment has not been trouble-free, however. Atkinson, Staso, and Hosford (1978) described problems in meeting federal standards for admitting minority applicants to counseling while maintaining a single admission standard on test scores and selection following the Bakke decision in California. Jaslow (1978) described some of the problems in the desegregation of schools and the difficulty in retraining school personnel, students, counselor educators, and communities in the skills for working in a racially mixed school.

Casas (1984) pointed out that professional and institutional apathy were clearly implicated in the low number of persons of ethnic or racial minorities studying or teaching counseling or therapy. Chapter 6 will document the disproportionately small number of minority persons in counseling. Most graduate schools preparing counselors, however, would be quick to defend their emphasis on affirmative action and their genuine interest in a culturally diverse student/faculty community. Unfortunately, far fewer schools are making a strong and concerted effort to recruit, admit, and retain ethnic or racial minority students (Atkinson & Wampold, 1981). The University of Michigan (Casas) is cited as having an excellent record for recruiting Hispanics by providing funds to recruit them to psychology. Columbia University recruits a large number of minority students by providing extensive remitted tuition for their education. Western Washington University and, until recently, Boston University managed training grants with well-funded stipends for graduate students studying multicultural counseling, many of whom were from minority groups. The University of California at Santa Barbara has an innovative admissions procedure that provides extra credit for graduate study to applicants with multicultural backgrounds (Atkinson, Staso, & Hosford, 1978).

The recommendations by the Education and Training Committee of APA's Division 17 are discussed in chapter 10. These recommendations provide widely quoted guidelines on what would be necessary to develop multicultural awareness in programs of counselor education. A more extensive discussion of the weaknesses in the field of counselor education is available in Casas (1984).

2. The International Perspective

Although culture as a concept is ancient, the systematic study of culture and psychopathology is a phenomenon of the 20th century. Initially the fields of psychoanalysis and anthropology were the focus of interest in studying culture and mental health, later expanding to include epidemiology and sociology and more recently the subspecialty of social psychiatry. The focus of study has shifted from the anthropological study of remote cultures to the cultural variations in modern pluralistic and complex societies.

Through the work of men like Kiev (1972), Prince (1976), Kleinman (1980), and Torrey (1986), the indigenous approaches to mental health in non-Western cultures began to be taken more seriously, replacing the "crazy shaman" notion of curiosity and fascination with indigenous healers' techniques, and sometimes even integrating them with other modern mental health services. Major cross-cultural studies of psychiatric evaluation and diagnosis (WHO, 1979) have resulted in a more careful assessment of culture beyond the exotic, dramatic, and more conspicuous manifestations (Draguns, 1980) to a "near-to-home" phenomenon of everyday life as well. Torrey (1986) went so far as to draw direct parallels between the techniques of witch doctors and psychiatrists in naming their treatment, identifying a cause, establishing rapport, developing client expectation for improvement, and demonstrating legitimacy. Kleinman (1980), among others, opposes any conclusion that would imply shamans and psychiatrists do the same thing and considers this identification an oversimplification that does "a profound disservice to both psychiatry and anthropology" (p. 99).

There is likewise more emphasis on what "developed cultures" can learn about providing mental health services from less-developed cultures. Prince (1976, 1980) demonstrated how the activity of all healers and healing institutions depends on endogenous self-righting mechanisms for healing to occur, rather than on exogenous experts. In non-Western cultures with fewer formal healing institutions, there is more dependence on endogenous self-righting mechanisms such as dreams, sleep or rest, altered states of consciousness, religious experience, or even psychotic reaction as healing resources. Some of the renewed interest in learning how these self-righting mechanisms work is because of their proven effectiveness is managing psychiatric disorders, the shortage and expense of modern psychiatric facilities, the high prestige of some endogenous approaches in their home cultures, and the evidence that modern treatment methods tend to be culture-bound and ineffective (Prince, 1980; Higginbotham, 1979a, 1979b).

Kleinman developed ethnomedical models from his work in China and other non-Western cultures that contrast with the biomedical models of modern medical treatment. Kleinman (1978) attacked the "discipline-bound compartmentalization" of medical research through ethnography, ethnoscience, epidemiology, and cultural systems analysis.

The cultural context does not tell us merely about the social and cultural environment of a particular local system of medicine but also about its specific cognitive, behavioral, and institutional structure and the cultural constructional principles (values and symbolic meanings) underlying and determining that structure (Kleinman, 1978, p. 415).

David Reynolds (1980) has adapted *Naikan, Morita,* and several other systems of traditional Japanese therapy to Western cultures as uniquely appropriate to mental illness in Western as well as Asian society. Although Reynolds is careful to acknowledge the unrealistic claims in much of the popular literature about meditation, Zen-related therapies, and other non-Western approaches, he demonstrates the value and adaptability of these therapies when appropriately presented. Many other non-Western derived therapies have gained popularity but frequently without documentation and careful standards of delivery (Pedersen, 1979).

As a consequence of being culturally relevant, phenomena are inevitably culturally perceived, so that even in psychobiological processes such as the perception of space and cognition there are cultural differences (Diaz-Guerrero, 1977; Marsella & Golden, 1980). These culturally specific characteristics challenge the universality of psychology, not its scientific character. There are alternative assumptions from our cultural perspectives not related to the ''American ideal'' (Sampson, 1977) or to the premises of the Protestant ethic (Rotenberg, 1974; Draguns, 1974) and the pervasive assumptions of individualism (Hsu, 1972; Pedersen, 1983a; Watts, 1963). It is increasingly clear that Western style mental health services are inappropriate, too expensive, too dependent on technology and are frequently destructive to the non-Western host setting. There are numerous assumptions, beginning with individualistic biases, that require us to look to non-Western alternatives (Pedersen, 1983b).

Watts and Herr (1976) discovered that societies that are prescriptive about individual talents being used for the state provide different counseling services than societies with less social control and more individual freedom of choice. Most international counseling theories are rooted in either psychological or sociological perspectives (Herr, 1985), with the psychological perspective emphasizing individual choice and the sociological perspective emphasizing the obligation.

Triandis (1985) separated countries that are more individualistic from those that are more collectivist in their social norms. Self-concept and self-esteem measures vary a great deal across different cultures, as do other cognitive structures and habits, as a result of an individualistic or collectivist orientation. In the same vein, in what Triandis (1985) called ''tight'' cultures, people have a greater aversion to uncertainty than do people in ''loose'' cultures, again according to prevailing social norms. Kleinberg (1985) discussed other social psychological aspects relevant to international counseling.

The international perspective puts the problems of developing a multicultural awareness in a world context. Many of the problems being researched across countries highlight parallel problems across ethnic or socially defined groups within each country as well. By studying international differences we can identify differences closer to home that otherwise might escape examination.

3. The Theoretical Perspective

There is no agreement on a theoretical or conceptual framework for matching therapy interventions with culturally complex personal problems to facilitate intercultural adjustment. In several recent comprehensive reviews of the literature, Marsella (1979), King (1978), and Strauss (1979) commented that there is no paradigm to focus the increasing research studies or to test the consistency of contradictory theories offered to explain the relationship of personality and culture. LeVine (1972) provided a useful classification for organizing the theories of culture and personality. First, *anticulture and personality* states that culture determines personality and that the individual has little influence on the culture. Second, *psychological reductionism* states that all human activity can be explained by studying individuals. Third, *personality as culture* equates personality dynamics with culture. Fourth, *personality mediation* assumes a chain reaction where culture creates an individual personality who in turn changes the culture. Fifth, the *"two systems" approach* avoids the question of whether culture or personality is more basic, but assumes a continuous and parallel interaction and compromise between the two.

Culture and mental health research has failed to develop grounded theory based on empirical data for several reasons. First, the emphasis has been on abnormal behavior across cultures isolated from the study of normal behavior across cultures (Katz & Sanborn, 1976). Second, only in the 1970s has a pan-cultural core emerged for the more serious categories of disturbance such as schizophrenia and affective psychoses, so that they are recognizable according to uniform symptoms across cultures even though tremendous cultural variations continue to exist (Draguns, 1980). Third, the complexity of research on therapy across cultural lines is difficult to manage beyond prequantificated stages (Draguns, 1981a, 1981b). Fourth, the research that is available has lacked an applied emphasis related to practical concerns of program development, service delivery, and techniques of treatment (Draguns, 1980). Fifth, there has been insufficient interdisciplinary collaboration from psychology, psychiatry, and anthropology among the more directly related disciplines, each approaching culture and mental health from different perspectives (Favazza & Oman, 1977). Sixth, the emphasis of research foci has been on the symptoms as a basic variable to the neglect of the interaction of persons, professions, institutions, and communities (Ivey, 1980b). Cultural differences introduce barriers to understanding in those very areas of interaction that are most crucial to the outcome of therapy through discrepancies between counselor and client experiences, beliefs, values, expectations, and goals. Multicultural counseling describes conditions that are most unfavorable for successful therapy (Lambert, 1981). It is no wonder therefore that there is disagreement concerning the theoretical criteria of interculturally skilled counseling.

4. The Therapist Perspective

Wrenn (1962, 1985) defined the "culturally encapsulated counselor" as one who has substituted stereotypes for the real world, disregards cultural variations among clients, and dogmatizes technique-oriented definitions of counseling and therapy. Counselors can become "addicted" to one system of cultural values, which results in the same disorientation and dependence as with any other addiction by analogy (Morrow, 1972). Pluralistic therapy then recognizes a client's culturally based beliefs, values, and behaviors and is sensitive to the client's cultural environment and network of interacting influences.

Sue (1978, 1981) suggested that culturally effective counselors have at least five characteristics. First, they recognize their own values and assumptions in contrast with alternative assumptions, with the ability to translate their own values and assumptions into action. Second, they are aware of genetic characteristics of counseling that cut across schools, classes, cultures, and any other contextual variables that influence the counseling process. Third, they understand the sociopolitical forces that influence the attitudes of culturally different minorities or otherwise oppressed groups. Fourth, they can share a client's world view without negating its legitimacy and without cultural oppression of their client's viewpoint. Fifth, they are truly eclectic in their own counseling style, generating a variety of skills from a wide range of theoretical orientations.

Tseng and Hsu (1980) discussed how therapy might compensate for culturally different features so that highly controlled and overregulated cultures might encourage therapies that provide a safety valve release for feelings and emotions, whereas underregulated or anomic cultures would encourage therapies with externalized social control at the expense of self-expression. There is a constant readjustment of the balance between interacting therapeutic and cultural variables. It is as though the individual were participating in a social game based on conventional rules that define boundaries between the individual and the cultural context. Watts (1961) defined the duty of the therapist as involving participants in a "counter game" that would restore a unifying perspective of ego and environment so that the person can be liberated in a balanced context.

To the extent that the therapist is distanced from the client, culture becomes a more significant barrier. Kleinman (1980) described the problems that result when the explanations of the clinician and the patient are in conflict. Kleinman characterized most clinicians as schooled in the biomedical paradigm to recognize and treat *disease* as the malfunction or maladaptative biological or psychological process. By contrast, the patient is more likely to experience *illness* as an interruption in his or her social and cultural network. Patients evaluate treatment as a "healing process" more than as a "cure outcome," recognizing that there are no clear beginnings or endings in the complex interaction of variables. The best a clinician can hope to do, therefore, is to help restore balance.

Draguns (1977) suggested several guidelines for adjusting therapy modes to fit the culture. The more complex the social and cognitive structure, the more a society will prefer hierarchy and ritual characterized by elaborate techniques for countering psychological distress. The stronger a society's beliefs are in the changeability of human nature and plasticity of social roles, the more it will favor therapy techniques as vehicles of change. Where attitudes toward psycho-

Research on Multicultural Counseling

logical disturbance reflect deep-seated prejudices about human nature, people are less tolerant and accepting of the mentally ill.

The therapist needs to form a facilitative relationship with culturally different clients so that, ideally, the client will experience being warmly received, deeply accepted, and fully understood (Lambert, 1981). To establish that relationship the client needs to perceive the counselor as a credible expert (well informed, capable, and intelligent) and trustworthy (Sue, 1981). The counselor needs to accommodate a wide range of therapist and client roles, integrating them with the client's world view without at the same time losing his or her own cultural integrity (Sue, 1977). These prerequisities incorporate a blend of the goals of helping through insight, self-actualization, behavior change, and immediacy with the appropriate process. A client may be exposed to appropriate process and appropriate goals, appropriate process and inappropriate goals, inappropriate process and appropriate goals, or inappropriate process and inappropriate goals (Ivey, 1981). Neimeyer and Gonzales (1983), in their archival study on counselor-client similarity and perceived effectiveness, found that White clients attributed change more to counseling than to other factors whereas non-White clients expressed lower levels of overall satisfaction with counseling.

Ultimately the counselor characteristics listed in the above paragraph result in rapport and empathy with and interest and appreciation of the client's culture. The counselor understands its special terms and language, and knows the client's community and the problems of living in a bicultural world (Sundberg, 1981a, 1981b). Given that therapists are recipients of the same amount of stereotyping and ethnocentrism as is the general public (Bloombaum, Yamamoto, & James, 1968; Korchin, 1980; Wampold, Casas, & Atkinson, 1981; Casas, 1984), our expectations for the multicultural therapist's effectiveness seem somewhat unrealistic. In his update of Harrison's (1975) findings that tended to support prejudices by White therapists, Atkinson (1983) found no conclusive evidence that minority clients are better served by minority counselors than by White counselors. Multicultural counselors frequently assume it is better for minorities to counsel other minorities because cultural barriers are so formidable. Vontress (1981) suggested that few counselors really want to change themselves. Most are products of a racist socialization, and this condition is not likely to change as a result of a few courses without the impact of affective confrontation such as that experienced through cultural immersion. Sometimes it would seem that the advancement of multicultural counseling implies the abandonment of counseling theory, therapy techniques, and our traditional understanding of a client's psychological processes when counseling techniques we have learned don't seem to work. Wohl (1981) criticized the "super-flexibility" and "elastic modifications" of sound principles of some multicultural counselors. Even before students acquire the fundamentals of counseling and therapy they are urged to abandon them in favor of some unorthodox method that is presumed to be multicultural. Patterson (1974, 1978) also argued that the proper approach is not to be "flexible" in modifying the method to fit the client's expectations and wishes, even though this is the most popular attitude among multicultural counselors, because it subverts the counseling goals of self-actualization.

5. The Client's Perspective

Atkinson (1984a, 1985b), Atkinson and Schein (1986), Abramowitz and Murray (1983), Harrison (1975) and Sattler (1977) reviewed the literature on the effects of race in psychotherapy. There is considerable controversy on the issue of whether counselors and clients ideally should be culturally similar. This area of research much too frequently has addressed distal factors and ignored proximal ones. Carkhuff and Pierce (1967) are frequently cited as providing evidence for the belief that counselors who are most different from their clients in ethnicity and social class or who are not of the same sex have the greatest difficulty effecting constructive changes. LeVine and Campbell (1972) likewise are cited as supporting evidence that groups who perceive themselves similarly are more likely to relate harmoniously. Mitchell (1970) suggested that most White counselors can't help Black clients because they are part of the clients' problem. Stanges and Riccio (1970) demonstrated that counselor trainees preferred clients of the same race and culture, and Harrison (1975) and Berman (1979) demonstrated that Black counselors preferred Black clients. Other factors, however, have tended to exaggerate the apparent importance of racial similarity and have resulted in contradictory research findings. Parloff, Waskow, & Wolfe (1978) concluded that cultural matching of counselors and clients is not clearly preferred. Other research also indicates lack of support for the preference for matching clients and counselors by culture. Some research (Gamboa, Tosi, & Riccio, 1976) has demonstrated special conditions where the clients actually preferred culturally different counselors. Atkinson (1983) cited 12 studies from a variety of ethnic groups that reported no client preferences for the race or ethnicity of the counselor. Sanchez and Atkinson (1983), and Parham and Helms (1981, 1985a, 1985b) reported that those subjects with the strongest commitment to their own ethnic group are more likely to prefer counselors from the same ethnic background.

Several issues are involved. First, as Peoples and Dell (1975) demonstrated, the preference for counseling style may be more important than racial match among Black and White clients, among Asian-Americans (Atkinson et al., 1983), and among lower-class clients as compared with middle-class clients (Aronson & Overall, 1966). Black counselors used more active expression skills and fewer attending skills than did White counselors. Muliozzi (1972) also indicated that

White counselors felt more genuine and empathic with White clients, although Black clients didn't see White counselors as less genuine in understanding. In other research (Ewing, 1974) Black students were shown to react more favorably to Black and to White counselors than did White students. Bryson and Cody (1973) indicated that Black counselors understood Black clients best, but that White counselors were more acceptable than Black counselors to *both* Black and White clients. The preference for skilled and competent White counselors by non-Whites might be explained by Acosta and Sheehan's (1976) finding that Mexican Americans and Anglos attributed more skill, understanding, and trust to Anglo professionals than to Mexican-American professionals.

It seems that variables such as more active intervention styles for positive change through counseling are more important than is racial similarity in building rapport (Atkinson, Maruyama, & Matsui, 1978; Peoples & Dell, 1975). Kinloch (1979) included physical, cultural, economic, and behavioral characteristics in his analysis of cultural difference because these characteristics function in ways similar to those of nationality and ethnicity. Erickson and Schultz (1982) formed a concept of ''comembership'' between client and counselor based on any shared interest, status, or characteristic. Comembership provided a basis for shared identity and solidarity that was stronger than ethnicity or nationality in predicting successful counseling outcomes. Hilliard (1986) criticized psychological research for not specifiying within-group differences of sex, socioeconomic status, and age in the study of ethnic groups.

Second, Korchin (1980) criticized the tendency to decide on an a priori basis that membership in one particular ethnic group, cultural group, or class relegates a client to less qualified therapists for shorter periods of time. Warheit, Holzer, and Areye (1975) and Ambrowitz and Dokecki (1977) identified socioeconomic status as the most powerful predictor of poor mental health conditions. Fierman (1965), Korchin (1980), and Gomes-Schwartz, Hadley, and Strupp (1978) attacked the assumption that therapy cannot be successful with lower socioeconomic groups. Lorion (1974) and Lorion and Parron (1985) provided a comprehensive review of other literature on the relationship between therapy and low economic status or poverty as a predictor of mental health. Lower-income persons are less likely to be in therapy, or are in therapy for shorter periods of time with symptoms similar to those of clients of other socioeconomic groups, even though those symptoms typically are described as more severe among lower-class clients. Lower-class clients are treated by less experienced staff and through less sophisticated modes of therapy.

Third, minortity clients may respond even with anger when confronted by a minority counselor (Jackson, 1973) either because they perceive the minority counselor to be associated with a majority-controlled institution, because they perceive majority counselors as more competent, or becuse they are jealous of the minority counselor who has "made it" (Atkinson, Maruyama, & Matsui 1978). The minority counselor may also prefer not to work with a minority client because of a tendency to either deny identification with to or overidentify with minority client problems, or because he or she views counseling minority clients as lower-status work (Gardner, 1971; Sattler, 1970; Calneck, 1970). Helms (1984) criticized the counselor-client racial/ethnic matching research for emphasizing the minority client and not the dominant-culture counselor. Casas (1984) criticized even more strongly research on whether minority clients should or should not be matched with minority counselors.

Fourth, a compromise solution might be to introduce two counselors, one similar and one dissimilar to the client's culture. Bolman (1968) advocated the approach of using two professionals, one from each culture, collaborating in crosscultural counseling with traditional healers from the minority culture as cocounselors. Weidman (1975) introduced the alternative notion of a "culture broker" as an intermediary between client and counselor for working with culturally different clients. Slack and Slack (1976) suggested another alternative—bringing in a client who already has effectively solved similar problems to work with chemically dependent clients. Mediators have been used in family therapy for problems of pathogenic coalitions (Satir, 1964), with the therapist and mediator mediating to change pathogenic relating styles. Zuk (1971) described counseling itself as a "go-between" process where the therapist mediates conflict between parties. In these various examples, the use of at least three persons in therapy provides an additional "cultural punch" (Opler, 1959) that may be uniquely suitable for working with some cultures. Trimble (1981) recommended that bringing in a third person frequently is suitable for working with Native American clients to help the client become more comfortable in therapy.

Fifth, when the counselor is indeed bilingual or bicultural, the process of counseling might itself become a process of mediation. Meadows (1968) went back to the early Greek notion of the counselor as a mediator between the client and a "superordinate world of powers and values." Mediation is not without its own unique problems. Miles (1976) pointed out how these "boundary spanning activities" of counselors can result in role ambiguity and role diffusion for either the counselor or the client, who are expected to coordinate the conflicting demands of multiple membership. To some extent the problems of Stonequist's (1937) "marginal person" apply to the role of a mediator. Mediation also presents opportunities. Ruiz and Casas (1981) described a bicultural counseling model for a blending of majority and minority cultural affiliations. This model was to help counselors become both more bilingual and bicultural in response to their clients' needs. Berry (1975) suggested that bicultural individuals have a higher potential to function with cognitive flexibility and are more creatively adaptive to either culture than are monocultural or monolingual individuals or counselors.

Szapocznik, Rio, Perez-Vidal, Kurtines, and Sanisteban (1986) and Szapocznik and Kurtines (1980) further suggested that bilingual and bicultural individuals are better adjusted and perform at a higher level than monolingual or monocultural individuals in either of their two cultures. As a mediator, the counselor serves to interpret either culture, and it is therefore important for the counselor to be accepted in a well-defined role by both cultures to be effective (MacKinnon & Michels, 1971).

Given the complications in understanding and communicating with culturally different clients, and given that few therapy variables other than client-counselor relationship correlate with outcome, Lambert (1981) suggested the possibility that multicultural therapy is not only difficult but even contraindicated in most circumstances.

6. Conclusion

The future will require us to advance in blending culture and mental health in four areas. First, we will need to advance the conceptual and theoretical approaches to the interaction between culture and mental health beyond the diffuse and incomplete theoretical alternatives now available. Second, we will need to sharpen our research efforts to identify those primary variables that will allow us to explain what has happened, interpret what is happening, and perhaps predict what will happen in the migration of persons and ideas across cultures. Third, we will need to identify criteria of expertise for the education and training of professionals to work multiculturally so that they be adequately prepared to deal with the problems of a pluralistic society. Fourth, we will need to revolutionize our mode of providing services based on new theory, new research, and new training so that mental health care can be equitably and appropriately provided to members of a pluralistic society.

It is in the appropriate and accurate *application* of multicultural counseling services that we have the ultimate criteria of effectiveness. Although considerations of the delivery of services should no doubt be foremost in our examination of the field, most emphasis has, in fact, been on basic research questions unwittingly, yet effectively, separated from the practical concerns of program development, service delivery, and techniques of treatment (Draguns, 1980). We need to draw practical implications from the available information. This may include redefining the domain of counselors to include outreach workers, consultants, ombudsmen, change agents, and facilitators of indigenous support systems (Atkinson et al., 1983).

The constraints of multicultural counseling include elements from theory, research, and training as well. We need to place more attention on cultural variables to increase counseling's measured accuracy and effectiveness, to accommodate ethical imperatives of culturally different consumers, and to measure counselor competency in communicating with culturally different clients. We need to increase our understanding of the multicultural dimension within all counseling contacts. We need to integrate multicultural variables into the core curricula of counselor education programs rather than to teach them as a sub-specialty. We need to introduce more multicultural materials into the reasearch literature of mainline professional journals of counseling and therapy. We need to develop alternatives to counseling based on practices in other cultures. We need to match more accurately counseling intervention skills with different cultures, and we need to translate counseling and mental health into the language of other diciplines, fields, and professions of social management. Counselor education plays an important role as the new popular ideology and religion to justify and solve social programs (Sampson, 1977).

CHAPTER 6

The Need for Multicultural Counseling

The multicultural counselor faces a modern dilemma in the United States. Sensitivity to cultural variables is recognized as valuable and even ethically essential for appropriate mental health services, and yet the dangers of cultural encapsulation are more serious now than they have ever been in history. There is a need to resolve this dilemma in a way that will reflect and respect more than one perspective (Pedersen & Marsella, 1982).

1. Ethnocultural Representation in Counseling and Therapy

The rhetoric of support for multicultural issues in counseling and therapy has not been reflected in the data describing the professions of counseling and therapy in the United States. First of all, racial ethnic minorities are underrepresented in clinical and counseling psychology. Second, this underrepresentation is particularly true in applied and academic settings. Third, racial ethnic minority persons are represented most heavily in the lower and less influential academic ranks (Casas, 1984). Finally, publications and professional presentations about culturally different perspectives are underrepresented in the primary professional journals as well as in the annual programs of the American Psychological Association.

There is increased pressure in the United States for the fields of counseling and therapy to acknowledge the importance of consumers' cultural environment. The National Institute of Mental Health (Fields, 1979), the American Psychological Association (Korman, 1974), the American Psychological Association Council of Representatives (APA, 1979), and the recent Presidential Commission on Mental Health (Fields) all have emphasized the ethical responsibility of counselors and therapists to know their clients' cultural values before delivering a mental health service to those clients.

The Vail conference (Korman, 1974) on levels and patterns of professional training in psychology in 1973 gave visibility to multicultural issues in counseling and therapy. The Dulles Conference in 1978 allowed mental health providers from a variety of ethnic and cultural backgrounds to work out guidelines for cooperation and some sense of consensus that resulted in a Minority Affairs Office in APA. By 1979 the APA accreditation criteria demanded cultural diversity among faculty and students in APA-approved programs of counseling and clinical psychology. Casas (1984) suggested several reasons for the recent increased interest and concern for racial/ethnic minority groups in the United States. First, there is a pragmatic understanding and acceptance of demographic changes and socioeconomic political events that have given cultural minority groups more power. Second, many minorities such as Blacks, Hispanic- , and Asian-Americans are demographically visible. Third, the civil rights movement has led to legislation favoring legal rights of minority groups. Fourth, White counselors and therapists have economic incentives for attracting non-White clients.

Lee, Trimble, Cvetkovich, and Lonner (1981) analyzed the program contents of the APA 1960, 1970, and 1980 convention programs to discover that program titles relating to ethnic groups or cultural differences consistently constituted only about 3% of the program offerings for any of the APA divisions, including clinical (Division 12) and counseling (Division 17) psychology. In a replication of this methodology, Inouye and Pedersen (1985) analyzed the APA convention programs and program supplements from 1977 to 1982. The content of APA convention program offerings, as described by their titles, was assumed to reflect the level of interest in cultural and ethnic issues by the APA. Program titles dealing with general topics relating to culture and ethnicity, those focusing on the nationalities of the world, or those examining the various racial and ethnic minority groups in the United States were tabulated in terms of their proportion of actual program times allocated to each APA division according to evenly divided shares of time for each event.

Table 2 shows that by comparing the hours allocated from 1977 to 1982 for cultural and ethnic content, the 4.7 overall average percentage of hours allocated by Division 17 (counseling) and the 2.9 overall average percentage of hours allocated by Division 12 (clinical) make it clear that ethnic and cultural content is extremely underrepresented in APA programs. The 1977–1982 average percentage allocated to that content by all APA divisions was 5.0%. Although counseling psychology provided proportionately slightly more time to cultural and ethnic programs than did clinical psychology, both divisions did so somewhat less than the ratio of ethnic and cultural content across all APA divisions.

TABLE 2

Cultural and Ethnic Content of Programs Sponsored by Division 12 (Clinical) and Division 17 (Counseling) at the American Psychological Association Annual Meetings from 1977 to 1982

	1977		1978		1979		1980		1981		1982	
	C/E*	%**	C/E*	%**	C/E*	%**	C/E*	%**	C/E*	%**	C/E*	%**
Division 17 (Counseling)	1.78	3.9%	0	0	1.55	3.9%	3.49	8.3%	2.43	8.3%	1.65	4.0%
Division 12 (Clinical)	1.07	1.2%	4.01	4.0%	3.48	4.5%	1.99	2.4%	2.73	3.0%	1.10	1.2%
All Divisions Combined	33.36	3.6%	52.69	5.1%	54.72	5.1%	57.64	5.7%	68.92	6.1%	50.03	4.4%

*C/E equals hours allotted to cultural and ethnic content.
**% equals percentage of C/E content hours of total program hours for each division.
Note: From *Cultural and Ethnic Content of the 1977 to 1982 American Psychological Association Convention Programs* (p. 25) by K. Inouye and P. Pedersen, 1983. Unpublished.

Russo, Olmedo, Stapp, and Fulcher (1981) surveyed the representation of racial/ethnic minority groups and women as clients of psychologists generally. By examining the data related to clinical and counseling psychologists, it is clear again that ethnic minorities and women are seriously underrepresented at all levels, especially at the more professionally advanced levels of psychology. As shown in Table 3, the data on faculty in U.S. graduate departments of psychology are classified by sex and race/ethnicity. The 1,571 White faculty and especially the 1,258 White male faculty greatly outnumber the 110 minorities as well as the 347 women in clinical psychology. Likewise the 598 White faculty and especially the 467 White male faculty greatly outnumber the 52 minorities as well as the 152 women in counseling psychology.

The data on U.S. resident master's level student members of APA are tabulated by sex and race/ethnicity. The 2,360 White students and especially the 1,353 White male students greatly outnumber the 126 minority students as well as the 1,056 female students in clinical master's programs. Likewise the 848 White students and especially the 475 White male students greatly outnumber the 39 minority students as well as the 377 female students in counseling master's programs.

Russo, Olmedo, Stapp, and Fulcher (1981) also provide data on U.S. resident doctoral level student members of APA, tabulated by sex and race/ethnicity. The 15,885 White students and especially the 4,186 White male students greatly outnumber the 634 minority students as well as the 4,346 female students in clinical doctoral programs. Likewise, the 3,939 White students and especially the 937 White male students greatly outnumber the 173 minority students as well as the 997 female students in counseling doctoral programs.

Russo et al. (1981) also provide data on the sex and race/ethnicity of 1980 doctorate recipients in psychology to discover that 917 White and 120 minority students received their doctorates. The proportion of women, however, has increased to 43% doctorate recipients, suggesting a trend toward increased representation of women. Racial and ethnic minorities, however, continue to be represented at the same low rate.

Many other studies document how Native Americans, Asian-Americans, Blacks, and Hispanics are seriously underrepresented as both students and faculty in clinical and counseling psychology programs (Kennedy & Wagner, 1979). Although minority students may be proportionately increasing in numbers (Kennedy & Wagner, 1979; Banikiotes, 1977), other data suggest that minority admissions have already peaked and are in fact decreasing (Smith, 1982; Super, 1977). Doctoral graduates from minority backgrounds have decreased from an already small 8% in 1981 (Russo et al., 1981) to a mere 5% in 1983 (Stapp, Tucker, & VanderBos, 1985). Atkinson et al. (1983) documented in data from 305 counselor education programs that ethnic minorities are less underrepresented as students than as faculty members. This would suggest that some progress is

TABLE 3
Faculty in U.S. Graduate Departments of Psychology: Subfield by Sex by Race/Ethnicity

Subfield	Race/Ethnicity						Total	% Women	% Minorities
	White	Black	Hispanic	Asian	Native American	Not Specified			
Clinical									
Men	1,258	38	12	8	0	14	1,330		
Women	311	28	5	1	1	1	347		
Not Specified	2	0	0	0	0	2	4		
Total	1,571	66	17	9	1	17	1,681	20.6	5.5
Counseling									
Men	467	13	4	4	2	6	496		
Women	130	14	4	1	1	2	152		
Not Specified	1	1	0	0	0	0	2		
Total	598	28	8	5	3	8	650	23.4	6.8

Source: 1980–1981 Survey of Graduate Departments of Psychology, American Psychological Association and Council of Graduate Departments of Psychology. The numbers in this table are based on the responses of 364 graduate departments of psychology and are not intended as estimates of the population of faculty.
Note: From "Women and Minorities in Psychology," by N. Russo, E. Olmedo, J. Stapp and R. Fulcher, 1981, *The American Psychologist,* 36, p. 1349. Copyright by American Psychological Assoc. Reprinted by permission.

being made toward greater minority representation in counseling and clinical psychology.

Still one more indication of underrepresentation was documented by Sundberg (1981a, 1981b) in his tabulation of APA research journals from 1975 to 1979. The four APA journals most likely to have reports on counseling and therapy—with 1% to 3% of the articles giving some indication of cultural or ethnic materials—were the *Journal of Abnormal Psychology*, the *Journal of Consulting and Clinical Psychology*, the *Journal of Counseling Psychology*, and *Professional Psychology*. Most of these articles were reports of programs or reviews, research reports on assessment techniques, or correlational group difference studies unrelated to counseling or therapy. Other journals reporting multicultural articles, such as the *International Journal of Psychology* or the *Journal of Cross-Cultural Psychology* and the *Transcultural Research Review* or *International Journal of Social Psychiatry*, seldom reported studies of counseling or therapy. Casas (1984) indicated that the same general pattern of underrepresentation applies to journals of the American Personnel and Guidance Association (American Association for Counseling and Development) as well.

2. Historical Background in Cultural Awareness

How did we get into such an inequitable multicultural imbalance? To some extent our domestic perspective of counseling and therapy may reflect historical racial and ethnic relations in the United States characterized by heightened group consciousness, government mandated affirmative action in employment and education, court-ordered busing to achieve racial integration in public schools, and demands for bilingual education in public school systems. In comparing ethnic/racial relations in the United States with those in other cultures, Lambert (1981) found the U.S. perspective to be ''unusual compared with that of other countries in its growing salience of ethnic/racial relations, its bipolarity, its emphasis on hierarchy over cultural contrast, the casting of government in the role of protagonist for the underclass, and the ethnic specificity and direction of violence'' (p. 189).

The civil rights movement of the 1950s resulted in a militancy of minorities for change toward greater equity. The growing community mental health movement of the 1960s supported equitable services by affirming that mental health care was the right of all citizens and not just the wealthy or middle-class dominant majority (LeVine & Padilla, 1980). The issues of feminism and popular dissent from the anti-Vietnam War movement further promoted a climate of discontent where protest against inequitable treatment was accepted and even encouraged by the media and general public. The stigma of discrimination became synonymous with any attempt to treat groups differently. Sue (1981) suggested that this obsession with equality might itself be discriminatory. Minority groups may not be asking for equal treatment as much as for equal access and opportunity. Differential treatment is not necessarily discriminatory or even preferred. Appropriate mental health services are almost inevitably differentially defined across cultures.

By the 1970s the underutilization of mental health services by minority groups had become a serious issue. One reason for the apparent underutilization might be that behavior such as individualistic assertiveness, described as pathological in a minority culture, might be viewed as adaptive in a majority culture client (Wilson & Calhoon, 1974; Grier & Cobbs, 1968). Sue (1977) demonstrated that Asian-Americans, Blacks, Chicanos, Native Americans, and other minority group clients terminate counseling significantly earlier than do Anglo clients and are diagnosed as more seriously ill. These measures of underutilization were largely credited to cultural barriers hindering counseling and therapy such as language barriers, class-bound values, and culture-bound attitudes. Others (Pedersen, 1982) suggested that minorities might be avoiding dominant culture mental health services to prevent the erosion of their own values and cultural identity where those services might in fact *increase* acculturative stress among consumers. Casas (1984) concluded that whether or not mental health services are being underutilized by minorities depends almost entirely on how the data are collected; a number of studies suggest that these services are not being underutilized at all.

Now in the 1980s the U.S. perspective includes the large numbers of refugees both from Cuba and the Caribbean as well as from Vietnam, Laos, and Cambodia. Initially funds were provided for special services to these culturally different groups. More recently former refugees are being served by the regular mental health services. Especially in the Southeast but elsewhere as well, the rapidly growing Hispanic population is likewise dependent on regular mental health services. Our regular mental health services, however, still are not prepared to serve these culturally different populations in appropriate ways (Atkinson et al., 1983).

In the past we have tried four different demographic approaches to multicultural awareness, without success. The paradox of pluralism is that on the one hand we are more dependent on one another than ever before while at the same time needing to prove our economic, social, cultural, and political independence with renewed vigor. *Assimilation* of the minorities by a dominant group has been the most popular mode of accommodation. As discussed earlier, assimilation requires that the minorities seek acceptance and are in turn accepted. *Integration* has also been suggested as promising a heterogeneous society where ethnicity has lost significance and has been absorbed into class stratification. Integration has led to the desperate inequalities of a society where some persons are considered more equal than others. The concept of *multiple ethnic colonies* presents an extreme solution that would fragment society into encapsulated and independent sectors. *Pluralism* seeks to maintain a delicate balance, assuming the continued and distinct self-identities of the various ethnic groups through shared political and socioeconomic institutions. There are few, if any, successful examples of pluralism in the world, although this finally may be the only acceptable alternative for survival.

The "melting pot" metaphor for assimilation, introduced through a play by Israel Zangwill in 1908, assumed that a new and unique culture would emerge as each immigrant group gave up its "old world" values in exchange for the values of a "new world" (Atkinson et al., 1983). There were "lumps" in the melting pot that refused to dissolve as some cultural groups maintained their original identity. Some legislation, such as the Chinese Exclusion Act, discouraged immigrant cultural groups from assimilating. Although the explicit policy for assimilation is no longer popular, there is some evidence of implicit assimilationist policies in practice (Marsella & Pedersen, 1981; Pedersen, Draguns, Lonner, & Trimble, 1981).

The difficulty with integration as an alternative is its implicit hierarchical bias in favor of the dominant culture. The results of integration have been an implicit paternalism at best and arbitrary domination at worst. Integration has evolved into class and ultimately caste structures where the minority group must resort either to conflict or subservience. Atkinson et al. (1983) described the language used to describe minority groups as denoting implicit cultural bias. Anthropological, sociological, and psychological data have contributed to an implicit cultural bias by assuming: (a) that problems result from social pathology or deviance, (b) that problems result from social disorganization or the disintegration of values, (c) that solutions require a dominant culture perspective because of the cultural deficit of other groups, or (d) that culturally defined levels of adequacy are limited by the genetic deficits of some cultural groups.

As the roles of counselors and therapists are defined more rigidly in a cultural context, we tend to isolate ourselves along the lines of a particular cultural bias of institutionalized racism, with less and less pretense toward either assimilation or integration of values.

From an international perspective, the culturally specific characteristics of counseling and therapy in the U.S. perspective challenge the universality of psychology but not its scientific character. Alternative cultural assumptions in other cultural settings do not follow the "American ideal" (Sampson, 1977; Diaz-Guerrero, 1977), the premises of the Protestant ethic (Rotenberg, 1974; Draguns, 1974), or the other pervasive assumptions of individualism (Hsu, 1972; Pedersen, 1979).

Jones and Korchin (1982) described mental health as having two different orientations. On the one hand, mental health is perceived as *political*, with the basic tenet that mental health as well as social welfare, economic status, political power, personal dignity, and other facets of well-being of minority group members depend on the acquisition of power and control over their personal and collective destinies. On the other hand, there is a *multicultural* perspective of mental health that begins with the assumption that there are indeed differences among groups, each of which has its own unique tradition.

In many instances it has been easier to "explain" or rationalize problems of cultural differences than to adapt. A variety of social science theories have been presented in the past to explain the racial-ethnic components of maladaptation by minority cultures (Sue, 1981). (a) The biological-racial explanation has been around the longest in the popular myth that explains the lack of achievement by some cultures in terms of genetic inferiority. The weakness of this position is the assumption that biological and sociocultural factors can be separated. (b) Physiological explanations focus on neurological deficiencies as by-products of poverty and deprivation. The weakness of this position is that diagnosis of mental deficiencies is ambiguous and the rationale can be used as a substitute for hereditary inferiority. (c) Demographic theories look for explanations in environmental conditions, but there is no clear evidence that persons migrating from poverty or disadvantaged areas are permanently unable to achieve when later presented with appropriate opportunities. (d) Psychological explanations emphasize individual motivation, self-image, delay of gratification, anxiety, achievement expectancy, and so forth. Motivational and behavioral handicaps are blamed for failure in school, although these handicaps may be a consequence of educational deprivation as well as its cause. (e) Sociological explanations emphasize cultural, class, and environmental differences but without clear evidence of a causal relationship between sociocultural status and achievement.

3. The Complexity of Social System Variables in Counseling and Therapy

Many of the historical mistakes indicated in the last section were the result of oversimplifying culture. Culture is complicated.

The definitions of culture are increasingly likely to include demographic, status, affiliation, as well as ethnographic variables of ethnicity and nationality. Kinloch (1979) included physical, cultural, economic, and behavioral characteristics in his analysis. These special variables function in ways similar to ethnic and nationality variables in the analysis of interaction. Erickson and Schultz (1981) introduced the concept of "comembership" to describe the broader perspective of cultural variables. "Comembership is an aspect of performed social identity that involves particularistic attributes of status shared by the counselor and student—for example, race and ethnicity, sex, interest in football, graduation from the same high school, acquaintance with the same individual" (p. 17). Comembership provides a basis for special solidarity between counselors and clients, drawing from the same perspective, using the same language, and sharing the same in-group references. In their analysis of empathy, Erickson and Schultz demonstrated that comembership is stronger than either race/ethnicity or social class as a predictor of rapport.

An adequate understanding of knowledge in developing multicultural awareness is necessarily complicated. Maruyama (1978) described persons who depend on one authority, one theory, or one truth as victims of monopolarization. Monopolarized persons tend to be trapped in one way of thinking, believing theirs is the universal way. They are trapped in an inflexible structure that resists adaptation to alternative ways of thinking. The alternative is what Maruyama calls "transpection," which goes beyond any single viewpoint to include many complex variables at once to describe an event.

It would be a serious mistake to assume that all members of a particular ethnic group take the same perspective of each issue, problem, or event. The differences of age, sex, life style, socioeconomic status, and a long list of variables in addition to ethnicity and nationality influence each individual's cultural perspective. Rather than characterize cultural groups in rigid categories, the U.S. perspective needs an alternative framework that will combine the many different cultural identities each person presents to the different situations or events encountered (Dillard, 1983).

4. Cultural Encapsulation

The culturally encapsulated individual is just as able to evade reality through ethnocentricism, ("mine is best") as through relativism, ("to each his own"). Maintaining a cocoon is accomplished by evading reality and depending entirely on one's own internalized value assumptions about what is good for society. Isolation is accentuated by the inherent capacity of culture-bound and time-honored values to prevail against the tentativeness of present knowledge.

It is therefore necessary for the culture-sensitive individual not only to learn new knowledge and skills, but also to reorganize the old knowledge that no longer applies. The encapsulated individual is singularly unable to adapt to a constantly changing sociocultural context. The same sociological data with which we inform ourselves can be used to reinforce tendencies toward stereotyped images of cultural groups, separating and "encapsulating" the individual from social reality.

One escapes from cultural encapsulation through training. The arguments against learning unfamiliar cultures are often quite familiar, especially as implicit assumptions in priorities where multicultural education and training are given a lower priority than education and training from an "established" cultural viewpoint. Some of the more familiar arguments against multicultural education and training include the following:

1. All multicultural training is a waste of time and money when any intelligent individual should be able to adjust in a foreign culture without any preparation.
2. Training is actually harmful because the trainee learns half-truths and develops stereotypes that have to be unlearned when arriving in the foreign culture.
3. Only training programs that teach factual information about the foreign culture are valuable in learning about what to expect.
4. Failure to make an emotional adjustment to another culture is a sign of weakness and mental instability, and consequently is unlikely to be prevented by training.
5. It is a waste of time to focus on one's own cultural assumptions and biases; more time should be spent looking at the values of the foreign culture.
6. The intelligent person already knows his or her own assumptions or biases and is in control of them.
7. There is one right answer for each situation in the foreign culture, and it does not change from time to time or place to place.
8. Any reasonable person from the foreign culture will be able to identify what would be an appropriate response to an ambiguous situation.
9. It always will be possible to identify rewarding experiences in the foreign culture because they will remind the visitor of rewarding situations back home.
10. If you can become less sensitive to a simulated embarrassing situation, you will become less caring in the real situation later.
11. Just being in spontaneous contact with foreign nationals will enable you to learn about them and their values.
12. You don't have to learn about a foreign culture once you get the feel of the way they do things.
13. Diversity creates disunity in a society—all people should be taught to believe the same way to produce a homogeneous society that has strength.
14. The differences that separate us from one another somehow are a regression to some primitive earlier stage of evolutionary progress and are out of place in the ideal future where differences of ethnicity, religion, and race will be eliminated.
15. When we take particular differences of race, religion, nationality, and sex as reasons for treating people differently, we are being prejudiced.

These differences have no legal binding force and should be regarded as irrelevant by responsible citizens.

16. The long-range drift toward secularization and rationality demands that we ignore nonrational or irrational factors inherent in religious, ethnic, and racial diversity in the name of human progress.

17. To emphasize ethnic diversity while our society is going through the present crisis would be to aggravate the dangers of fragmentation that would allow us to destroy ourselves from within.

Encapsulation is a result of several basic and familiar processes in our professional activity (Wrenn, 1985). Wrenn's five-point description of encapsulation demonstrates how counseling *as a profession* has protected itself against the complex threat of multiculturalism.

(1) We define reality according to one set of cultural assumptions and stereotypes that becomes more important than the real world outside. (2) We become insensitive to cultural variations among individuals and assume that our view is the only real or legitimate one. It is not surprising that the assumption that "I know better than they do what is good for them" is offensive to the target audience. (3) Each of us has unreasoned assumptions we accept without proof. When these assumptions are threatened by another religion, political view, or culture, we can easily become fearful or defensive. When persons of the host culture are perceived as threatening, they quickly become an "enemy" to be opposed and ultimately defeated in the name of self-preservation. (4) A technique-oriented job definition further contributes toward and perpetuates the process of encapsulation. The world is simplistically divided into a polarity of friends and enemies, us and them, with each relationship being evaluated according to whether or not it contributes to getting the job done. (5) When there is no evaluation of other viewpoints, individuals may experience encapsulation by absolving themselves of any responsibility to interpret the behavior of others as relevant and meaningful to their own life activity.

Some people have developed a dependency on one authority, one theory, one truth. These encapsulated persons tend to be trapped in one way of thinking, believing that theirs is the universal way. They are trapped in an inflexible structure that resists adaptation to alternative ways of thinking. In contrast, a liberated mode of thinking represents an effort to establish empathy with other persons different from ourselves. Empathy is a process of learning foreign beliefs, assumptions or perspectives, feelings, and consequences in such a way that the outsider participates in the host culture. Through multicultural contact, people can be liberated to cope with constant change and to feel empathy with other alternatives available to them.

5. The Argument for Multicultural Training and Evaluation

Why might a person seek education and training about other cultures? There are several widely accepted assumptions about the social value of transferring knowledge across cultural boundaries and evading encapsulation. Each reason is partially true but, as will be apparent, oversimplifies the benefits.

1. More knowledge leads to more empathy, more empathy will ultimately lead to more sympathy, and more sympathy will finally lead to improved multicultural relations.

2. Increased multicultural knowledge will stretch people's imaginations with a net result of increased tolerance of other cultures—this will contribute toward a more secure world.

3. The diffusion of knowledge about other cultures will lead toward a more homogeneous world, mixing the different cultures with one another in a "melting pot."

4. The demonstration of how people from different cultures are interdependent on one another might contribute toward world peace as we learn to exchange what we have for what we need from others.

5. Learning about persons different from ourselves clarifies our knowledge of who we are as we learn about ourselves through others' perception of us.

6. The meeting of cultures and minds is hoped to enhance all participants' development toward some sort of progress. To say that multicultural openness in these terms is a good and desirable outcome can be extremely naive unless we also look at the dangers of multicultural openness.

In many instances it has been easier to "explain" or rationalize cultural differences than to understand them. A variety of demographic, social, and historical theories have been presented to explain cultural differences in contemporary society.

6. Conclusion

Pluralistic perspectives are needed to accommodate the range of differences in the culturally learned assumptions by which each individual interprets events. The more obvious cultural differences of nationality and ethnicity provide an opportunity to develop multiple perspectives that will increase our accuracy in dealing with the sometimes less obvious differences of age, sex, life style, socioeconomic status, and affiliation. Until the issues of multicultural counseling are seen and described in terms of increasing accuracy for all counseling and therapy rather than for special interest groups, we are unlikely to see more than a token acknowledgment of cultural variables on the part of mental health professionals.

PART THREE

Skill for Multicultural Action

Skill is based both on awareness and on knowledge to bring about appropriate and effective change in multicultural situations. Skill learning is both the most difficult and the most important of the three levels in multicultural development discussed in this book.

First of all, it is important to examine each cultural group's method as well as context in which it prefers to give and receive help. The method of counseling and the context of counseling are both culturally defined. The many errors illustrated in previous chapters usually occurred when a dominant culture imposed its own unique method and context for counseling on minority groups whose preferred method and context were quite different. Although counseling is a product of Euro-American mental health and educational institutions, the functions of counseling are universally familiar, but in different methods and contexts.

Some of the many different training approaches for preparing skilled multicultural counselors already have been cited in previous chapters. Rather than superficially reviewing these approaches, the focus on skill development in this book entails examining one method, the Triad Model, in greater depth. The Triad Model is suitable in that it allows a broad definition of culture, promotes the management of complexity in simulated multicultural counseling interviews, and demonstrates the dynamic ever-changing perspective of a client's culturally learned response to counseling. A set of four different skills is described for development through simulated triad interviews with culturally different clients.

The development of multicultural awareness is a continuing and unending process that requires learning and relearning. The complex range of skills generated by culturally different clients is illustrated in the guidelines suggested by the APA's Division 17 (Counseling) Education and Training Committee, as described in chapter 10. This last chapter should be viewed as a beginning for developing a multicultural awareness.

CHAPTER 7

The Role of Method and Context in Multicultural Counseling

There are as many different methods of helping persons as there are cultural groups. Each group defines its own criteria of appropriate helping methods. In a similar way, each culture has its own requirements regarding the formal and informal context in which help may appropriately be provided. By examining the role of method and context in multicultural counseling, it is possible to avoid many of the errors illustrated in the previous chapters about multicultural awareness and knowledge.

Multicultural counseling is not simply learning to work with exotic populations; it is a different way of looking at all counseling relationships. As a result of ethnographic, demographic, status, and affiliation variables, each client will differ—to a greater or lesser extent—from each counselor. Furthermore, the salient cultural difference, whether a difference of nationality, ethnicity, age, or sex, may change even within the same interview. As a result of many counselors' disregard of the importance of culture in counseling relationships, three serious errors have frequently occurred in counseling.

The first error has been overemphasizing the importance of a person's behavior and underemphasizing the importance of the expectations or values that give those behaviors meaning. Categorical interpretations of behaviors have resulted in the naive imposition of narrowly defined criteria for normality by a dominant culture on culturally diverse people.

The second error has been oversimplifying various social system variables in counseling by emphasizing the most obvious aspects of a client's background. Authenticity requires that counselors consider ethnographic, demographic, status, and affiliation variables as they interact with one another in a constantly changing configuration. Culturally skilled counselors can understand the cultural complexity of their clients and thereby avoid the dangers of cultural encapsulation (Wrenn, 1962).

The third error has been describing counseling as a primarily formal process that emphasizes trained professionals' specialization in mental health services. Kleinman (1980) contrasted the specialized view of a perspective focused on the malfunctioning body part with the more systemic "illness" perspective that includes contextual variables in mental health care, such as a person's family and friends. An alternative approach incorporates a three-stage gradual continuum of formal, nonformal, and informal client contexts into the counseling process and, consequently, into the healing process. A multiculturally skilled counselor can balance formal and informal approaches in the treatment of culturally different populations (Pedersen, 1981, 1982, 1986a).

1. The Balance of Formal and Informal Support Systems

In each person's identity different social support systems are woven together in a fabric where formal and informal elements, like texture or color in a weaving, provide a pattern or design that is unique. In each person's identity, a balance of formal and informal support systems is essential to good mental health.

The pattern or design of social systems in Western cultures is significantly different from that in non-Western cultures (Pearson, 1982). In a world perspective, the formal context of counseling and therapy is an "exotic" approach. In most non-Western systems there is less tendency than in Western societies to locate the problem inside the isolated individual than to relate a person's difficulty to other persons, the cosmology, or informal support systems.

Counseling can occur in an informal as well as a formal mode. The place where counseling occurs as well as the method by which counseling is provided are defined by a balance of formal and informal support systems. In the literature on nonformal education, Jordan and Tharp (1979) contrasted formal schooling with the more informal, nonschool environment, pointing out that the institution of formal education results in a picture of the school itself as a "culture." The combination of formal and informal methods and contexts creates a dynamic balance of indigenous support systems and defines our personal cultural orientation.

Although most research on support contains similar assumptions, definitions of support vary greatly (Caplan, 1976; Cobb, 1976). The kinds of support frequently mentioned include emotional support (feelings of closeness, intimacy, esteem, and encouragement), tangible goods and assistance, intellectual advice or guidance, and supportive socialization (Pearson, 1985). Social support networks prevent disorder by early detection of problems and referral to appropriate helpers (Gottlieb & Hall, 1980) and by meeting basic human needs for affiliation and attachment. The literature on counseling and therapy is now providing more data on the importance of indigenous support systems to mediate the functions of counseling (Pearson, 1982, 1985).

An examination of Figure 7, which shows the full range of methods and contexts through which support systems function, from the most formal (where rules, structures, and definite expectations apply) to the more informal (where spontaneity and the lack of defined structures apply), reveals a paradigm for describing the range of formal and informal support systems. Although the incorporation of formal and informal support systems has been included in previously published literature, no single paradigm has been presented that incorporates the full range of possibilities for analyzing how the formal and informal systems complement one another. These combinations include a range of alternatives appropriate in various culturally diverse settings.

Each cell of Figure 7 depicts a different combination of formal and nonformal features of counseling methods in various counseling contexts. Each cell in the figure illustrates a different meaning.

1. A formal method and formal context are involved when the counselor-specialist works with a fee-paying client in a scheduled office interview. Counseling as a professional activity occurs mostly in this cell.

2. A formal method and nonformal context are involved when the therapist-specialist works by invitation or appointment with a client in the client's home, office, or community. Semiformal meetings with individuals, families, or groups of foreign students are often best scheduled for locations outside the counseling office. A location that is more familiar to the client can make it easier to establish rapport when discussing personal problems.

3. A formal method and informal context are involved when the counselor-specialist is consulted about a personal problem by a friend or relative at a party or on the street. In some cultures it is important for the person requesting help to be accepted as a friend before it is appropriate for that person to disclose intimate problems. When I counseled foreign students at the University of Minnesota, I first would have to be "checked out" at nationality-group parties or conduct interviews about personal problems on street corners while crossing campus. For various reasons the students wanted counseling but not in an office or formal setting.

4. A nonformal method and formal context are involved when a person not trained to do counseling (by degree or experience) is asked for psychological help when providing a professional service, training, or presentation. When I counseled for 6 years in Asian universities, it became clear that the functions of a counselor were not well understood. The concept of a medical doctor was

Method

		Formal	Nonformal	Informal
Context	Informal	1 Office-scheduled therapy	4 Mental health training	7 Mental health presentation
	Nonformal	2 Community mental health service	5 Support groups	8 Family & friends
	Formal	3 Professional advice	6 Self-help groups	9 Daily encounter

FIGURE 7

A Three-Dimensional Model of Counseling Services Methods

clear, but the counselor was more a special kind of "teacher." To accept help from a teacher was honorable and increased one's status in the community. Consequently it was frequently useful to describe counseling as a teaching and learning interaction. An Asian student would be quite likely to ask his or her teacher for advice and help on a personal problem.

5. A nonformal method and nonformal context are involved in the various support groups organized by persons to help one another through regular contact and an exchange of ideas, even though none of the participants is trained as a therapist. When I had Asian or other foreign students as clients who were unfamiliar with counseling, I frequently would ask them to bring a friend to the interview. The friend, although not trained as a counselor, would function almost as a cotherapist by providing constant support, clarifying the content of formal counseling interviews, and helping me to understand the client by acting as mediator and interpreter. This can be especially useful if there is a language problem between the client and counselor.

6. A nonformal method and informal context are involved when self-help groups and popular psychology are used as resources. A frequent indicator of

culture shock is withdrawal from support groups and increased isolation from groups of others. There are various self-help groups, such as Alcoholics Anonymous and other organizations for addicts, single persons, veterans, or those who share the common bond of a traumatic experience. Similarly, there is much literature on positive thinking or advice giving that is a frequent source of help. My Chinese clients frequently first consulted the Confucian proverbs for advice, and sought counseling only when the proverbs seemed inadequate.

7. An informal method and formal context are involved when a listener receives considerable assistance in solving a psychological problem from a formal, scheduled presentation or activity even if that was not the explicit intention of the program. In non-Western cultures, much of what we call counseling in Western settings occurs through religious institutions. Family meetings and activities also provide valuable support for the mental health profession and leave a great vacuum by their absence. These institutions are not primarily psychological, nor is their primary purpose to promote mental health. The ritualistic context, however, is often formal and contributes significantly to healthy mental attitudes.

8. An informal method and nonformal context are involved when family and friends provide help to an individual. In many Asian cultures it would be unacceptable to go outside the family or a very close circle of friends to disclose personal problems. In some situations a foreign student under stress while in the United States may be helped by making contact with relatives or close friends who can serve as a resource and context for casual and indirect conversations that can promote healthy mental attitudes.

9. An informal method and informal context are involved in daily encounters in which individuals receive help spontaneously and unexpectedly from their contacts with other people, whether that help is intended or unintended. As mentioned earlier, Americans have a saying: "If you don't know what to do at least do something." The Chinese, however, have a contrary saying: "If you don't know what to do at least don't do anything." Spontaneous recovery from crises or stress takes many forms. Imagine, for example, that it is a nice day and you are walking down the street. Someone smiles. You smile back. You feel better. Each culture teaches its own repertoire of self-help mechanisms for healing.

A comprehensive picture of formal and informal support systems helps to classify the different sources of psychological help. Without an adequate framework to identify the resources, counselors are likely to rely too heavily on more formal, obvious support systems and ignore the less obvious, informal alternatives. If counselors seek to translate counseling and therapy to culturally different populations, they will need to understand the relative importance of each formal or informal combination of helping alternatives. Formal interventions to provide psychological help need to complement the diverse informal influences in clients' support systems. The formal and informal framework highlights the complexity of clients' indigenous support systems and also indicates the importance of matching the right method and context so that culturally skilled counseling can occur.

2. Cultural Complexity

In attempting to understand the complexity of multicultural contact, counselors have developed simplified models to explain and understand selected aspects of reality. Counselors' imbedded rationality leads them to construct simplified models of complex reality in order to manage reality. If counselors behave rationally regarding the simplified model, they assume the behavior is appropriately generalized to the real world. The danger is that counselors confuse the labels with reality.

Culture has contributed profoundly to our understanding of human behavior by complicating explanations of interpersonal contact in ways that guarantee complexity. Pedersen and Pedersen (1985) developed a Cultural Grid to help identify and describe the cultural aspect of a situation, to help form hypotheses about multicultural differences in explanations, and to help train persons for culturally appropriate interaction. The Cultural Grid is an open-ended model that matches social system variables (demographic, ethnographic, status, and affiliation) with personal variables (behavior, expectation, and value) in a personal and cultural orientation.

Various other researchers also have studied multiple roles within the definitions of culture. Kinloch (1979) included physical, cultural, economic, and behavioral categories as separate cultures. These special groups function in ways similar to ethnic and nationality groups within the perspective of a situationally defined role. Consistent with his notion of a "subjective culture," Triandis, Vassiliou, Vassiliou, Tanaka, and Shanmugam (1972) developed an elegant model that combines behavioral intentions with social cognitions through roles and emotional attachments and perceived consequences. Erickson and Shultz (1982) reported that comembership affiliations defined by contextual roles are even more cohesive than are cultural affiliations defined exclusively by similar nationality or ethnicity.

There are several specific implications for counselors in examining the cultural role of methods and context of multicultural counseling. First, the counselor is encouraged to differentiate formal and informal counseling approaches in terms of method and context. The client may prefer counseling in an informal context but not necessarily through an informal method, or prefer a formal context and a formal method. Second, the paradigm of formal and informal alternatives provides a comprehensive range of possibilities for counselors to consider, especially in working with persons from cultures unfamiliar to them. Each culture favors different levels of formality in methods and contexts as the preferred mode of giving or receiving counseling. Third, by presenting a comprehensive description of the resources through which a client may receive help, the counselor is encouraged to coordinate the goals of a more formal counseling intervention with the advice and resources available in the range of less formal alternatives.

3. Cultural Competencies for Counselors

In the variety of research literature on intergroup or multicultural contact, the one consistent finding is that groups or individuals who perceive themselves to be quite similar in some way are more likely to relate in harmony. On the other hand, if they perceive themselves to be dissimilar, they are more likely to relate through conflict. It is important to look at specific areas of competency that would promote a shared world view between the visitor and the host culture. More research has been done on competencies for mutlicultural education than on competencies for multicultural counseling. It may be useful to apply some of the educational competencies to the development of multicultural counseling competencies.

The evaluation and assessment of internationalism in higher education relates to both cognitive and affective competencies as educational objectives. Using the guidelines suggested by Benjamin Bloom (1956) and McCraw (1969) the following goals can be applied to the teacher or counselor:

- is aware of the other cultures;
- is willing to receive information about value systems different from her or his own and voluntarily selects articles and books about a different culture;
- is willing to respond to instructional materials about a different culture by asking questions and offering comments;
- obtains satisfaction from responding to information about another culture;
- accepts the idea that it is good to know and understand other people of other cultures;
- prefers the above idea to any competing dogma, rejecting cultural isolationism;
- is committed to the value of international understanding and cooperation; and
- conceptualizes this value into the total value system by weighing alternative international policies and practices against the standard of international understanding rather than against narrow special interests.

As an example of what a teacher or counselor should know about the other culture under discussion, a checklist of skills and information found in Bloom's guidelines would be known by the multiculturally skilled educator. The teacher or counselor:

- knows much of the history, customs, language, and geography of one or more cultures other than his or her own;
- knows contributions of various cultures to the world;
- knows where and how to find additional information about other cultures;
- demonstrates constructive ability to solve problems involving international understanding;
- sees the implications in data regarding social and economic circumstances;
- understands that people and peoples are more alike than different;
- applies general ideas regarding culture to a particular cultural context;
- analyzes a culture into component parts;
- forms generalizations from cultural data and observes exceptions;
- observes differences in wealth, values, and behavior among cultures and understands the reasons for the differences;
- sees the necessity of world trade and the value of world travel;
- understands the causes for changes in alliances among nations;
- sees the implications of shortened travel and communication time between countries;
- understands the nature of international interdependence; and
- evaluates ideas on the basis of their effect on world harmony.

Like California, Pennsylvania, North Carolina, and many other states, Minnesota has recently required all teachers to complete a training program in human relations to develop multicultural skills. The law requires that applicants demonstrate an ability to:

- understand the contributions and life styles of the various racial, cultural, and economic groups in a society;
- recognize and deal with dehumanizing biases, discrimination, and prejudices;
- create learning environments that contribute to the self-esteem of all persons and to positive interpersonal relations; and
- respect human diversity and personal rights.

Filla and Clarke (1973) developed a series of skill descriptions to meet the human relations requirements; these descriptions provide guidelines for multicultural development for social institutions outside the school as well. Although these skill descriptions do not claim to be the "best" statements or to be all-inclusive, they do provide some examples of how the theory of multicultural teaching can be applied to practical problems of counselor education.

The first cluster of competencies aims at understanding the contributions and life styles of various cultural groups. An effective program should cover: the history, social development, unique life style, outstanding leaders, subcultures, intergroup harmony, educational values, and daily life activities of host culture residents. These skills demonstrate a balance of cognitive, or "knowing," goals, affective, or "feeling," goals, and behavioral, or "doing," goals. The process of understanding applied to an multicultural training design needs to include all three aspects among its competency objectives. Likewise, the competencies demonstrate a balance of learning new ideas or skills and reorganizing the obsolete, inaccurate views or misinformation from previous experience. A balanced program also needs to include persons from different cultural backgrounds beyond the narrowly defined viewpoint of any single culture. The resources for learning about multicultural communication are the persons from the cultures being studied, who are therefore readily available as foreign or international students in the trainee's host culture.

A second cluster of competencies involves the recognition of dehumanizing biases, discrimination, or prejudices and the skills to change them in the trainee. An effective program should cover: positive and negative cultural labels, positive and negative role models, examples of prejudice, role of the outside observer, rights of the local resident, examples of multicultural harmony, local stereotypes, local contributions, and strategies for dealing with cultural bias.

The primary benefits of multicultural communications training are to increase a trainee's degree of freedom, not to change trainees in ways they may not want to be changed. There is a significant difference between understanding or accepting another's values and choosing to adopt those values for oneself. Bias, discrimination, and prejudice have become "bad" words in our vocabulary; the benefits derived from cultural stereotypes that contribute to our sense of cultural identity, however, are not readily recognized. The emphasis in these skills is on becoming aware of our cultural bias and then making a deliberate rather than accidental decision about whether we wish to retain our prejudices or not. Cultural bias becomes most dangerous when it is implicit in the attitudes of an individual or policies of an institution, without sufficient consideration of consequences and without intentional awareness.

A third cluster of competencies relates to creating learning environments that contribute to the self-esteem of all persons and to positive interpersonal relations. An effective program should cover: the variety of teaching and learning styles, positive contributions of learning, the role of emotional expression, the role of creativity, the role of competition and cooperation, the direct or indirect communication style, the function of rules and regulations, examples of human relations problems, means of giving and receiving feedback, accurate descriptions of local motives, the role of dependence and independence, and conflict situations.

The basis of a pluralistic society depends on the ability to share power on some equitable basis. The contrary policy has been one of "helping" persons less "fortunate" than ourselves labeled as "disadvantaged" rather than sharing power with them on any equitable basis. The teacher must first deal with preconceived views of people from other cultures, views that have generated both antagonism and fear as defenses against open communication both between teacher and student and among students. Programs of preservice training have not been sufficient in preparing teachers to cope with cultural aspects of education or in providing a supportive collegial community. The implicit constraints of White-dominated "Anglo" values and the militant response of separatists both politicize multicultural communication and inhibit the open exchange of learning.

A fourth cluster of competencies teaches respect for human diversity and personal rights. An effective program should cover: culturally unique values, ways to exchange ideas that promote harmony, respect for cultural diversity, importance of core values, respect for human rights, accommodation of local values and rights, ability to contrast local and visiting cultural values, responsibility of listening carefully, ability to guide other visitors into the culture, the role of cultural diversity in harmony, and the role of visitors in the local culture.

The training process to learn these competencies goes through several stages of progressive development. First, trainees assess personal *motivation* and relationship to the target multicultural population in specific ways. Each person needs to know self, the host population, and his or her own limitations in bringing about desired changes. Second, trainees need to design a plan for changing after they have identified the *need* for specific changes. Participants need to know resources in making changes, attitudes of populations toward those changes, and methods likely to produce changes. Third, trainees need to *define* a task objectively. They need to develop change-agent skills, project the impact of proposed changes, clarify roles in relationship with the target population, and develop a sensitivity to the target population's perception of its own role. Fourth, trainees need to *plan* an approach involving members of the target population in the planning, develop necessary techniques or tools, try out parts of the plan, allow for feedback and continuous reevaluation of the task, and limit objectives to those that later can be evaluated in terms of specific outcomes. Fifth, trainees need to *carry out* the plan. Trainees need to build and maintain morale, monitor the effects of changes on the target population, and maintain congruence between methods and goals. Sixth, trainees need to *evaluate* or assess progress in the project. They need to anticipate problems and diagnose the reason for unexpected results, modify methods, and otherwise learn from mistakes. Finally, trainees need to ensure continuity and transference of positive results that come from applying what was learned through training. Trainees need to motivate others to take responsibility in participating toward a solution, to generate a wider support for changes, and to appreciate the contribution of others applying the training results to the host population.

In developing training materials that are realistic, relevant, and readily available, it is useful to rely on critical incidents that actually occur in multicultural counseling. The critical incident approach is widely used as abbreviated case studies that highlight a crisis or required decision.

4. Critical Incidents in Human Relations

Although the critical incidents cited below provide examples of incidents suitable for the four competency areas, they overlap to a considerable degree. Whenever possible critical incidents should be drawn from the participant's own multicultural experiences or experiences he or she is likely to have in the future.

I. To Understand the Contributions and Life Styles of Various Racial, Cultural, and Economic Groups in Our Society

1. You are acquainted with a student whose life style does not emphasize "time consciousness." The student's failure to meet deadlines had downgraded his otherwise adequate assignments and alienated him from his teacher. Neither the school nor the student seems willing to adapt their style to one another. The student's father asks you what to do.

2. You find that the inhabitants of a small village where you are staying resent Americans a great deal because of previous bad experiences with the U.S. military and tourists. You discover that you have been grossly overcharged at your hotel and taken advantage of in other ways. Your plan was to spend the whole summer in one place rather than tour around so that you would get to know the people and not be an ordinary "tourist." Now you find that people are taking out their hostility toward "Americans" on you as an individual. You seek the advice of a casual friend who seems better accepted by the people than you are.

3. The person with whom you are traveling, a friend from back home, seems to be turning into an "ugly American," being condescending in his treatment of others, suspicious that he is being cheated, concerned that nothing is "clean" enough, and generally obnoxious toward non-Americans. You want to help him make a better adjustment both for his sake and because his behavior is embarrassing. You take him aside for a "little talk."

II. To Recognize and Deal With Dehumanizing Biases, Discrimination, and Prejudices

1. You are in a mixed group of new acquaintances. Elections have just been held, with the political parties divided along Protestant and Roman Catholic

lines. The discussion is intense and likely to erupt into violence. You are not well enough acquainted with the issues to recognize which of the persons in your group belong to which political party or religious group. One of the leaders in the group asks you for your opinion.

2. In becoming acquainted with your host family you discover that the women in this society have a very subservient role, have to work very hard, and are completely dominated by men. Cautious inquiries suggest that this style of life is well accepted and normal even though it seems extremely unfair to you as a woman. Your anger over this unfair treatment is beginning to show, and the members of your host family are starting to make fun of you for being a "women's lib" type.

3. Despite your best efforts in learning the foreign language, you find yourself inadequate in your ability to express yourself. The persons with whom you talk on the street seem impatient and somewhat irritated by the way you do violence to their language. You refuse to use English, even though their English is adequate, but you are beginning to resent their lack of sympathy with your attempts to enter their culture. You catch yourself becoming unreasonably angry with a complete stranger who doesn't understand you when you ask him a simple question.

III. To Create Learning Environments That Contribute to the Self-Esteem of All Persons and to Positive Interpersonal Relations

1. You are Jewish and find yourself in a large German city where everyone seems prejudiced against you. You had many relatives who suffered under the Germans in concentration camps, but you were never aware of any strong anti-German bias until now. It seems impossible to separate your feelings against Germans as a group from your relationship with them as individuals. You can understand and explain your bias, but you cannot seem to control your feelings that are coming out in your behavior toward Germans. A German casual acquaintance asks you if you are Jewish because you "look" Jewish, and you become extremely angry with him.

2. You are Black and have been invited to speak before a class of secondary students who have never seen or talked with a Black. A friend of yours invited you to come and explain to the students the racial problem in the United States and what is being done to combat racism.

3. The leader of your group is an authoritarian man who succeeds in dominating, planning, and controlling the activities of the group. He is jealous of any threat to his control. Other members of the group are able to tolerate his domination but you find it increasingly impossible. The other group members have begun looking to you, a woman with considerable international experience, for advice and guidance on what to do. You believe that the leader is doing a

bad job and resents your threat to his authority. You sit down to "have it out" with him for the group's sake as well as your own.

IV. Respect Human Diversity and Personal Rights

1. One of your friends is planning to marry a foreign national who is of a different religion as well as a different nationality than your friend. Neither set of parents agrees to the marriage, and the engaged couple is not sure they will be able to overcome the differences of both culture and religion. At the same time they are unwilling to separate and hope that once they are married their families will somehow come to agree. They ask your advice.

2. Your new friends insist on borrowing things from you and neglect to return them unless you ask for them back. They seem much more casual about "ownership" of personal belongings than you would like and assume that they have a right to your things as your friends. You try to set an example by not borrowing anything from them, but they continue to borrow from you and don't acknowledge the subtle hints you make. They seem to be using you to their own advantage, although among themselves they seem to have developed a satisfactory arrangement.

3. You have been caught with a group of friends who were in possession of marijuana. The police have placed all of you in jail and are not allowing you to contact anyone outside the jail. The conditions are impossible, and you feel that you are entirely at the mercy of the jailor. You are ready to do just about anything to get out of jail and are angry because you didn't even break the law in the first place. You need to find some way to get help.

5. Conclusion

There are prerequisites for counselors for examining multicultural criteria in terms of balance and complexity. One prerequisite is a need to reexamine their assumptions that stem from their cultural background. A second prerequisite is a need to accept the multiplicity of variables that constitutes an individual's cultural identity. Counselors may learn even to measure their competence by each client's ability to handle increasingly complex relationships. A third prerequisite is to develop a balance of indigenous support system variables. The ecology of mental health includes both formal and informal perspectives mediated by both the methods and context of counseling.

Counselors are at a starting point in understanding the role of formal and informal support systems in culturally complex counseling relationships. The next step will be either to develop a specialized and separate field of "multicultural counseling" or to illustrate the importance of cultural variables in all counseling relationships. The balanced integration of formal and informal sources of support will help counselors match the right method with the right context. The culturally accurate interpretation of behaviors from the perspective of expectations and values will help counselors manage both the complexity and the dynamism of a client's personal cultural orientation. Both balance and complexity will become more important as criteria for measuring competence in multicultural counseling.

CHAPTER 8

The Triad Model of Multicultural Counselor Training

The function of counseling is essentially to establish a temporary, means-oriented coalition with the client against the problem. Unless such a coalition can be established, the problem will continue to control the client and isolate the counselor. The client-counselor coalition provides a temporary, means-oriented vehicle for counselor effectiveness. The greater the cultural difference between a client and counselor, the less likely a counselor is to establish a coalition with the client against the problem.

The Triad Model describes counseling as a three-way interaction between the counselor, the client, and the problem from the client's perceptual world view. The problem is seen as both good and bad, especially from the client's point of view, not simply as bad. Each problem has rewarding as well as punishing features, which presents a dilemma for the client. The problem is complex, like a personality, and not limited to a single presenting symptom. The problem is actively changing, drawing its identity from the client's total environment of relationships. In the counseling relationship the problem sometimes resembles a personified enemy with a secret strategy of its own. The problem is concrete and not abstract, defined by its own threats and promises in the perceptual world view of the client.

1. Counseling as a Triad

When two persons communicate with one another in counseling, there are three conversations going on at the same time. The first conversation is the exchange of verbal and nonverbal messages that both partners see and hear. This is the least ambiguous and the most open of the three conversations. The second conversation or dialogue takes place within the counselor's mind as he or she processes the messages and observations. The counselor thinks about the alternative meanings of the messages the client communicates. Ideas and thoughts about totally irrelevant information also intrude into this internal conversation. The counselor monitors both the first conversation (what is being said by both persons) and the second conversation (what the counselor is thinking but perhaps not saying). The third conversation or dialogue takes place within the client's mind as he or she processes the messages and observations. The client will also think about alternative meanings of the messages the counselor communicates as well as irrelevant information that comes into the client's mind. The counselor does not know what this third conversation or internal dialogue within the client's mind is about. The client, however, probably debates both positive (procounselor) and negative (anticounselor) interpretations of the counseling interview.

The Triad Model for multicultural training is an attempt to make those positive and negative messages more explicit. As the counselor becomes more skilled in interpreting accurately the client's positive and negative messages from this third internal dialogue, the counselor will be in a better position to make appropriate decisions. The Triad Model brings a third person into *simulated* interviews to represent the anticounselor and sometimes a fourth person to represent the procounselor. The interactions of these three or even four persons provide insight into the client's internal dialogue. Counselors working with culturally different clients will have a particularly hard time in discerning the client's internal dialogue accurately.

Counseling can be described as an interaction of push and pull factors in which the counselor seeks fulfillment in being helpful, the client seeks to reconcile internalized ambiguity, and the problem either does or does not survive in its control over the client. Pepinsky and Karst (1964) contended that the counselor-client interaction is basically a social interaction that follows the same laws and principles as other social interactions. Pedersen (1968, 1976) described this force field in a conceptual model, characterizing counseling as a dynamic interaction of contrary forces in the mode of social power theory (Strong, 1978) and in the context of an equilibrium between the counselor seeking a coalition with the client against resistance by the problem (Caplow, 1968). The counselor-client coalition requires identifying action in accord with a shared goal. Just as the client has called in a counselor for assistance, the counselor must also depend on the client for knowledge about the problem. Negotiating a coalition between the client and counselor describes the task functions of counseling, which are subject to frequent maintenance and modification.

The use of three persons in therapy is not new. Bolman (1968) suggested that at least two therapists, one representing each culture, be used in multicultural therapy to provide a bridge between the client's culture and the therapist's culture. Slack and Slack (1976) also advocated triads by suggesting involving a third person, who had already coped effectively with a problem similar to the client's, in the counseling relationship. Triads have been applied in family therapy to illustrate pathogenic coalitions (Satir, 1964) where the therapist employs mediation and side-taking judiciously to break up and replace pathogenic relating. Counseling becomes a series of negotiations in which all three parties vie for control. Zuk (1971) described this approach as a "go-between" process where the therapist catalyzes conflict in a crisis situation that is favorable for change and in which all parties can take an active role.

The simulated multicultural counseling interview between a counselor from one culture and a coached client/anticounselor team from the same other culture was adapted to the techniques of video self-confrontation and microcounseling for teaching interviewer skills in attending behavior, reflection of feeling, and summarization of feeling (Ivey & Authier, 1978; Kagan, Krathwohl, & Farquhar, 1965). Videotaped interviews have demonstrated their effectiveness in identifying and strengthening positive facilitative behaviors and changing nonfacilitative behaviors; the supervisor is used as a third person who interrogates and debriefs the trainee after the interview. Other studies (Revich & Geertsma, 1969; Solomon & McDonald, 1970; Walz & Johnson, 1963) indicated that videotaped self-confrontation promotes behavioral change. Bryson, Renzaglia, and Danish (1974) also described how simulated racial encounters can be used in training.

Appropriate behavioral change is more likely to result when the videotape playback serves as a source of information feedback to the trainee by modeling the desired skills. Simulated "role-play" techniques have been widely used for some time, and the successful use of coached clients in simulated interviews also has been well documented (Whitely & Jakubowski, 1969).

Hosford and Mills (1983) reviewed an impressive data base demonstrating the importance of videotape as a therapeutic and training medium of choice, comparing the technological breakthrough of videotape in training with that of the microscope in the biological sciences. Video-based training and intervention approaches are being used in a wide variety of therapy and pretherapy training as well as research settings. Video-augmented interventions have proven effective in treating alcoholism, drug addiction, sexual dysfunction, suicidal intent, disruptive behavior of children, anorexia nervosa, anxiety, employment interviewing skill difficulties, assertiveness difficulties, phobias, marital social skills deficiencies, and a wide range of other psychological or behavioral problems (Hosford & Mills, 1983).

Video has numerous unique advantages in training. First of all it provides a permanent visual and auditory record that can be replayed. Second, it includes a mosaic of multilevel perspectives of the simplest to the most complex behaviors. Third, video is a highly personal medium encouraging participation. Fourth, video communicates rapidly, providing the basis for lengthy and detailed feedback. Fifth, video involves multiple information processing capabilities of the brain. "With the unique properties of videotape to involve major brain systems simultaneously, therapists can develop very potent interventions which can be used effectively to help clients ameliorate a variety of problems for which they seek counseling." (Hosford & Mills, 1983, p.126)

Pedersen (1976, 1977, 1978) developed a Triad Model for multicultural training. This model matches a therapist-trainee from one culture with a coached team of two other persons from a contrasting culture, one as a client and the other as an "anticounselor," for a videotaped simulation of a multicultural therapy session. The therapist seeks to build rapport with the culturally different coached client, while the anticounselor seeks to represent the problem element from the client's cultural viewpoint. The anticounselor is opposed to any successful intervention from a culturally different counselor. The anticounselor makes explicit the otherwise implicit resistance of culturally different clients. The Triad Model views counseling as a three-way interaction between the counselor, the client, and the problem where the counselor seeks to establish a temporary, means-oriented coalition with the client against the problem.

The unique element of this model is the personified role of the problem in the anticounselor, who actively tries to prevent the counselor from coalescing with the client toward solving the problem. Along with the anticounselor, there is also a "procounselor" in the client's internal dialogue, attempting to facilitate the counseling process in positive ways. Every counseling communication therefore contains three dialogues: first, the explicit verbal exchange; second, the counselor's internal dialogue; and third, the client's internal dialogue. Although counselors don't *know* the client's internal dialogue, we may assume that the dialogue has a negative (anticounselor) and a positive (procounselor) aspect. The Triad Model is merely an attempt to make the client's internal dialogue more explicit to the culturally different counselor.

The key element in the Triad Model is a balance of power between the *counselor* and *client* on the one hand and the *problem* on the other hand. The model grew out of 3 years' counseling in an Asian university where the problem element was frequently anthropomorphized as an externalized force in the interview. First, the problem is perceived as both good and bad, not just bad, judging from the client's perspective. For an alcoholic, a bottle of cheap wine may provide more immediate relief than advice. If the problem were unambiguously bad, the client would have an easier time disengaging. Second, a problem is complex, much like a personality in its dynamic, ever-changing, and adaptive capability to elude simplistic labels. Third, the problem is active rather than passive, with an ability to change and constantly adapt, so that what seems to be the problem at one point may change even during the course of an interview, as though the problem had a life of its own, independent of either counselor or client. Fourth, a problem is not abstract but, from the client's point of view, very concrete. The therapist must learn to work within the client's perceptual framework in order to be effective.

Figure 8 describes this triadic interaction between the counselor, client, and problem in which the client is initially dominated by the problem and the counselor intervenes to restore a balance of power in the client. Counseling then becomes a process whereby a client's contribution of power or influence increases and, as an inverse function of this process, the problem's capacity for power or influence decreases. The counselor intervenes to encourage the client's progress up the slope through a client-counselor coalition that balances the power influence of the problem.

As Figure 8 illustrates, at any point along the scale the power of the counselor plus the power of the client should be approximately equal to the power of the problem (Co + Cl = P). The effective counselor needs to vary the power of intervention according to the client's changing needs. If a counselor assumes too much power, the client will withdraw from counseling in preference for the problem, which will seem less threatening. If the counselor assumes too little power, the client will also withdraw back to the problem in response to ineffective counseling.

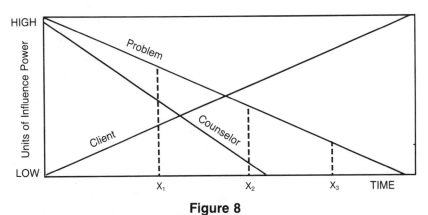

Figure 8
A Schematic Description of the Ratio of Power Influence Over Time for Counselor, Counselee, and Problem With Three (X$_1$, X$_2$, X$_3$) Points in the Counseling Process Indicated

The three situations (X_1, X_2, X_3) are indicated in Figure 8. In X_1, the client has little power and is dominated by the problem, requiring the counselor to exert more power than the client. In X_2 the client is able to exert enough power so that the counselor may reduce power. Situation X_3 shows the client as being able to manage the problem almost independently and maintain a balance. The measures of high and low power influence are relative and not absolute to accommodate a relatively effective client facing a difficult problem or a relatively ineffective client facing a mild problem.

The counselor needs to coordinate the power of intervention according to the variable rate and direction of a client's movement in order to maintain a client-counselor coalition and balance in the interview. Counselors might exert more power through confrontation and interpretation and less power through reflection and nondirective accommodation. To the extent that a counselor and a client come from different cultures, it is particularly difficult to maintain the appropriate balance of power in a counseling interview. The research indicating that a positive relationship is the most important predictor of success in therapy, however, suggests that this balance of power must be maintained. The Triad Model provides a conceptual framework for activating the counseling interaction and for defining the goal of training as increasing a counselor's skill in maintaining an effectively balanced relationship in counseling.

2. Research on the Triad Model

There are several advantages to applying the conceptual system of the Triad Model to the training setting. First, the anticounselor provides an opportunity for persons from different ethnic groups to role play critical incidents likely to arise in multicultural counseling under controlled conditions that maximize safety. Second, the use of an anticounselor makes the cultural problems and values less abstract and less diffuse for the naïve counselor. Third, the anticounselor immediately identifies inappropriate counselor interventions with direct and explicit feedback to the counselor trainee by whatever means would be appropriate to the client's culture. Fourth, the counselor trainee becomes more aware of the unspoken thoughts and feelings of the client from another culture. Fifth, the simulated interviews can be videotaped to analyze specific ways in which cultural differences affect counseling.

The Triad Model seems to work best when there is both positive and negative feedback to the counselor from the client and resource persons during or after the interview. For that reason, variations in roles for the client's partner have been developed in the roles of a "procounselor" and an "interpreter" as interchangeable with the "anticounselor." The procounselor and interpreter roles are introduced to complement the anticounselor model in more comprehensive multicultural training programs. When the client-anticounselor team is highly motivated and feels strongly about the issue under discussion, and when the anticounselor has a high degree of empathy for and acceptance by the client, more relevant insights about multicultural counseling result. The anticounselor needs to provide direct, immediate, and articulate feedback to the trainee, with the client being free to reject an inauthentic anticounselor. The simulated interview is spontaneous and not scripted. The selection and training of coached client/anticounselor teams are of primary importance. The teams should be as similar as possible, matching ethnicity, socioeconomic status, age, life style, sex roles, and other significant variables.

As a procounselor, the third person attempts to facilitate a coalition within the interview by reinforcing and encouraging positive counselor behaviors. As an interpreter, the third person attempts to increase the accuracy of communication between counselor and client, irrespective of positive or negative outcomes for counseling. Sometimes the incorporation of a resource person in an actual role from the client's background in a naturalistic mode is less confusing or abstract that the disembodied notion of an anticounselor, procounselor, or interpreter who represents "perspectives" rather than real persons. As a third-person-friendly, the third person becomes a friend or relative who encourages the counseling relationship in a naturalistic mode. As a third-person-hostile to counseling, the third person becomes a friend or relative who discourages the counseling relationship. A sixth training adaptation is being developed that includes both a procounselor and an anticounselor in a four-member simulated interview. The interaction between four persons can become quite complicated, but it clearly demonstrates both positive and negative aspects of the force field in a multicultural interview.

Research with prepracticum counseling students at the University of Hawaii showed that students trained with the Triad Model achieved significantly higher scores on a multiple-choice test designed to measure counselor effectiveness, had lower levels of discrepancy between real and ideal self-descriptions as counselor, and chose a greater number of positive adjectives in describing themselves as counselors than did students who were not trained with the Triad Model. Students trained with this model also showed significant gains on Carkhuff measures of empathy, respect, and congruence as well as on the seven-level Gordon scales measuring communication of affective meaning (Pedersen, Holwill, & Shapiro, 1978). Bailey (1981) compared a traditional mode of teaching human relations/multicultural skills with two modes using simulated interviews of two persons, as client and counselor in the first mode, and three persons, with a client, counselor, and an anticounselor in the second mode. She used Ivey's Counselor Effectiveness scale, a revised Truax Accurate Empathy scale, and the Revised Budner Tolerance of Ambiguity scale as dependent measures. In a three-way analysis of covariance, all tests were found significant between the lower-scoring traditionally trained group and both high-scoring treatment groups. No significant differences were found between the triad and dyad training groups on effectiveness, suggesting that both approaches were equally effective but similarly superior to the traditional lecture method of multicultural training for counselors.

Hernandez and Kerr (in press) trained three groups of students using (a) a didactic mode, (b) a didactic plus role-play with feedback mode, and (c) a didactic plus triad training mode. After training, videotaped interviews of all students were scored by six professionals on the Global Rating Scale, the Counselor Rating Form-Short, and the Cross Cultural Counseling Inventory. "The findings support experiential training and especially the continued use of Pedersen's Triad Model which is geared towards sensitizing and preparing counselors to work more effectively and efficiently with clients from diverse ethnic backgrounds" (p. 14). Neimeyer, Fukuyama, Bingham, Hall, and Mussenden (1986) compared the reactions of 20 counseling students who participated in either the procounselor or anticounselor conditions of Pedersen's Triad Model. Results indicated that participants in the more confrontational anticounselor version felt more confused and less competent than did participants in the procounselor version. No differences in objective ratings of response effectiveness were noted, however, suggesting a differentiation between perceived expertness and actual effectiveness. Neimeyer et al. suggested that the more confrontational anticounselor model is better suited to more advanced students who already have developed some confidence for multicultural interactions, which is consistent with other research on the Triad Model (Sue, 1980; Ivey & Authier, 1978).

Derald Sue (1980) field-tested the anticounselor and procounselor training models with 36 counseling students at California State University, Hayward. Sue reported that students felt the anticounselor model was more effective than the precounselor model in achieving self-awareness, developing cultural sensitivity for contrasting cultural values, and understanding political/social ramifications of multicultural counseling. The anticounselor model tended to be most effective in giving participants awareness of their cultural values and biases, engendering cultural sensitivity to other ethnically defined groups, and helping them understand the political/social ramifications of counseling. The procounselor model was most effective in helping students obtain specific knowledge of the history, experiences, and cultural values of ethnic groups, and helping them develop multicultural counseling skills. Students were more comfortable with the procounselor model, whereas the anticounselor model was more anxiety provoking. When asked to rate the most effective model for learning about multicultural counseling in the shortest period of time, however, the anticounselor model was seen as far superior. Confrontation by the anticounselor brought out issues of racism, bias, and conflicting values through immediate feedback to the counselor trainees, whereas the procounselor tended to facilitate acquisition of skills. The anticounselor showed trainees' mistakes, and the procounselor helped remedy counselor trainees' multicultural style. Ideally, a good training design would incorporate both an anticounselor and a procounselor.

3. Multicultural Training of Counselors

The Triad Model has been used in several hundred workshops throughout the United States. Persons who have used the model report that they are able to articulate the problem better after a series of multicultural interviews with the client/anticounselor teams—"The client's problem as I see it from my own cultural viewpoint is almost certain to be different from the way that problem is viewed from within the client's culture." Participants also reported increased skill in anticipating resistance to counseling from persons of other cultures. Otherwise, counselors might complete a multicultural interview knowing they failed but never knowing *why* they failed. Immediate feedback from the anticounselor confronts a counselor with mistakes even before the counselor has finished a poorly chosen intervention. There are indications that participants in the counselor role become less defensive after training and are less threatened by working with clients from other cultures after training. Finally, there is less anxiety about making mistakes in counseling clients from other cultures when trainees have rehearsed "recovery skills" for getting out of trouble when they make a mistake.

The Triad Model has been used both for preservice training as a unit in a prepracticum counseling course and for a series of inservice training workshops. A demonstration 1-hour videotape with four triad interviews accompanied by a training manual has been produced by Media Resources at the University of Minnesota for counselors who want to use the Triad Model in their own training program. Selection and training of coached client/anticounselor teams is of primary importance. These teams of resource persons should be as similar as possible, with matching ethnicity, nationality, socioeconomic group, age level, life style, and sex role. Ordinarily, an unusually articulate and knowledgeable resource person from the target population is invited to participate as an anticounselor and asked to select a culturally similar teammate as a coached client. The client/anticounselor teams are trained by viewing and discussing the 1-hour model videotape and then rehearsing their roles with the trainer as the counselor. Usually one client/anticounselor team is trained for every 10 participants in the workshop or classroom module. Each team represents a different cultural viewpoint, so the more teams, the more culturally varied the training experience.

In the inservice training workshop for smaller groups of counselors, two teams are trained, and the 10 to 15 counselors are assembled in a meeting room with a video monitor. Following an introduction and presentation of the video demonstration tape of the triad model, the facilitator answers questions while one of the counselors leaves the room with a client/anticounselor team to make the first videotape. The counselor and team return to the group after having produced a 10-minute videotape of a simulated counseling interview and a 5-minute videotape of the three participants debriefing one another. This 15-minute videotape is shown to the larger group for comments and discussion. While the first tape is being viewed and discussed, another counselor leaves the room with the second client/anticounselor team to produce a second videotape. Throughout the day there is always one counselor and one team making a tape while another videotape is being viewed or discussed, until all counselors have had a chance to produce a videotape and receive feedback on their performance. Each counselor misses the viewing and discussion on one colleague's videotape. The advantages of immediate feedback of videotaped counseling interviews provoke stimulating discussions on the variety of cultures as well as presenting problems in counseling relationships. The videotapes produced during such a workshop can also provide a valuable resource (Pedersen, 1976).

The inservice training workshop for larger groups of counselors requires one trained team for every 10 participants and a room large enough for everyone to meet together in small groups. After the introduction and presentation of the demonstration videotape, the Triad Model is demonstrated to the group. The model can be demonstrated by one team to the whole group, or participants can be asked to break up into triads and experience the triad model directly, with guidance from the circulating facilitators and team members. Once the participants have a clear notion of the model, they are divided into groups of 10 according to prearranged assignments to ensure that each group will be as culturally heterogeneous as possible. A different team will be assigned to each group for a period of 45 minutes. During this time the team will elect a volunteer from the group to role play the counselor. The team will have prepared three or four problems for simulated counseling interviews with the volunteer. They will role play the interview for 5 or 10 minutes and then go out of role for a 5- or 10-minute debriefing period. If there is time, a second volunteer may be chosen and the process repeated. After each 45-minute period, the teams rotate to another group in ordered sequence until each team has met with each group. A general discussion period at the end of the day is used to share insights and answer questions.

The preservice example of using the model was used in prepracticum courses at the Department of Guidance and Counseling, University of Minnesota, University of Nebraska, Virginia Polytechnic, University of Hawaii, Harvard University, and Syracuse University. Thirty students were randomly paired with another classmate from the opposite sex or different ethnic group. Each pair made two videotapes of simulated counseling interviews, switching roles for the second tape as a premeasure of multicultural counseling ability. These tapes and a similar series of posttraining tapes were scored to measure changes in skill resulting from training. The 30 students were assembled into triads so that each triad contained two subjects of one sex and the third member of an opposite sex. Five of the 10 triads were also multicultural in ethnic composition. The objective was to have triads where two persons were much alike and one person was as different as possible, using sex role and ethnicity as indicators of differences. During the first phase of training, one student in each triad was assigned to the counselor role, one to the client role, and one to the anticounselor role. They met for 3 hours in the same roles, simulating and discussing three different multicultural interviews. During the second phase of the training 1 week later, the students rotated roles in the triad and the 3-hour procedure was repeated. During the third phase in the third week of the project, students again rotated their roles so that each student had experience in each of the roles for a third 3-hour session for a total of 9 hours, using the Triad Model with feedback on nine crosscultural interviews (Pedersen et al., 1978).

Adaptations of these training designs have been used in a wide variety of workshop or classroom situations. The Triad Model seems to work best (a) when there is positive as well as negative feedback to the counselor, (b) when all three persons rather than just the counselor and client interact with one another, (c) when the client/anticounselor team is highly motivated and feels strongly about the issue under discussion, (d) when the anticounselor has a high degree of empathy for and acceptance by the client, (e) when the anticounselor is articulate and gives direct, immediate verbal or nonverbal feedback to the counselor, (f) when the client has *not* selected a real problem from his or her current situation where counseling might be appropriate, (g) when the discussion is spontaneous and not scripted, (h) when the counselor has a chance to role play the model and receive feedback three or four times in sequence, (i) when the client feels free to reject an inauthentic anticounselor, and (j) when the facilitator introducing the model and leading the discussion is well acquainted with how the model operates.

4. Triad Resource Persons

Three different variations of the Triad Model include the use of an anticounselor, procounselor, or an interpreter. In each case the three-way interaction helps to make a culturally different client's internal dialogue more explicit. All of the following interview examples are transcripts of *simulated* counselor interviews.

As an example of the anticounselor at work, let us consider a situation where a White American male counselor (CO) is working with a 24-year old Japanese-

American female client (CL) who is troubled about whether or not to move out of her parents' home. The anticounselor (AC) is also a Japanese-American woman. The perception of a parent/daughter relationship is quite different for the client than for the counselor, making it difficult for the counselor to see the problem accurately. A portion of the interview transcript illustrates the contrasting perceptions, as illuminated by the anticounselor.

CL: What do you think I should do? I mean, what's correct? Do you think . . .?

CO: Well, I guess if you're going to play by your parents' rules, staying home and suffering, I think . . . .

AC: You see! He thinks you're suffering at home and that you should move out. Your parents! Remember!

CL: Do you think I'm suffering at home?

CO: Well, I think something brought you here to talk to me about the dilemma you're in about wanting to move out and being very uncomfortable in having a rough time bringing it up with your folks in such a way that uh . . . you can do that.

CL: If your folks felt that you didn't like them because you moved out and you were ungrateful . . .

AC: Ask him when he moved out; when he actually moved out of his house.

CL: Yeah, when did you move out of your house?

CO: I moved out of my folks' house when I was 16.

AC: Why did he move out so young, you know? I mean 16!!! After all that his parents did for him and everything! You know? He moved out at 16!

CO: Well, I went away to school. And, it was important to live at school. It was in another town.

CL: Didn't your parents get mad that you went to another school?

CO: No, they wanted me to go to school. Education is pretty important.

AC: See! He's implying that your parents don't think education is important!

In this brief example the anticounselor demonstrates what the client might be thinking but would probably not say in the interview. Through the anticounselor, the counselor has direct access to an implicit level of meaning from the client's cultural point of view.

By contrast, the procounselor attempts to provide every opportunity for the counselor to do a better job. Sometimes a procounselor ends up replacing the counselor and taking over the interview rather than facilitating the counselor's own effectiveness. A skilled procounselor will help the counselor do a better job without distracting or threatening the counselor. An example of a skilled procounselor at work illustrates some of the ways of providing help within the interview.

The counselor in this situation was a White man (CO), the client was a White lesbian (CL), and the procounselor (PC) was a White woman. The client was a female graduate student in her early 20s. She had recently had a fight with her female roommate/lover and the lover left the state. The client was left with much anger, loss, and anxiety over the situation. It began to affect her schoolwork and that brought her to counseling. The cultural difference in this interview relates to sex role rather than ethnicity.

CO: What else is going on? What other kinds of issues are bothering you? Is it mainly school?

CL: Well, just, you know, I wouldn't say anything is bothering me . . . I guess everything is bothering me . . . I guess everything is bothering me right now because of school. But, ah, you know, if you don't think you can help me, just say so. I don't expect . . .

PC: Look at how nervous I am and look at how I am shaking.

CO: You're really, really concerned about things . . .

CL: Wouldn't you be?

CO: Sure, yeah, yeah. And yet you're not sure that I can help you. You won't let me hear . . .

CL: Why? You haven't helped me yet!

PC: Maybe it has something to do with your being a man.

CO: Do you think, ah, can you think of what kind of help you'd like me to be? Can you think of some ways I can be of help to you?

CL: Ah, yeah, I guess I don't think you can help me much.

PC: Sarah, give him a try. I know he's a man, but give him a try.

CL: I, ah, who are you, anyway?

CO: I'm a psychologist and, ah . . .

CL: Where did you go to school?

CO: Where'd . . . I went to Brown as an undergraduate and to the University of Colorado as a graduate student, and I had some problems in graduate school, too.

PC: He might understand your problems, you know.

CO: I'd like to try to help you if I can, and if I can't there's always the possibility that another therapist might be better, but I'm willing to give it a try if you want to try working with me a few sessions.

CL: Yeah, you really don't get a whole lot of choice here at Counseling and Testing. I just got signed up and I didn't know if you were going to be a man or woman or social worker or what.

CO: Would you rather be working with a woman?

CL: Ah, yes.

After the interview, the procounselor commented on how she provided support for the client.

As a procounselor, it was extremely frustrating working with a counselor who used a different style than I would use. The counselor did not seem interested in the clues that I gave him and ignored my suggestions. At times I felt angry with the counselor. Timing of my comments seemed disharmonious and the session felt disjointed. I was attempting to facilitate problem clarification by focusing on the "here and now" situation by comments on the client's expectation of sessions and nonverbal behavior occurring in the present. When I realized the direction I was going in—providing data to the therapist—wasn't working, I switched to supporting the client, e.g., putting my arm around her, suggesting she level with the therapist, and so forth. This change of approach felt better than the first direction.

The interpreter acts as *both* procounselor and anticounselor in providing feedback. As an example of the interpreter role, consider an interview between a Black male counselor (CO), a Laotian male client (CL), and a Laotian male interpreter (I). The problems in this simulated role play relate to a Hmong refugee (the client) living in Honolulu. Hmong are highland people of Laos. There are several concerns of a physical, psychological, and spiritual nature. Physically, the client had suffered abdominal pains and backaches that led to an unwanted operation. "Strange" behavior suggests that the client's psychological state has been affected. For example, he has been seen walking down the street wearing two or three pairs of pants, sometimes forgetting to look at traffic lights or cars. He also has followed strangers in town. The most significant problem, however, is the loss of everything familiar in having had to flee to a new country. This has disrupted his spiritual well-being. The client, consequently, attributes all his present problems to the ill-doings of spirits. Thus, the counseling dilemma, which is broached in the simulated role play, is how to treat this person within the context of his cultural beliefs and expectations when no traditional healer from the client's culture is available.

Consider how the interpreter acts as a teacher for the counselor through neutral feedback that is neither clearly negative nor positive:

CO: Uh, have I left anything out?
CL: No, I think you covered what I had told you. And, in addition to that, I also have some other problems because after the operation, I began to worry about myself and my future life, very, very, much. I do not know what to do, so I spend days and nights thinking about what am I going to do with myself? And, I could not eat, as I said before, I could not sleep, so I kind of stay "half-way" (half-awake) all the time. And this leads to a lot of things that I have in my mind: At times I can see my grandparents who died many years ago, or my friend who was in the army together with me who was killed. And they are all there happily and they keep calling my name, and waiting to see me.

I: What he's saying is he's stuck because he worries so much about his life and so forth that . . . this culture, when you start seeing things— especially a member of your family or your close friend who has died— that means that his life is also going down the drain. That he will die soon. If it were back home, that's what would happen.

CO: OK. So that's what having those visions means in your culture. Maybe what I can do is give some feedback to you about what that would possibly mean in this culture, and you might have a better understanding of how that's handled. And maybe you can help me out. Uh, it seems like what you experience could be seen as visions of your grandparents or hallucinations. Or some psychologists might use the word delusions— things like that. People have been helped in the Western culture a lot of times just through talking therapy or getting into some new type of occupation; some new type of environment might relieve those visions. (*To Interpreter*) I don't know if I'm getting this across to him, but maybe you can . . .

I: What he's saying is that things like that happen in this country also, but it's not as serious as it would be if it happened in our country. Because they can do things, patients with that kind of problem can be helped . . . Is that what you are saying?

CO: It can be just as serious; I wouldn't put it off, saying that it's not as serious, it can be just as serious—but work can be done to help make life a little bit easier for you. Uh . . .

CL: If anything can help me, I will appreciate it very much. You see, back home, when we have something like this, we usually go to the traditional medicine man and he will either give us some medicine or he will chant. And, with his chant, all the spirits will go away and that way, he can save our life. But here, I do not know of anybody who can do these sorts of things. So I hope that you can help me.

CO: Well, Uh . . .

I: What he's saying is that in his particular culture, when you see those things—the spirits coming close to humans—it can cause harm to the living. So, we have traditional healers (or whatever you call them in this country). We have a whole ceremony to chase the spirits away or whatever, and then he would be cured. That means he would not see those spirits again and so forth.

These several examples show how training culturally different resource persons as coached clients provides direct and immediate feedback for counselor trainees in simulated multicultural interviews. When resource persons are authentic to a particular culture and articulate in that culture's viewpoint, the impact of their comments has a powerful influence on the counselor's attitudes. By including representatives of the client's population in training counselors to work with that population, the client's cultural perspective is directly valued as an important part of counselor training.

5. Specific Guidelines for Using the Triad Model

Meichenbaum's (1974) cognitive behavioral approach and subsequent research have demonstrated the importance of knowing a client's internal dialogue. Other research has also indicated that the more culturally different the client the more difficult it will be to interpret that client's internal dialogue accurately. The Triad Model is an attempt to articulate a client's internal dialogue through the role of an anticounselor and a procounselor from the client's cultural perspective. In summarizing this approach it is important to describe the procounselor and the anticounselor role, review the advantages of each role in multicultural training, and provide examples of what someone role playing each role might say or do.

Description of the Anticounselor Triad Design

1. The anticounselor is deliberately subversive in attempting to bring out mistakes of the counselor trainee.
2. The counselor and the anticounselor are pulling in opposite directions, with the client choosing among the same-culture anticounselor, who most likely understands but is opposed to counseling, and a different-culture counselor who is likely to understand the client but is working toward a counseling solution.
3. A counselor-client coalition against the problem, or anticounselor, becomes the vehicle of effective counseling whereas ineffective counseling results in a client-problem coalition that isolates the counselor.

Advantages of the Anticounselor Triad Design

1. The anticounselor forces the counselor to be aware and attune to the client's cultural perspective. If the counselor fails to establish the client's trust in the counselor's ability to solve the problem, a counselor-client coalition against the problem will not occur.
2. The anticounselor articulates the negative, embarrassing, and impolite data that would otherwise remain unsaid.
3. The anticounselor forces the counselor to examine the counselor's own defensiveness and raise the counselor's threshold for nondefensive responses.

4. The anticounselor quickly points out a counselor's inappropriate intervention and mistakes. This allows the counselor to become skilled in recovering from mistakes with increased rather than diminished rapport.
5. The anticounselor often attempts to sidetrack the discussion and distract the counselor. This forces the counselor to become skilled in focusing on the client's problem.

Examples of What an Anticounselor Might Say or Do

1. Build on the positive things a problem has to offer, which may anchor one end of a client's ambivalence about giving the problem up.
2. Keep the interaction on a superficial level or attempt to sidetrack the counselor toward inconsequential conversation.
3. Obstruct communication by getting "in-between" the counselor and the client both physically and psychologically.
4. Attempt to distract and annoy the counselor in order to draw attention away from the client.
5. Emphasize the importance of "cultural differences" between the counselor and client to undermine a counselor's faith in his or her ability to intervene appropriately.
6. Demand immediate, specific, and observable results from counseling.
7. Exclude the counselor by communicating privately with the client by whispering, using their shared foreign language, or playing cultural "in jokes."
8. Find a scapegoat and ride it to deflect all blame away from the problem.
9. Insist that someone more expert be called in to replace the counselor.

Description of the Procounselor Triad Design

1. The procounselor helps the counselor and client articulate the presenting problem from the client's cultural reference point.
2. The third person, procounselor, functions as a facilitator for the multicultural interview.
3. The procounselor identifies with the client's culture and thus is able to provide relevant cultural information to the counselor.
4. The procounselor is not a cotherapist but serves as an immediate resource person who can guide the counselor by suggesting specific therapeutic strategies and supplying information the client may be reluctant to provide.
5. The procounselor can reinforce the counselor's strategy both verbally and nonverbally.

Advantages of the Procounselor Design

1. The counselor has an immediate resource person to consult when confused about the problem or needing support.
2. The procounselor makes cultural information explicit with the intention of facilitating the interview.
3. The procounselor gives the advantage of another person working on the problem without taking on a cocounseling role with the client (this could happen, but is not an objective of the procounselor triad design).
4. The procounselor helps lower the client's resistance to counseling by helping the counselor approach sensitive issues in a culturally appropriate style.
5. The procounselor can provide beneficial feedback to the counselor if and when the counselor seems defensive in the interview.

Examples of What a Procounselor Might Say or Do

1. Restate what either the client or counselor says in a positive fashion.
2. Relate statements by the client or counselor to previous content, e.g., "Like what he said before . . ."
3. Offer approval or reinforcement of client or counselor affective states, e.g., "You seem to be feeling more relaxed now."
4. Reinforce what a client or counselor says by nodding when the procounselor feels something desirable is being discussed.
5. Reinforce what a client does, e.g., saying "That's good" to a client who volunteers a lot of information.
6. Aid the counselor by making suggestions, e.g., "We should focus on this problem because the client has the most trouble with this."

A number of models are being used for therapy that involve three persons, such as conjoint family therapy, therapy with cocounselors, work with interpreters/translators, or work with a client's friend who is brought into the therapy interview. The Triad Model differs from those alternatives in the unique characteristics of the anticounselor and procounselor.

The Triad Model has been used for about 10 years with several hundred groups of counselors. Persons who have used the model report that they are better able to articulate the problem after a series of crosscultural interviews with the client/anticounselor teams. The client's problem, from the counselor's viewpoint, is almost always different from the way that problem is viewed in the client's culture. Participants also report increased skill in specifying the resistance in the counseling interview. Immediate feedback from an anticounselor confronts the counselor with mistakes even before the counselor has finished a wrongly chosen sentence. Other research indicates statistically significant growth on the three Carkhuff scales of empathy, respect, and congruence as well as on the Gordon seven-level measures of understanding affect. There are indications that participants in the counselor role become less defensive after training and less threatened by working with clients from other cultures. Finally, there is evidence that participants' real and ideal views of themselves as counselors become more congruent after training.

5. Conclusion

The Triad Model seems to offer a number of advantages over alternative training approaches. It provides an opportunity for persons from different cultures to accomplish a training goal. By a simulated interview format, the model offers greater safety to demonstrate strong feelings and provide direct feedback. Separating the roles of client and anticounselor makes the problem less diffuse and abstract to counselor trainees. The anticounselor models and encourages negative feedback to the counselor in a less threatening mode. Inappropriate counselor intervention is immediately apparent in feedback from the anticounselor. Members of the client's culture become resource persons for teaching counselors to work with individuals of the client's culture. In this way the client population has an expert role in training counselors. In the balance of power between counselor and anticounselor, the trainees are reminded that the determination of success or failure ultimately lies with the client and not with the counselor. More data are being collected on strengths and weaknesses of the Triad Model by developing alternative triad modes using a procounselor, instead of the anticounselor, for example, to reinforce and facilitate appropriate multicultural counseling skills. Although the model emphasizes multicultural training of counselors, the focus is on training any counselor to work better with any client. Culture is only a label for one of the many sources of influence that affect counseling relationships.

CHAPTER 9

Four Dimensions of Multicultural Skill Training

We already have demonstrated the importance of defining culture to include the perspectives of age, sex, life style, socioeconomic status, and other special affiliations. From this perspective all counseling is to a greater or lesser extent multicultural because the client and counselor are almost certainly somewhat different in their affiliations. We also have seen how standard counseling skills create problems when they are applied indiscriminately across cultural groups. This chapter is an attempt to identify four areas, each incorporating many different skills, that are designed to adapt standard counseling skills to multicultural counseling.

The four skill areas discussed in this chapter are designed to complement and not substitute for good counseling technique. The training model requires a simulated multicultural counseling interview between a coached client-anticounselor team from one culture and a counselor trainee from a different culture. The interview is videotaped and rerun for a debriefing discussion among the three participants and a counselor trainer. The anticounselor role is similar to that of an alter ego in psychodrama, except that the anticounselor is not neutral but rather is deliberately subversive in attempting to bring out mistakes in the counselor trainee. The counselor and the anticounselor are consequently pulling in opposite directions, and the client chooses between the same-culture anticounselor, who most likely understands the client but is opposed to counseling, and a different-culture counselor who is less likely to understand the client but is working toward a counseling solution. A counselor-client coalition against the problem, or anticounselor, becomes the vehicle of effective counseling, whereas ineffective counseling results in a client-problem coalition that isolates the counselor.

1. Multicultural Skill Areas

Four skill areas have emerged from working with the Triad Model in simulated multicultural interviews. These skill areas are: (1) articulating the problem from the client's cultural perspective; (2) recognizing resistance from a culturally different client in specific rather than general terms; (3) being less defensive in a culturally ambiguous relationship; and (4) learning recovery skills for getting out of trouble when making mistakes in counseling culturally different clients. These skill areas are in the process of being tested and validated.

The four areas share some face validity, however. First, we each perceive the world from our own culturally biased viewpoint. If the client does not share the counselor's cultural background, the client's viewpoint is likely to differ from the counselor's. Second, it is important to recognize resistance in specific rather than general terms as it relates to cultural differences between the counselor and client before the interview can be expected to proceed. Third, the multicultural interview is frequently ambiguous for the counselor and can easily cause even a skilled counselor to become uncertain or defensive. If the counselor is distracted by becoming defensive, the rapport with a client is likely to diminish. Constant attack by the anticounselor is most likely to bring out a defensive response in the counselor that can be viewed, controlled, and diminished. Fourth, skilled counselors make perhaps as many mistakes as do unskilled counselors. Skilled counselors are, however, able to get out of trouble and recover from mistakes with increased rather than diminished rapport with the client. The function of training is not only to train counselors how to avoid making mistakes, but also to help those who make mistakes to recover effectively. The Triad Model provides opportunities for the counselor to recover from mistakes in a relatively safe environment and to develop recovery skills that fit the counselor's own style and a variety of different situations.

In developing specific abilities within each of these four general areas, Ivey's microcounseling skills (Ivey, 1980a) were extremely influential. More information on the microskills is available in Ivey's (1980a) several publications. Each of the four areas includes a series of specific skills.

Excerpts from four triad interviews will illustrate the four skill areas of articulating the problem from the client's cultural perspective; anticipating resistance from a culturally different client; diminishing defensiveness by studying the trainee's own defensive responses; and learning recovery skills for getting out of trouble when counseling the culturally different client.

In each interview the counselor was instructed to do the best job of counseling he or she could, the client was instructed to be objective and to accept help from either the counselor or anticounselor, and the anticounselor was instructed to use cultural similarity with the client in preserving the problem and diminishing the counselor's effectiveness. The three participants were allowed to speak directly to one another, the counselor was encouraged to use feedback from the anticounselor to modify counseling behaviors, and the anticounselor was encouraged to confront any inappropriate intervention by the counselor. All interviews were simulated and role played.

2. Unit One: Articulating the Problem

Each of us perceives the world from our own culturally biased point of view. To the extent that a client does not share the counselor's cultural background, the client is less likely to share the same point of view regarding the problem being discussed. The following excerpts from the demonstration videotaped interview illustrate how the Triad Model assists counselor trainees in discovering how the counselor and client might have different points of view regarding the problem. There is a brief discussion following each interview excerpt.

SKILL AREA: Articulate the Problem

The following excerpts from transcripts illustrate how the three-way interaction among client, counselor, and anticounselor helps articulate elements of the problem under discussion.

Problem 1

Client: Like I am a liberal arts major and a lot of times most of the classes are a lot of White kids. There aren't many Black kids on campus. And not in GC, General College, you know, so the ones I do know I have to go elsewhere to meet them, talk to them and stuff.

Counselor: Is it White gals you have a problem relating to and White guys or . . .?

Client: Well . . .

Anticounselor: Right now, the question is can you relate to him? (*pause*) Yeah, what are you doing here?

Client: Well, uh, you got a good question there. I mean . . .

Counselor: Do you have difficulty relating to me now? I'm White, you're Black.

Anticounselor: Remember all the things that happen when White folks deal with Black folks.

At this point the anticounselor almost seems to contribute to the counselor's own resources both regarding the content, Black-White relationships, and the client's process of relating to the counselor in the present. Sometimes the process almost resembles a cocounselor triad, with the client benefiting from both the counselor and anticounselor.

Problem 2

Client: And I'm here on a scholarship studying Portuguese. And, well, I'll guess I'll just try to . . . Do you want to explain what you are all about since you're the problem?

Anticounselor: Sure. We're horny! (*laugh*)

Counselor: That's . . .

Anticounselor: Since we've been down in this country I've never seen so many teasers before in my life. (*laugh*) Remember the one you met in the swimming pool the other day? (*laugh*)

Client: I guess he's pretty well explained it, but what it amounts to is, ah, I study all day and of course in the evenings I want to take a break and do something fun and so I've been visiting some of your night spots and I find a lot of beautiful women down here; they're really nice. So we have a few drinks and we talk, maybe we go to the theater or something, and we go home up to my apartment, and I start making some passes toward them because they are giving me all these come-on signs, you see . . .

Counselor: Oh.

Client: And as soon as I start making these passes they get scared, and they either split or break down and start crying, and I just don't understand it.

In Problem 2, there is a clear division of responsibility between the client and the anticounselor in explicating the problem, the client acknowledging what the anticounselor says as true but being unwilling to say the same thing himself. It's as though the client can rest assured that the negative, embarrassing, and impolite data that need to be brought out in a counseling interview can be turned over to the competent anticounselor. As the interview develops, the negative feedback from the anticounselor models negative statement making for the client as well, so the overall effect is explicating more of the negative and difficult aspects of the problem than would be likely to emerge in a multicultural counseling dyad. Although those negative aspects might not have been brought out explicitly, they would nonetheless have been there and, even unexplained, would have had a profound effect on counseling.

Problem 3

Anticounselor: You chose to be in graduate school. Since you chose to be in graduate school, why complain about it?

Client: Yeah, I know about it and she knows about it as well, but, I mean that . . . we don't know that it is going to turn out like that.

Counselor: Uh-huh . . . You don't deny the fact that you put these pressures on yourself. You accept that.

Client: Yeah, yeah.

Counselor: But at this point you're saying, my god, I didn't think that when I was taking these responsibilities on myself that it would lead to this.

Client: And moreover when you are in graduate school you have all kinds of pressure on you that you have to pass this prelim and that and ah . . .

Anticounselor: School is more important than love affairs.

Client: That's what they think, but . . .

Anticounselor: Your parents won't want you to lose yourself over a love affair and give up your work.

In explicating the problem, the anticounselor on occasion may attack the client as well as the counselor in order to keep the interview off balance and retain control. The distracting elements of a client's problem can be brought out by the anticounselor to overwhelm both the client and the counselor.

The skill area of "articulating the problem," or perceiving the problem from the client's cultural point of view, contains many microskills in the tradition of Ivey (1980a). It is useful to consider the following components, many drawn from the literature on counselor skills training, in describing the ability to articulate the problem.

1. Perceiving the problem from the client's cultural viewpoint

Cognitive rational insight: The counselor develops the ability to define accurately the feelings related to a client's presenting problem.

Paraphrase: The counselor gives back to the client the essence of past verbal statements by selective attention to the content of client verbalizations.

Reflection of feeling: Selective attention is given to key affective or emotional aspects of client behavior.

Summarization: The counselor reflects a client's feelings over a longer period of time and gives several strands of thinking back to client.

Concreteness: The counselor's statements are less vague or inconclusive and more concrete or specific.

Immediacy: The counselor matches the client's statements by using the same time perspective—whether past, present, or future.

Respect: Enhancing statements by the counselor about self or others are considered to represent respect, whereas negative statements or "put-downs" indicate an absence of this dimension.

Genuineness: There is an absence of mixed verbal and nonverbal messages. In particularly effective communication, verbal and nonverbal message synchrony between client and counselor may be noted.

Positive Regard: The counselor gives selective attention to positive aspects of self or others or to the demonstrated belief that people can change and manage their own lives.

Tracking: The counselor is able to follow accurately and even anticipate what the client will say next in the interview.

3. Unit Two: **Recognizing Resistance**

It is important to recognize resistance in specific rather than general terms as it relates to cultural differences between a counselor and a client. When resistance arises in an interview it is important to identify and deal with it before proceeding to control the problem dimension of the counseling interview. It is important to watch the interaction between a client and anticounselor partner to determine the nature of resistance in the simulated interview. If the client accepts and validates what the anticounselor says, it is important for the counselor to modify his or her intervention to accommodate what the anticounselor says.

SKILL AREA: Anticipate Resistance

The following excerpts illustrate how the Triad Model helps a counselor anticipate the kinds of resistance or barriers likely to occur in an interview with clients from other cultures. In a crosscultural dyad, many of these insights would not be brought out or would be assumed to be understood without explication.

Resistance 1

Anticounselor: Make sure you really want to share that with him now.
Client: Well, he's the counselor; he's supposed to be helping me.
Anticounselor: Yeah, OK, I agree with that. But do you really want to share me with him? I mean—wouldn't somebody else be better able to deal with this whole situation rather than somebody on that side of the tracks who doesn't know what we're all about?
Counselor: Are you getting a little uncomfortable, Terry? Perhaps because I'm White—in sharing some of these things with me?
Client: Uh—not really, and it's like I said, you know. I try to be pretty openminded about what I'm talking about. But the thing I want to know is can you really understand where I'm coming from? What kind of things I'm really dealing with?
Counselor: Try me.
Client: OK. Like I said, most of my classes have uh—you get tired of being the only Black kid in classes. Well, I can't change that because I can't get more sisters and brothers on campus. Right? So the thing is, I would like to know— what is it about myself that people find so funny that they can make jokes at and not expect me to really feel bad when somebody makes a Black joke?
Counselor: Yeah, but I don't think there is anything about you that is so funny . . . (*pause*) I don't laugh at you.

Anticounselor: Listen to the hesitation, listen to the hesitation—did that sound like it came from the heart to you? Did you hear the hesitation in that?

Client: What exactly—what exactly do you think my problem is? (*pause*) If you think I don't understand it . . .

In the struggle to establish trust with a client from another culture, the counselor is sometimes perceived as one of the enemy group of White, middle-class men who seem to be to blame for what has happened. It is enormously hard to break through that predisposition as an individual. Even so minor a distraction as a hesitation by the counselor will have a potentially negative interpretation.

Resistance 2

Anticounselor: We've been here 5 or 6 minutes and how much trust do we have in him? What has he done so far that can make us say that we can trust him to deal with the whole situation? You heard him hesitate. You heard him stumble around; we've heard him take the uniqueness out of the problem.

Counselor: Terry . . .

Anticounselor: We've heard him say deal with the jokes. How much trust can we put in this man?

Counselor: Terry, why don't you ah—try to ah—eliminate (*pause*) not eliminate, certainly not eliminate . . .

Anticounselor: I'm beginning to think trust is getting less and less.

Counselor: I asked you a question on . . .

Client: Well, it's like the questions you are asking don't stick in my mind as well as what he is saying to me. It's like he can relate with what I'm, you know, the thing I'm going with and you gave me a lot of stuff about how a lot of Black people are approaching the same problem. But the thing is what I want to know is—how do I deal with it?

There is a buildup of data in which counselor mistakes or insights contribute toward an overall perception. Mistakes in particular contribute toward a losing score for the counselor. The client in likely to move toward a conclusion that is either positive or negative in trusting the counselor. If the conclusion is negative, however, the counselor would be less likely to get that feedback in a crosscultural dyad than in the triad.

Resistance 3

Counselor: It seems to me that what you are saying is that you want to be able to relate to those people, have a good time, enjoy yourself, ah—have good relationships with the girls . . .

Client: But, you see, one real serious problem I seem to have is—we've talked about it . . .

Anticounselor: Ummmm . . .

Client: Is, in a sense, your culture is asking me to change. They don't want to do any of the changing. These girls I go out with, in a sense, they are demanding that I change. I can't be me. I can't be my culture.

Anticounselor: That's a lot of bullshit!

Client: Why do I have to do all the changing? Why can't we have a compromise of some sort?

Anticounselor: Why should he be forced into these Victorian standards that he doesn't see as natural?

One basic source of resistance is the whole question of whether the client should change to fit the new environment or the environment be changed to fit the client. The counselor is likely to be perceived as wanting to change the client rather than the environment, especially by clients from foreign cultures. Somehow the counselor is going to have to work through that resistance before counseling can have an acceptable outcome for the client.

The skill area of "anticipating resistance," or recognizing resistance in specific rather than general terms, recognizes the importance of dealing with negative affect before proceeding with the content in a client's response. The skill area also recognizes the difficulty of identifying negative affect in specific and accurate terms for culturally different clients. It is useful to consider the following microskills, many of which have been validated elsewhere in the literature about counseling skills, as important in identifying resistance in specific rather than in general terms.

2. Recognizing resistance in specific rather than in general terms

> *Stress-coping insight:* The Counselor is able to define accurately the client's response pattern to the problem.
> *Values conflict:* The counselor is able to identify ambiguity in the client's basic beliefs.
> *Questioning:* The counselor is able to use either open or closed questions in a culturally appropriate mode.
> *Directions:* The counselor is able to tell the client(s) what to do in a culturally appropriate way.
> *Confrontation:* The counselor is able clearly to note discrepancies within the self or between the self and others.
> *Interpretation:* The counselor is able to rename or relabel the client's behaviors or verbalizations accurately.
> *Focus on Topic:* The counselor clearly identifies the subject of the client's special topic or problem.
> *Focus on group:* The counselor is aware of the role of natural support groups for the individual client.

Mirroring: The counselor is able to reflect and adjust voice tone, body position, or other communication style so that it is in synchrony with that of the client.

Self-awareness: The counselor has an explicit awareness of what he or she is doing that might antagonize a client.

4. Unit Three: Diminishing Counselor Defensiveness

The multicultural counseling interview is frequently ambiguous for the counselor and can easily cause even a skilled counselor to become less sure of him or herself, leading to defensive counselor behavior. It will be important for the counselor in any interview to avoid the distraction of defensive counselor behavior and to focus on the client's message, which may not be intended as an attack on the counselor personally. If the counselor allows him- or herself to be distracted by becoming defensive, the rapport with a client is likely to diminish. If a counselor is ever going to be defensive, it is more likely to occur in the presence of an anticounselor seeking to sabatoge the interview. The Triad Model allows counselors to examine their own latent defensiveness and raise their threshold for nondefensive responses.

SKILL AREA: Diminish Defensiveness

The following excerpts from trial interview transcripts illustrate defensive and nondefensive counselor responses to a potentially threatening situation. Counselor defensiveness is an extremely important variable in training but exceedingly difficult to define operationally. The effect of counselor defensiveness is clearly destructive in its various forms, and these several examples should highlight how the triadic interaction with an anticounselor tends to bring out residual or latent defensive responses.

Defensiveness 1

Counselor: How do you feel in terms of your relationship now? You came here and we have been talking for about 2 or 3 minutes. How do you feel about the way we've been talking?

Client: Well, you haven't helped me for one thing. I mean you just . . .

Anticounselor: Do you think he can help you?

Client: I don't know.

Anticounselor: What makes him different from anybody else?

Counselor: Do you feel uncomfortable with me?

Client: Uh, not now, not yet.

Counselor: I uh—I ah (*pause*) I don't feel any discomfort with you at all.

Client: Oh, well, 'cause I'm a friendly person I suppose (*laugh*).

Anticounselor: Remember how White folks like to tell you things that sound good so they can get on the good side of you for a little while. (*pause*)

The counselor has a great need for reassurance even though the interview has just started. This need is no doubt exaggerated because the interview is being videotaped and the counselor thinks he has only about 10 minutes to show his stuff. With the anticounselor present, the client is likely to be less polite than if the counselor and client were alone together. The counselor's obvious discomfort despite his denial only emphasizes the defensive stance. The anticounselor turns the counselor's defensiveness to his own advantage.

Defensiveness 2

Client: Yeah, you see this thing, these things for me are very intense for me right now because I just came. I've been here for only about a month.

Counselor: Would you feel better if I got back behind the desk and we sort of had that between us?

Client: No, then you remind me of my father.

Counselor: OK, I don't want to do that (*laugh*). OK, is this more comfortable?

Client: Yeah, it is.

Counselor: OK. (*pause*)

Client: Then you make me feel like you are rejecting me. You are not rejecting me!

Counselor: I'm in a box here. On the one hand I want to do the things that will make you comfortable and on the other I don't want to get too distant and make you feel like I'm rejecting you.

Anticounselor: He's manipulating you little by little 'til he gets to a point that he's going to say that you got to be just like American girls. That's the best way.

Counselor: How do you feel now as opposed to when you came in?

Client: Well, I'm kind of feeling uncomfortable. It was OK for a while and now I feel like, I don't know—I feel like I want to go.

The counselor is trying to deal with his own discomfort as well as the discomfort of the client and is scrambling to establish a comfortable rapport. The harder the counselor struggles to regain the client's confidence the more anxious the client becomes. As the resistance increases, the anticounselor consolidates her position and the counseling intervention is blocked. Perhaps if the counselor had dealt with the resistance directly instead of indirectly it might have been possible to recover.

Defensiveness 3

Counselor: Why did you come here today? Can you tell me something about what concerns you?
Client: Uh—I came . . .
Anticounselor: What's the use of coming anyway?
Client: I don't know how to put it, this . . .
Counselor: Uh-huh—it's difficult to talk about?
Anticounselor: He probably won't understand.
Client: I don't know what to say.
Counselor: I guess in a way you are thinking, "What good does it do me right now? Whatever I say is going to be kind of confusing for him."
Client: Yeah, yeah.
Counselor: Why don't you try and tell me something of what concerns you? And let's see if I can try to understand.
Anticounselor: It's too complicated. (*pause*)
Client: Perhaps it isn't.

The counselor provides an example of a nondefensive response to the client even when the counselor is under direct attack, although the openness and self-disclosure modeled by the counselor may in themselves be threatening to a client from another culture. The anticounselor's accusations are accepted as relevant and do not distract the counselor from the task at hand. By dealing with the resistance openly, directly, and nondefensively, the resistance seems to diminish considerably and the interview is allowed to proceed.

The skill area of "diminishing defensiveness," or helping the counselor to control the impulse to feel threatened in culturally ambiguous situations, is another widely recognized characteristic of good counseling in all settings. The increased ambiguity of multicultural settings, however, increases the potential for threat. The following microskills, drawn from the counseling literature, provide measures for diminishing defensive reactions for counselors.

3. Reducing counselor defensiveness in multicultural counseling

Sense of humor: The counselor is able to facilitate rapport through an appropriate use of humor in the interview.
Self-disclosure: The counselor is able to disclose information about him- or herself in a culturally appropriate way to increase rapport.
Evaluation: The counselor is able to evaluate a client's expression, manner, or tone of response to get at hidden agendas.
Descriptive: The counselor is able to describe the client's response without evaluating it as good or bad.

Spontaneity: The counselor is able to be spontaneous rather than strategic in a way that increases rapport.

Receptivity: The counselor is able to accept advice or help from the client in a culturally appropriate way.

Admitting to being defensive: The counselor is able to admit openly to defensive counselor behaviors in a nonapologetic way.

Apologizing: The counselor is able to accept responsibility for a counselor error and apologize in such a way that it strengthens rapport.

Planning: The counselor is able to develop and explicate a plan of action to the client for the period of an interview.

Manipulation: The counselor is able to bring the client to accept what the counselor perceives as being clearly in the client's interest.

5. Unit Four: Recovery Skills

Skilled counselors make perhaps as many mistakes as do unskilled counselors, with the difference that skilled counselors are able to get out of trouble and recover from the mistake with increased rather than diminished rapport. The function of training is then perhaps not to teach counselors how to avoid making mistakes but rather to help counselors who make mistakes to recover effectively.

SKILL AREA: Recovery Skills

If a counselor is not making mistakes while counseling a client from a culture that is totally unfamiliar to the counselor, then the counselor may well not be taking enough personal risk. Counselor training should not merely prevent the counselor from making mistakes but should help the counselor recover from mistakes once they have been made. The triad provides opportunities for the counselor to make mistakes and experiment with various recovery strategies. The counselor who feels confident that he or she can recover from any mistakes made in counseling is likely to be less apprehensive about making the mistakes in the first place. The recovery skills cover a range of strategies, and the following examples show a range of recovery methods by counselors who have gotten themselves in trouble.

Recovery 1

Anticounselor: You know what he is trying to do? He is going to try to get everything out of you and then convince you that you have to be the way Americans are and just screw around . . .

Counselor: Well, I'm just thinking that you—I don't understand much about your country—what you have been used to . . .

Anticounselor: And you know what will happen when you go back home.

Counselor: So I need to find out first of all what you have been used to and what pleases you, and then I can help you learn how to get men to respond to you in the same way here. It is not necessary, you see, that you do respond as they demand. It is perfectly possible, and I guess you have to take this kind of on faith—this is, I might say, a problem not just foreign girls have but American girls have this problem too.

Client: No, you know, they don't have that problem. They seem to enjoy that type of thing and they don't seem to have a problem with it.

Counselor: I don't want to argue about that. What we want to do is deal with your problem.

Client: That's right.

Counselor: And I guess I need to understand—I'm asking you to understand that there are ways that you can avoid being a helpless person in a relationship. And maybe I can help you a little bit to learn how to avoid being helpless. Does that sound useful?

In the process of exploring the client's problem, the counselor tries to generalize the problem to include American women as well as foreign women. Both the client and the anticounselor totally reject that generalization and obviously resent being lumped together with American women in this instance. The counselor could have defended his statement, he could have gotten into a discussion with the client on the topic, he could have argued or apologized, but he did none of these things. Instead, he put the focus directly back on the client and the client's problem and very neatly avoided what might have been a serious problem.

Recovery 2

Counselor: Have you ever talked to the girls about these double messages you are getting and . . .

Client: I tried a few times. They seem to be so upset that they don't want to talk. They just want to split and go home. But I did talk to one girl and she said I don't understand ah—what is going on down here. Apparently I don't understand the customs or the values or something.

Counselor: Ummmm . . .

Client: It's so unnatural to me—it is so different. I don't know whether I can understand it.

Counselor: Yeah, it's quite different from America. I've been to America and the whole approach to male-female relationships there is different and . . .

Anticounselor: Why don't you explain to us the value of virginity? Try that. Isn't that a winner? (*laugh*)

Client: Apparently there is some value on that type of thing here. I don't know . . .

Anticounselor: Why, what do you get from it?
Counselor: Why don't you explain to me your perception of how virginity is seen here? Maybe I can clarify it for you.

The counseling interview becomes intense when the client's relationship with women in Brazil is discussed. The anticounselor brings up the topic of virginity as an oversimplification of the issues involved, and the client reinforces the comment as relevant. The counselor does not get sidetracked into a discussion on virginity, however, nor does she try to defend or explain her own culture. Rather, she asks the client to clarify his understanding of virginity and maintains her facilitative role.

Recovery 3

Anticounselor: I was saying that since you are not from our culture that you are no use to him.
Counselor: Uh-huh, I think that's right, at this point I don't know what it means yet. But what I would like to do is develop an appreciation and an understanding so that I am in a position to help Sung.
Anticounselor: I think that you are getting frustrated.
Counselor: Not yet. I could. (*pause*) Could you tell me—you see you're right. I really don't know a great deal about your culture at all, and in order to help you I really have to have more of an appreciation of it.
Client: You see the problem is that engagement is important, and my family is important, and your degree is important as well.
Counselor: So with so many things coming at the same time that are so important you feel that you have to make choices between them and leave out some of them?

It is extremely difficult for a counselor to admit confusion or frustration in the middle of an interview even though those feelings may be very real at the time. In this excerpt the counselor is very self-disclosing in sharing his confusion while at the same time emphasizing his willingness to work toward a more complete understanding. Considerable risk is involved in being that open. The counselor might endanger credibility, increase the client's anxiety level, or otherwise inhibit the counseling interview. Bluffing and pretending to understand when the counselor really doesn't understand is perhaps even more risky, however.

The skill area of "recovery skills" is not otherwise reported in the literature on counseling skills and frequently is overlooked as a teachable/learnable skill area. However, it is clear in viewing examples of expert counseling that the experts make as many—and perhaps more—mistakes than the novice. The difference is that the experts, having taken a chance and failed, can recover more expertly than the novice. It is therefore important to examine microskills that might contribute to the counselor's ability to recover in a multicultural counseling interview.

4. Recovery skills for getting out of trouble

Changing the topic: The counselor can redirect the interview appropriately following a controversial interaction.

Focusing: The counselor can refocus the counseling interview on the basic problem instead of on the controversial issue.

Challenging: The counselor confronts the client with the counselor's perception of what is really happening.

Silence: The counselor is able to tolerate periods of silence in the interview that contribute to multicultural rapport.

Role reversal: The counselor can solicit consultation from the client as a resource for generating solutions and alternatives.

Referral: The counselor is able to refer the client to another counselor in a culturally appropriate way and at an appropriate time.

Termination: The counselor is able to terminate the interview prematurely in a culturally appropriate way.

Arbitration: The counselor brings in a third person or "culture broker" to mediate the dispute in a culturally appropriate way.

Metaphorical analysis: Identifying and developing metaphors initiated by a client toward the explication of a client's perspective.

Positioning: Identifying an area of unmet need or opportunity not yet recognized by the client and building on it to the client's advantage.

This approach used in this model is limited to simulated counseling interviews for the purposes of training counselors and is not recommended for actual therapy. The approach is also not an example of successful multicultural counseling; the approach is geared rather toward helping counselors learn from their failures in the simulated interviews. A number of models used for therapy involve three persons, such as conjoint family therapy, therapy with cocounselors, and therapy in which the client brings a friend with him or her into the interview. This model differs from those alternatives in the unique characteristics of the anticounselor. Other approaches in Gestalt therapy or psychodrama resemble this simulation of a multicultural interview. Each of these theoretical positions, although significantly different, has contributed to this model.

This training model seems to offer a number of advantages over alternative training approaches. Under controlled conditions, the model provides an opportunity for persons from different cultures to accomplish a training goal they all need and want. As a simulated interview, the model offers participants greater safety to demonstrate strong feelings and provides direct feedback. Separating the roles of client and anticounselor makes the problem less diffuse and abstract to counselor trainees. The anticounselor models and encourages negative feedback to the counselor to clarify resistance. Inappropriate counselor intervention is immediately apparent in feedback from the anticounselor. The model is nontheoretical because it calls attention to good counseling without first requiring a theoretical knowledge of why a particular approach is good. The members of another culture become resource persons in learning to counsel persons from those same cultures without depending on expert outsiders. If members of the target audience have helped train their own counselors, they have more invested in the success of those counselors working among them. In the balance of power between counselor and anticounselor, the trainees are reminded how the determination for success or failure ultimately lies with the client and not the counselor.

CHAPTER 10

Conclusion: Developing Multiculturally Skilled Counselors

What are the different ways in which cultural backgrounds shape a counseling relationship? How can counselors evaluate their own cultural bias? How do problems and appropriate solutions vary from one culture to another? Is counseling itself, as a way of helping others, culturally encapsulated? If we consider age, sex, life style, and socioeconomic status as contributing to our cultural identity, then some aspect of any and every counseling interview is multicultural.

Members of the APA's Division 17 (Counseling) Education and Training Committee developed a position paper (Sue, Bernier, Durran, Feinberg, Pedersen, Smith, & Vasquez-Nuttall, 1982) entitled "Cross Cultural Counseling Competencies." The paper concluded that every counselor training curriculum should incorporate these elements of awareness, knowledge, and skill. The report was endorsed by the Executive Committee of Division 17. In this concluding chapter these competencies provide a framework for developing multicultural awareness.

1. Awareness

Four awareness competencies were identified by Sue et al. (1982). The *first* competency suggests that culturally skilled counselors are those who have moved from being culturally unaware to being aware and sensitive to their own cultural heritage and to valuing and respecting differences. By taking the broader perspective of culture in this book and by emphasizing self-awareness as the first stage of multicultural development, we have responded to this competency. The *second* competency is that culturally skilled counselors must be aware of how their own values and biases may affect minority clients. The awareness exercises in chapter 2 provide a means to understand your own values and biases as cultural patterns in your life. The chapters on previous research show how biases have affected cultural minorities as a group, and the chapters on skill building show how they affect face-to-face relationships. The *third* awareness competency is to become comfortable with differences between counselors and clients in terms of race and beliefs. The Cultural Grid provides a means to better understand the multicultural component of a conflict situation without either party forcing the other to betray his or her own cultural identity. The *fourth* awareness competency is sensitivity to circumstances (personal biases, stage of ethnic identity, socio-political influence, etc.) that may dictate referral of the minority client to a member of his or her own race or culture. The direct and immediate feedback from an anticounselor or procounselor provides a counselor clear and unambiguous guidelines for referring a client when cultural differences are too large to bridge in a constructive counseling session.

We know that cultural background influences both the way counseling is given and how it is received, but counselors have extremely few opportunities to train for work with culturally different clients. Rather there is a tendency to assume that clients and counselors share the same value assumptions despite abundant evidence to the contrary. There is an assumption that we all share the same meaning for "healthy" and "normal" when, in fact, we may be merely reflecting our own political, social, or economic values as culturally encapsulated counselors.

This book has described some of the different training models for developing multiculturally skilled counselors. Counselors should expect to increase their awareness of their own and others' cultural biases, to become familiar with research on multicultural counseling, and to learn specific skills that will help them work more efficiently with culturally different clients. Counselors should learn to understand better the mental health systems in other cultures, recognize cultural prejudices and biases, learn how environments contribute to self-esteem through positive interpersonal relationships across cultures, and respect cultural diversity across boundaries of nationality, ethnicity, age, sex roles, socioeconomic status, and other affiliations. Training materials described in this book have been used to train persons working with welfare clients, alcoholics, the handicapped, foreign students, prisoners, and other identity as well as nationality and ethnic groups where there is likely to be a difference in values between counselors and clients.

A multicultural training program for mental health professionals is needed for several reasons. They are:

1. Traditional systems of mental health services have a cultural bias favoring dominant social classes that can be counterproductive to an equitable distribution of services.
2. Various cultural groups have discovered indigenous modes of coping and treatment that work better for them and may usefully be applied to other groups.
3. Community health services are expensive when they fail; multicultural training might prevent some programs from failing.
4. Training methods that include indigenous people as resource persons directly in training counselors tend to reflect the reality of different cultures.
5. The constructs of healthy and normal that guide the delivery of mental health services are not the same for all cultures and might betray culturally encapsulated counselors to become a tool of a particular political, social, or economic system.
6. Increased interdependence across national ethnic and social-cultural boundaries requires direct attention to culture as part of mental health training.
7. Most therapists come from dominant cultures whereas most clients do not.

Although most mental health delivery services are provided by White middle-class men, the vast majority of clients receiving these services are non-White, are from lower socioeconomic levels, and differ significantly in their socialization and value assumptions from the counselors. The literature on how cultural values affect mental health services describes vividly mental health professionals' need for increased awareness. Value assumptions made by culturally different counselors and clients have resulted in culturally biased counseling with low utilization rates for mental health services.

Reviewing the literature leaves the reader with a clear impression that psychological services in the mental health field need to become more sensitive to cultural differences. Helpers who are most different from their clients, especially in race and social class, have the greatest difficulty effecting constructive changes, whereas helpers who are most similar to their clients in these respects have a greater facility for helping appropriately (Carkhuff & Pierce, 1967).

In multicultural counseling, there is a great danger of mutual misunderstanding, insufficient understanding of the other culture's unique problems, a natural hostility that destroys rapport, and negative transference toward the counselor (Vontress, 1971). A client's appropriate cultural response is often confused with neurotic transference. Ignorance of one another's culture by counselors and clients contributes to resistance in opposition to the goals of counseling. This resistance is usually accompanied by some feelings of hostility, threat, or unwillingness to allow the stranger access to a client's real feelings.

2. Knowledge

Four knowledge or comprehension competencies were identified by Sue et al. (1982) to guide culturally skilled counselors. The *first* competency requires a good understanding of the sociopolitical system's operation in the United States with respect to its treatment of minorities. Chapter 6 describes and documents this need in detail. The *second* competency requires specific knowledge and information about the particular group with which a counselor is working. Culture is complicated and dynamic, and although the background of each available culture cannot be presented, the skills for managing complex information can be taught. The *third* competency requires a clear and explicit knowledge or understanding of the generic characteristics of counseling and therapy. The basic skills discussed in the last three chapters are based on extensive research in the mainstream of counselor education. There is no attempt to substitute multicultural counseling techniques for basic counseling theory but rather an effort to integrate multicultural awareness into the developmental process. The *fourth* competency requires an awareness of institutional barriers that prevent minorities from using mental health services. Chapter 4 on culturally biased assumptions and chapter 7 on the need for multicultural awareness document the relevant sources for learning about these barriers.

Multicultural counseling occurs when the client and counselor are culturally different, working either in the client's culture, the counselor's culture, or in a third culture unfamiliar to both. The concept of culture is as old as organized society, but the systematic study of culture and mental health is a phenomenon of the 20th century. Initially the fields of psychoanalysis and anthropology were the focus of interest in studying "culture and personality." This focus was later expanded to include the more or less equivalent fields of social psychiatry, multicultural psychiatry, multicultural psychotherapy, and multicultural counseling. The emphasis has shifted from anthropological studies of remote societies to national and ethnic variations in modern, pluralistic, and complex communities. More recently, differences in physical, social, economic, and behavioral characteristics such as age, life-style, sex role, socioeconomic status, and other "comembership" affiliations have been recognized as contributing to the individual's "subjective culture" as well.

There has been much confusion regarding the labels of cultural difference. *Race* technically refers exclusively to biological differences, whereas *ethnicity* describes groups where members share a cultural heritage from one generation to another. People of the same ethnic group within the same race might still be culturally different. The terms *culturally deprived, culturally disadvantaged*, or *culturally different* were created to explain why a minority group is out of step with the dominant majority. The label *minority* is usually defined by the condition of being oppressed by a dominant majority.

Cultural features determine many counseling practices (Prince, 1980). Japanese therapies such as Morita emphasize the acceptance of mental suffering in Buddhist societies rather than its alleviation. Autogenic training with its drill-like procedures reflects the cultural values of Germany. Authoritarian cultures like those in the Soviet Union and Japan have not been enthusiastic about psychoanalysis, whereas it has been widely accepted in the United States. The more a society believes in the changeability of human nature and the plasticity of social roles, the more it will favor therapy as a vehicle of change. The more psychological disturbance reflects deep-seated prejudices about human nature, the less tolerant a society will be of mental illness. Each society has developed its own indigenous methods of maintaining this delicate social balance (Pedersen, 1983b).

There is a similarity across cultures in forms of counseling. Torrey (1986) drew direct parallels between the techniques of witch doctors and psychiatrists in naming treatment, identifying a cause, establishing rapport, developing client expectations for improvement, and demonstrating legitimacy. Although Western methods of counseling are increasingly popular in non-Western cultures, they are not necessarily more effective than indigenous approaches, where the emphasis is on self-righting mechanisms such as dreams, dissociated states, religious experiences, and psychological reactions rather than talk therapy (Higginbotham, 1979a, 1979b; Prince, 1980).

We need more multicultural research. Sundberg (1981a, 1981b) reviewed 15 research areas in need of exploration to advance multicultural counseling. These areas attend to outcome measures, contrasting expectations, counselors' cultural perception, clients' cultural predisposition, culturally appropriate alternatives, and natural support systems. More data are needed on the effectiveness of indigenous counseling approaches, comparisons of counseling techniques in different cultural settings, comparisons of different counseling approaches in the same culture, and the effect of cooperation between culturally different counselors.

For several reasons, a consensus of research methodology has not been developed in multicultural counseling (Draguns, 1981a, 1981b). First, the emphasis of research across cultures has been on abnormal rather than normal behavior. Second, only in the 1970s have universal core descriptions of symptom patterns begun to emerge, and then only for the more serious categories of disturbance such as schizophrenia and affective psychoses. Third, the complexity of research on multicultural counseling discourages empirical research. Fourth, available research lacks an applied emphasis related to practical concerns of program development, service delivery, and treatment techniques. Fifth, there has been insufficient interdisciplinary collaboration, with each discipline protecting its own insulated perspective. Sixth, the emphasis of research has been on the symptom rather than on interactions among people, professional institutions, and community.

3. Skill

Three skill competencies were identified by Sue et al. (1982). The *first* competency requires that the culturally skilled counselor be able to generate a wide variety of verbal and nonverbal responses appropriate to the cultural setting and skill level. The Triad Model provides one approach to training counselors in this competency through direct and immediate feedback from anticounselors and procounselors. The *second* competency requires that counselors be able to send and receive both verbal and nonverbal messages accurately and appropriately in each culturally different context. Some of the awareness exercises in chapter 2 and the discussion of matching context with method in chapter 7 directly attend to this competency. The *third* competency requires counselors to be able to exercise institutional intervention skills on behalf of clients as appropriate to each cultural context. Chapter 7 discusses how counseling functions can be adapted to different settings and chapter 6 discusses the consequences of non-responsive institutions where change is required.

The use of simulation "role play" techniques has been increasingly popular in microcounseling for counselor training programs. Psychodrama has long relied on simulation and role play of critical incidents as a mode less threatening to trainees and more motivating to clients. In a laboratory setting trainees can learn to facilitate client growth by increasing their awareness and sensitivity to their own reactions and to client reactions, communications, and possible alternative behaviors. In this relatively "safe" environment they can rehearse various response strategies without hurting real clients or themselves.

Most applications of microlab training have long used some form of recording such as videotape for self-confrontation by the trainees. Kagan (Kagan & McQuellen, 1981) effectively demonstrated how utilizing videotapes of a trainee's counseling session can help to identify and strengthen positive facilitative behaviors and change nonfacilitative behaviors. It has become frequent practice for counselor educators to develop simulation experiences to practice effectiveness in the functions they would be performing as counselors. Audio and video recordings are frequently used as simulation stimuli in a programmed learning format to train practicum students toward helping clients explore feelings.

Although there are many different multicultural training models, this book emphasizes only one model in depth. The Triad Model was developed to train mental health practitioners in working with culturally different clients through a microcounseling laboratory design. A therapist from *one* culture is matched with a coached client/anticounselor team from the same *other* culture for a videotaped simulation of a multicultural therapy session. The therapist seeks to build rapport with the culturally different coached client, offering a counseling solution to the problem. The anticounselor seeks to represent the problem element from the client's cultural viewpoint as opposed to intervention from a culturally different counselor. As a result of the role-played interaction, the therapist learns (a) to articulate the problem explicitly from the client's cultural viewpoint; (b) to anticipate resistance from clients from a different culture; (c) to diminish his or her defensiveness in working with culturally different clients; and (d) to practice recovery skills from inappropriate counselor responses made during the simulated interview.

The multicultural Triad Model sees counseling as occurring in the interaction of three elements: (a) the experiential world of the counselor; (b) the experiential world of the client; and (c) an anticounselor and procounselor who represent the internal dialogue of the client in the interview.

The Triad Model differs significantly from other approaches in limiting its application to *simulated* counseling interviews and *training* functions rather than direct therapy, and in the unique role of the anticounselor. Although research evidence is somewhat limited at this point, the Triad Model seems to offer numerous advantages that complement other training models (Ivey & Authier, 1978; Pedersen, 1986b).

The Triad Model has been used for the last decade in several hundred workshops throughout the United States. Persons who have used the model have reported that they are better able to articulate the problem after a series of multicultural interviews with the client/anticounselor teams. Participants also have reported increased skill in anticipating the resistance to counseling from clients of other cultures (Pedersen, 1977, 1986b). Otherwise counselors might complete a multicultural interview knowing they failed but never knowing *why* they failed. Immediate feedback from the anticounselor confronts a counselor with mistakes even before the counselor has finished a poorly chosen intervention. There are indications that participants in the counselor role become less defensive after training and are less threatened by working with clients from other cultures after training. Finally, there is less anxiety about making mistakes in counseling clients from other cultures when trainees have rehearsed ''recovery skills'' for getting out of trouble when they make a mistake.

Adaptations of these training designs have been used in a wide variety of workshop or classroom situations. The Triad Model seems to work best (a) when there is positive as well as negative feedback to the counselor; (b) when all three persons rather than just the counselor and client interact with one another; (c) when the client/anticounselor team is highly motivated and feels strongly about the issue under discussion; (d) when the anticounselor has a high degree of empathy for and acceptance by the client; (e) when the anticounselor is articulate and gives direct, immediate verbal or nonverbal feedback to the counselor; (f) when the client has *not* selected a real problem from his or her current situation where counseling might be appropriate; (g) where the discussion is spontaneous and not scripted; (h) where the counselor has a chance to role play the model and receive feedback three or four times in sequence; (i) where the client feels free to reject an inauthentic anticounselor; and (j) when the facilitator introducing the model and leading the discussion is well acquainted with how the model operates.

In their anecdotal comments about the Triad Model, counselors from other workshops emphasize the importance of "dealing with feelings" as well as content in the interview, "learning to deal with feelings of helpless frustration" in multicultural interviews in a nondefensive mode, learning "how to be in two cultures at the same time," and learning "the cues a client from another culture uses to communicate feelings." Coached clients report that "the questions you (counselor) ask don't stick in my head as well as what he (anticounselor) says," that "the anticounselor forces me to express myself more totally than I would otherwise," and that "having the problem objectified helped lay it out objectively from an outside point of view." Learning how to work with a counselor from another culture who doesn't understand the cues, hints, understatements, or appropriate omissions may force clients to betray their own cultural values. Coached anticounselors found they "could defeat the counselor by carefully attending to feelings." They described themselves as deliberately exposing "the personalized hidden self . . . exposing all the contradictions, value conflicts, fears, and expectations that are not supposed to come out." The Triad Model allows a counselor and client to reveal the barriers that culturally different clients and counselors erect against one another that might otherwise escape detection.

The Triad Model is only one of the many multicultural training models available to counselors. Many of the other models are cited in earlier chapters. Rather than review many models at a more superficial level, this book has examined one model at greater depth. Readers are encouraged to develop the multicultural awareness necessary to generate their own eclectic training approach that may combine many models.

4. Conclusion

By the 1970s there was abundant evidence that minority groups were underutilizing counseling services in many cultures and that behavior, such as individualistic assertiveness, described as pathological in a minority culture could be viewed as adaptive in the majority, or dominant, culture. In the United States, Asian-Americans, Blacks, Chicanos, Native Americans, and other minority groups terminate counseling significantly earlier than do Anglo clients because of cultural barriers, language barriers, and class-bound or culture-bound attitudes that hinder rapport (Sue, 1981). The National Institute of Mental Health, the American Psychological Association's Council of Representatives, the American Psychiatric Association's Task Force on Ethnocentricity among Psychiatrists, and the recent United States President's Commission on Mental Health all have emphasized the ethical responsibility of all counselors to know their clients' cultural values. Until recently, however, none of the mental health professions had actively developed multicultural approaches leading toward degree specializations in multicultural counseling (Aubrey, 1977). That situation is changing, however. Ivey (1980b), the architect of microtraining for counselors, has predicted that any successful treatment plan or community intervention that promotes intentionality through "self-awareness" and "other awareness" or any comprehensive program of counseling must consider the cultural factor. In most cases, multicultural counseling students design their own unique program with available courses and an appropriate faculty advisor at one or another of the larger universities. Guidelines for the multicultural training of psychologists are being designed by the American Psychological Association, Division 17 (Counseling Psychology) Committee on Education and Training.

Questions of controversy describe unresolved issues in counseling across cultures (Draguns, 1981a, 1981b; Pedersen, 1981, 1982). Should the therapist emphasize the culturally unique (emic) or the humanly universal (etic)? If the cultural element is underemphasized, the counselor will be insensitive to the client's values; if it is overemphasized, the counselor will stereotype clients. Should the counselor change the environment to fit the person or change the person to fit the cultural context? Dominant cultures tend to prefer the autoplastic mode of changing the person whereas many minority populations prefer the alloplastic style of changing the context. Is multicultural counseling a series of techniques that can be learned or is it dependent on a relationship in the more intuitive sense? Although there is a necessity to adapt techniques and be flexible, there is also a danger in disregarding the fundamentals of counseling and therapy in favor of unorthodox methods "presumed" to be multicultural. To what extent is all counseling multicultural? If we consider age, life-style, socioeconomic status, and sex-role differences in addition to ethnic and nationality differences, it is quickly apparent that there is a multicultural dimension in every counseling relationship. The goal should not be to establish a separate field of "multicultural counseling" but to validate the role of "culture" in all counseling and psychotherapy.

APPENDICES

APPENDIX 1

A Non-Test for Self-Evaluation on Questions Related to Multicultural Counseling

After reading *A Handbook for Developing Multicultural Awareness*, you should be able to discuss or respond to most of the following questions. You might find the list of questions useful to assess your own progress and multicultural development.

* * * * * * *

1. What are the ways that cultural differences between a counselor and a counselee affect counseling?

2. How serious is the implicit cultural bias among counselors and counselor training programs?

3. What are the indigenous alternatives in "counseling" in non-Western cultures?

4. How can counselors evaluate their own implicit cultural bias?

5. How could counselors be better trained to work in a multicultural population?

6. How do psychological problems vary with the culture of the clients?

7. Why are some methods better than others in working with persons from other cultures?

8. How can we learn from other cultures in sharpening our own skills as counselors?

9. Is "counseling" itself, as a product of Westernized, developed cultures, culturally encapsulated?

10. Can we assume that all counseling is to some extent "multicultural"?

11. What are the dangers of cultural encapsulation for a counselor?

12. What is meant by the model of multicultural analysis that includes international, interethnic, and social-role cultures, and how might such a model be useful for multicultural education of counselors?

13. What is meant by the "self-reference criterion"?

14. How might an anthropologist and a psychologist view the problems of culture and personality differently?

15. What are some of the ways in which culture and cultural systems might "cause" problems requiring counseling?

16. How do "shame" and "guilt" function through cultural values to shape the behavior of a population?

17. What are some of the ways in which cultures or cultural systems might help to "solve" personal problems?

18. In the research on rates of mental illness, which is a more significant factor—race or class?

19. What are some of the ways in which low-income persons are likely to be cheated out of equitable mental health care?

20. Why should more care be given to criterion data of predictive studies in research among multicultural populations?

21. What are some of the ways classroom tests are apt to be culturally biased?

22. Are tests to be used to adapt people individually and collectively to the presently dominant model of Western industrial society, or are they designed to uncover human potentialities to which cultures can be adapted?

23. To what extent is therapy a commodity or a means of social control and oppression by the comfortable over the distressed?

24. To what extent is a counselor committed to "changing" the environment and not merely helping a client adjust to it?

25. Discuss the meaning of acculturation, integration, adaptation, and isolation for counselors working with clients from other cultures.

26. Is there evidence that professional counselors are culturally conditioned in their responses?

27. What are the characteristics of "cultural encapsulation" for counselors?

28. How would you describe the values that are most likely to characterize the dominant American culture?

29. How would you characterize the concept of "subjective culture"?

30. What are some of the favorable conditions for multicultural contact likely to lead to increased harmony?

31. What are some of the unfavorable conditions of multicultural contact likely to lead to increased hostility?

32. What are some of the barriers to accurate communications across cultures?

33. What is the meaning of "self-fulfilling prophecy" for counselors working within a multicultural population?

34. What is "culture shock" and what are the behaviors that indicate its presence?

35. Describe the cycle of cultural adjustment.

36. In what sense are open-minded counselors likely to be more effective than more dogmatic colleagues as demonstrated in the research literature?

37. What is the "deficit hypothesis" and what has been its effect?

38. How might a counselor from a different culture than the client's face advantages and disadvantages in working with a client as compared to a counselor from the client's own culture?

39. What are some of the ways that Westernized systems of mental health care might be irrelevant to the needs of a Mexican-American population?

40. What are some of the values typical of a Native American client that might make counseling difficult?

41. In the adjustment of foreign students, which might be more important— relationships with host Americans or with their fellow countrymen?

42. What are some ways in which counseling with a foreign student might be more difficult than counseling with an American student?

43. What are some of the ways Western psychology and Eastern cultures might view counseling differently?

44. What are the similarities between therapy performed by "witch doctors" and psychiatrists?

45. What is the significance of the APA-sponsored Conference on Patterns and Levels of Professional Training held at Vail, Colorado, in July 1973 for multicultural counseling?

46. What is the importance of a client's and counselor's basic assumptions for the counseling process?

47. Is the person who claims to be healthy to be considered healthy by his or her own definition, or is some other criterion of "health" more suitable?

48. What are some of the explanations that have been popular to rationalize maladaptation by a minority culture in the United States?

49. Describe a counseling interview where the counselor, client, problem, and environment come from different cultures.

50. How would you differentiate paraprofessionals from professional therapists according to the advantages and disadvantages of each?

51. What might be some of the goals in "orienting" a foreign student to the U.S. university community?

52. Describe some of the difficulties teachers face in working with students in interracial classroom situations.

53. What are some of the ways that counselor education programs could be modified to make them more sensitive to multicultural value systems?

54. When you enter an unfamiliar culture do you use your own counseling methods or do you use the host culture methods?

55. What are some examples of how "triads" have been used in counseling and what might be some of the advantages of a triad?

56. What is an "anticounselor"?

57. Describe the counseling process from the point of "social power theory."

58. What might be some of the advantages of the Triad Training Model with an anticounselor?

59. What might be some of the disadvantages of the Triad Training Model with an anticounselor?

60. What are some of the tactics an anticounselor might find useful in simulating an interview with a counselor and a client?

APPENDIX 2

Draft Recommendations for Changes in the APA Ethical Principles November 1986

The following recommendations were developed at a Round Table session at the American Psychological Association meetings in Washington, DC in August 1986. These suggestions for changing APA ethical principles demonstrate the ethical implications of developing a multicultural awareness.

Preamble:

Psychologists respect the dignity and worth of the individual's fundamental human rights. To protect, preserve, and promote these fundamental human rights requires the psychologist to recognize that each individual lives in a sociocultural and historical context. The application of these fundamental human rights in practice, research, and writing requires the consideration of ethnographic, demographic, status, and affiliation variables with the sociocultural and historical context. It is the responsibility of every psychologist to be informed about the presence of cultural factors in his or her own conduct and perspectives, and in the areas of psychological endeavor in which he or she represents himself or herself as qualified to function. The implications of that responsibility need to be incorporated in all other policy statements and related guidelines of the APA.

Addition to Principle One: RESPONSIBILITY

Psychologists have a responsibility to intentionally, constructively, and approriately adapt their methods to culturally different populations, recognizing the different ways that cultural factors shape human behavior.

Addition to Principle Two: COMPETENCE

Psychologists should indicate and further develop their competence about the cultures of persons they are studying or serving.

Deletion from Principle Two: COMPETENCE

Item (d), second sentence. We recommend that the phrase, "When necessary . . ." be omitted. As long as that phrase is allowed to stand, the burden of proof with regard to the necessity of knowledge about cultural factors and the expertise in being responsive to them rest with the complainant, not the psychologist. In view of the present state of our knowledge about the presence of cultural factors in all forms of psychological functioning, we conclude that psychologists individually or collectively cannot justify the inclusion of the conditional phrase "when necessary."

Addition to Principle Three: MORAL AND LEGAL STANDARDS

Psychologists need to recognize culturally determined differences in moral and legal standards and in their interpretation of those standards, in terms of the consequences for themselves and for the person(s) being served.

Addition to Principle Four: PUBLIC STATEMENTS

Psychologists should specify their degree of competence and level of training about a particular culture in making public statements about that culture.

Addition to Principle Five: CONFIDENTIALITY

When the psychologist is serving persons from another culture, where the rules of confidentiality are even more strictly applied than in the psychologist's own culture, the psychologist is expected to define the rules of confidentiality in that culturally different client's more restrictive terms.

Addition to Principle Six: WELFARE OF THE CONSUMER

To "fully inform" consumers is defined in sociocultural terms appropriate to the consumer's cultural framework, and not exclusively from the psychologist's own culturally learned perspective.

Addition to Principle Seven: PROFESSIONAL RELATIONSHIPS

In professional relationships with culturally different populations, the psychologist needs to prevent the disparagement of cultural values held by that population and to actively promote a positive working relationship. If the psychologist cannot support any of a client's values, that information should be provided openly and directly, and a relationship should not be established unless a mutually satisfactory understanding can be reached.

Addition to Principle Eight: ASSESSMENT TECHNIQUES

Psychologists need to interpret assessment data accurately in the cultural context in which those data were gathered, or to whom information about those data are provided, recognizing the influence of cultural values on data being gathered or reported. Furthermore, psychologists are obligated to interpret those data in terms understandable to the relevant members of that culture.

Addition to Principle Nine: RESEARCH WITH HUMAN PARTICIPANTS

Psychologists doing research with culturally different populations must, in consideration of the sociocultural implications research may have for that population, become knowledgeable about the cultural values of that population in relation to the proposed research activity.

Addition to Principle Ten: CARE AND USE OF ANIMALS

Recognizing that different cultures have different norms and rules with regard to the treatment of animals, the psychologist working with animals in another culture will follow the rules of the more humane population, whether that be the psychologist's own culture or the host culture.

APPENDIX 3

Exercises Using the Triad Model of Multicultural Counselor Training Scoring Guide and Evaluation Form

EXERCISE: Chapter 8

The following brief excerpts from three multicultural counseling interviews include statements by counselors and by clients, followed by a space for you to write in what you would say next in the role of the *counselor and anticounselor*, keeping in mind that the procounselor and anticounselor are part of a culturally different client's internal dialogue.

Part I

The first set of statements is transcribed from an interview between a White male counselor and a Black female client discussing relationship problems the Black female client is having at the university.

1. *Client:* Okay, my problem is that I don't seem to be able to trust the White people here on campus. Being Black I seem to have sort of a problem with this sort of thing and I don't know what to do about it and somebody recommended you. Said that you were a good counselor so I decided to come, and get some help from you.

Counselor: Do you have any problems relating to the Black students on campus, Terry?

Client: No, not really. You know there are people everywhere. Some you don't like, some you do like.

Counselor:

Anticounselor:

2. *Client:* One thing about White males, you know, that there is a lot of trouble. Being a Black girl myself, a lot of White males get funny ideas about Black girls.

Counselor:

Anticounselor:

3. *Client:* Well uh . . . they go through life thinkin' that we're somewhat lower than White women because, you know, there is this great big thing about Black sexuality.

Counselor:

Anticounselor:

4. *Client:* Uh . . . (*laugh*) well, so that . . . it's not that I can't trust people . . . It's, I wonder . . . Now I forgot what I'm talking about. Uh . . . (*pause*) . . .

Counselor:

Anticounselor:

5. *Counselor:* Are you getting a little uncomfortable, Terry? . . . Perhaps because I'm White, in sharing some of these things with me?

Client: Uh . . . not really, and it's like I said, you know, I try to be pretty open-minded about what I'm talking about. But the thing I want to know is can you really understand where I'm coming from? What kind of things I'm really dealing with?

Counselor:

Anticounselor:

6. *Client:* Okay. Like I said, most of my classes have uh . . . you get tired of being the only Black kid in classes. Well, I can't change that because I can't get more sisters and brothers on campus. Right? So the thing is I would like to know, what it is about myself that people find so funny that they can make jokes at and not expect me to really feel bad when somebody makes a Black joke?

Counselor:

Anticounselor:

7. *Client:* What exactly . . . what exactly do you think my problem is? (*pause*) If you think I don't understand it.

Counselor: I think you understand your problem really well, I think your problem is simply ah . . . again, your problem . . . I don't think it's your problem at all. I think it's the problem that you're experiencing in relating to Whites on campus and ah . . . I think ah . . . many Blacks experience the same problem.

Counselor:

Anticounselor:

Part II

A second set of statements is transcribed from an interview between a Latin American client and a White U.S. male about male-female relationships.

1. *Counselor:* Could you tell me what you would rather have from them? How you would like a man to treat you when you go out with him?

Client: Well, it's just that, especially the first time . . . for some time,

Counselor: Uh-huh . . .

Client: I like to get to know the person in a different way.

Counselor:

Anticounselor:

2. *Counselor:* So you're really kind of in a bind. You want to meet guys and be friendly with them but you feel like they make you pay for it with your body.

Client: Yeah, and there's this whole stereotype about the hot Latin American . . .

Counselor: Uh-huh . . .

Client: And that makes them go even faster. And, of course, I flirt, I'm coquettish, you know? I know that I'm attractive . . .

Counselor:

Anticounselor:

3. *Counselor:* Before you came to this country, did you feel at peace with yourself when you were with men?

Client: Yeah.

Counselor:

Anticounselor:

4. *Counselor:* So I need to find out first of all what you have been used to and what pleases you and then I can help you learn how to get men to respond to you in that same way here. It is not necessary, you see, that you do respond as they demand. It is perfectly possible, and I guess you have to take this kind of on faith . . . this is, I might say, a problem not just foreign girls have but American girls have this problem too.

Client: No, you know, they don't have that problem. They seem to enjoy that type of thing and they don't seem to have a problem with it.

Counselor:

Anticounselor:

5. *Client:* Yeah, you see this thing, these things for me are very intense for me right now because I just came. I've been here for only about a month.

Counselor: Would you feel better if I got back behind the desk and we sort of had that between us?

Client: No, then you remind me of my father.

Counselor:

Anticounselor:

6. *Client:* Then you make me feel like you are rejecting me. You are not rejecting me?

Counselor:

Anticounselor:

7. *Counselor:* How do you feel now as opposed to when you came in?

   Client: Well I'm kind of feeling uncomfortable. It was okay for a while and now I feel like, I don't know . . . I feel like I want to go.

   Counselor:

   Anticounselor:

Part III

The third set of statements is transcribed from an interview between a White male counselor and a Chinese male client discussing relationship problems the Chinese male client is having at the university.

1. *Counselor:* So it seems to me, that what you are saying that even when you do get together, those infrequent times when you can get together, even those times don't seem like happy times.

   Client: Exactly, you see (*pause*) what happens at first when we get together ah . . . it is usually on some kind of vacation. We have 10 or 12 days and we have exams coming up and we are under all kinds of pressure, . . .

   Counselor: So with so many things coming at the same time that are so important, you feel that you have to make choices between them and leave out some of them?

   Counselor:

   Anticounselor:

2. *Client:* I mean right now I am not confident that I am going to hack it. (*pause*) I mean I have one more prelim to go through and there is this thesis thing . . . and I haven't any idea of what on earth it is going to be. (*pause*)

   Counselor: So that it is really at a point right now where you are saying can I make school. It is a question of breaking, in relation to your fiancee, breaking a strong important value that you have of being . . . of fidelity to her and it is also a question right now can I make it in school, can I fulfill my obligations to my family and to everyone else who put me here and to myself?

   Counselor:

   Anticounselor:

3. *Client:* Yeah, I guess I could come to you and we could talk about it but what good does that do to me?

   Counselor:

   Anticounselor:

4. *Counselor:* Sung, do you think you can solve some of your problems by working with other people? Sometimes it is more helpful to work with another person to solve a problem.

   Client: Yeah, sometimes it does . . . provided, I mean . . . provided that that person has a sympathetic understanding of the problem.

   Counselor:

   Anticounselor:

SCORING GUIDE FOR MULTICULTURAL TEST OF COUNSELOR RESPONSES

The counselor responses will be scored on a 10-point scale with regard to four skill areas.

1. *Cultural accuracy:* Perceiving the client's message from the client's cultural point of view. When a counselor's statement about the *client's* viewpoint includes *specific* reference to the exact words, concepts, concerns, or implications clearly related to the client's statement or background, it indicates a high level of cultural accuracy. When the counselor's statement is an extension of the *counselor's* cultural viewpoint, unrelated to the client's statement, a low level of cultural accuracy is presumed.

2. *Resistance identification:* Identifying resistance from the client in specific rather than general terms as it is presented by the client is demonstrated by clarifying, specifying, or otherwise organizing information from a client's ambiguously negative statement in a more specific counselor response. When the counselor's response to a client's ambiguously negative statement is specific to some source of criticism by the client of the counseling situation, a high level of skill is presumed. When the counselor's response does not clarify, specify, or focus in on a client's ambiguously negative statement, a low level of skill is presumed.

3. *Deferred defensiveness:* The counselor maintains focus on the client's needs even when receiving criticism and is not distracted by the need to defend the counselor's credentials. When the counselor maintains continuous focus on

the *client's* needs and purpose for being in counseling even under criticism, a high level of skill is presumed. When the counselor response focuses on the *counselor's* needs to become more secure in the counseling relationship and ignores the client's needs, a low level of skills is presumed.

4. *Recovery skill*: After having said or done something that aroused the client's anger or suspicion or otherwise distanced the client, the counselor recovers rapport by saying or doing something that is likely to reestablish a client's confidence in the counselor. When the counselor's response maintains both the counselor statement and the client response in furthering the purpose of the interview, a high level of skill is presumed. When the counselor does not focus on the client's viewpoint and is sidetracked or distracted by the client's response to an earlier statement, a low level of skill is presumed.

In scoring the responses you will indicate both the *presence* or absence of the designated skill and the degree to which that skill was *appropriately* used by the counselor. Although each item incorporates more than one skill, the item will be scored for only one of the four skill areas.

MULTICULTURAL COALITION TRAINING MODEL IN A MICROCOUNSELING TRIAD

EVALUATION FORM

Name _____ Telephone _____

Address _____

Date of Training _____ Number of hours spent in training _____

You role played the Counselor ( ), Client ( ), and/or Anticounselor ( ); you watched but did not role play ( ).

Please respond by circling one of the numbers in each dimension below to indicate *your feelings* about your own experience using the multicultural coalition training design. If the adjective at the extreme left describes your feelings, circle the number "1," and if the adjective at the extreme right describes your feelings, circle the number "7". If your feelings are somewhere in between these two extremes, circle the appropriate number between 1 and 7.

PLEASANT	1	2	3	4	5	6	7	UNPLEASANT
FRIENDLY	1	2	3	4	5	6	7	UNFRIENDLY
ACCEPTING	1	2	3	4	5	6	7	REJECTING
ENTHUSIASTIC	1	2	3	4	5	6	7	UNENTHUSIASTIC
LOTS OF FUN	1	2	3	4	5	6	7	SERIOUS
RELAXED	1	2	3	4	5	6	7	TENSE
COOPERATIVE	1	2	3	4	5	6	7	UNCOOPERATIVE
SUPPORTIVE	1	2	3	4	5	6	7	HOSTILE
INTERESTING	1	2	3	4	5	6	7	BORING
HARMONIOUS	1	2	3	4	5	6	7	QUARRELSOME
SELF-ASSURED	1	2	3	4	5	6	7	HESITANT
EFFICIENT	1	2	3	4	5	6	7	INEFFICIENT
OPEN	1	2	3	4	5	6	7	GUARDED

How would you describe the "Anticounselor" or "Problem" role? _____

_____

_____

_____

What are the most serious weaknesses in this training model? _____

_____

_____

What are the most promising advantages of this training model? _____

_____

_____

What new insights have you gained as a result of using this model? _____

_____

_____

Client, Counselor, Anticounselor, Procounselor, Interpreter

Which role is the most powerful? _____

Which role is the most interesting? _____

Which role is the most educational? _____

Which role is the most threatening? _____

The triads you saw emphasized "cultural differences" between persons:
from different countries (   )
from different ethnic groups (   )
from different sex roles (   )
from different life styles (   )
from different age groups (   )

Did the training help you anticipate resistance from clients of other cultures? _

_____

_____

_____

187

Did the training help you to articulate the problem from a client's cultural viewpoint? _____

_____

_____

Would you like additional training in this model? _____

_____

_____

Comments: _____

_____

_____

_____

_____

_____

_____

_____

APPENDIX 4

Exercises Using Four Dimensions of Multicultural Skill Training

1. EXERCISE: Chapter 9

As an introduction to multicultural counseling skills, please identify two contrasting "counselor statements" that would illustrate each of the following skills. *Each statement would be appropriate for one or another contrasting cultural setting.* The objective is to acquaint you with a range of contrasting intervention skills for the range of culturally different settings where counseling might be appropriate.

Label *cultural groups* for each response. These cultural groups may be labeled according to ethnicity, nationality, age, sex role, life style, socioeconomic status, or another appropriate identity group.

Label *counseling styles* for each response. These contrasting counseling styles may include contrasting labels from the examples below, or other examples from the student's own experience, as long as the two statements demonstrate two contrasting styles for demonstrating each skill.

The counselor styles might contrast in terms of:

focus on family or others	focus on self
differentiated emotions	undifferentiated emotions
direct communication	indirect communication
verbal	nonverbal

focus on content	focus on process
clear, precise	ambiguous
specific	general
active	passive
task focus	relationship focus

Example: Values Conflict: ability to identify ambiguity in the client's basic belief

CULTURE   STYLE

WASP Student   direct   a. Do you want to do what your mother says and alienate your friends?

                 indirect   b. Sometimes it's hard isn't it . . .

In this case, the example contrasts a direct with an indirect approach to counseling, recognizing that each approach might be appropriate in different cultural settings.

Please continue to generate counselor statements for each of the following skills.

Identify the cultural group and the contrast you are seeking to illustrate in your counselor statements.

CULTURAL GROUP   CONTRAST LABEL
    AND STYLE

1. Perceiving the problem from the client's cultural viewpoint

    1.1.   Cognitive rational insight: Ability to define accurately the feelings related to a client's presenting problem.

_____ a.

_____ b.

    1.2.   Paraphrase: Giving back to the client the essence of past verbal statements. Selective attention to key content of client verbalizations.

_____ a.

_____ b.

CULTURAL GROUP   CONTRAST LABEL
AND STYLE

    1.3.   Reflection of feeling: Selective attention to key affective or emotional aspects of client behavior.

_____ a.

_____ b.

    1.4.   Summarization: Similar to paraphrase and reflection of feeling, but represents a longer time period and gives back to client several strands of thinking.

_____ a.

_____ b.

    1.5.   Concreteness: The statement may be vague and inconclusive or concrete and specific.

_____ a.

_____ b.

    1.6.   Immediacy: Statements may be rated for tense—past, present, future.

_____ a.

_____ b.

    1.7.   Respect: Enhancing statements about the self or others are considered to represent respect, whereas negative statements or "put-downs" indicate an absence of this dimension.

_____ a.

_____ b.

CULTURAL GROUP   CONTRAST LABEL
AND STYLE

1.8.   Genuineness: An absence of mixed verbal and non-verbal messages. In particularly effective communication, in most cultures, verbal and nonverbal movement synchrony between client and counselor may be noted.

_____   a.

_____   b.

1.9.   Positive regard: Selective attention to positive aspects of self or others or demonstrated belief that people can change and manage their own lives. Content is culturally relevant.

_____   a.

_____   b.

1.10.   Tracking: Being able to follow accurately and anticipate what the client will say next in the interview.

_____   a.

_____   b.

2. Recognizing resistance in specific rather than general terms

2.1.   Stress-coping insight: Ability to define accurately a client's response pattern to the problem.

_____   a.

_____   b.

2.2.   Values conflict: Ability to identify ambiguity in the client's basic beliefs.

_____   a.

_____   b.

CULTURAL GROUP AND STYLE	CONTRAST LABEL

2.3.   Questioning: Using either open or closed questions in a culturally appropriate mode.

——————— a.

——————— b.

2.4.   Directions: Telling the client(s) what to do.

——————— a.

——————— b.

2.5.   Confrontation: Noting discrepancies in the self or between self and others.

——————— a.

——————— b.

2.6.   Interpretation: Renaming or relabeling the client's behaviors or verbalizations with new words from a new frame of reference.

——————— a.

——————— b.

2.7.   Focus on topic: The subject of the sentence is a special topic or problem.

——————— a.

——————— b.

2.8.   Focus on dyad (group): The predominant theme is an "I-You" focus by examining both client and counselor ideas on their relationship. In group settings the words "group," "family," or "we" may appear.

——————— a.

——————— b.

CULTURAL GROUP   CONTRAST LABEL
  AND STYLE

     2.9. Mirroring: Reflecting and adjusting voice tone, body position, or other communication style to be in synchrony with that of the client.

_____ a.

_____ b.

     2.10. Self-awareness: The counselor has an explicit awareness of what he or she is doing that might antagonize a client.

_____ a.

_____ b.

   3. Reducing counselor defensiveness in multicultural counseling

     3.1. Sense of humor: Facilitating rapport through an appropriate use of humor in the interview.

_____ a.

_____ b.

     3.2. Self-disclosure: Disclosing information about the counselor in a culturally appropriate way to increase rapport.

_____ a.

_____ b.

     3.3. Evaluation: Evaluating expression, manner, or tone of a client's response to get at hidden agendas.

_____ a.

_____ b.

CULTURAL GROUP   CONTRAST LABEL
AND STYLE

3.4. Descriptive: Describing the client's response without evaluating it.

———————— a.

———————— b.

3.5. Spontaneous: Being spontaneous rather than strategic or divisive in a way that increases rapport.

———————— a.

———————— b.

3.6. Receptivity: Accepting advice or help from the client in a culturally appropriate way.

———————— a.

———————— b.

3.7. Admitting to being defensive: Admitting openly to defensive counselor behaviors in a nonapologetic way.

———————— a.

———————— b.

3.8. Apologizing: Accepting responsibility for a counselor error and apologizing in such a way that it strengthens rapport.

———————— a.

———————— b.

3.9. Planning: Developing and explicating a plan of action to the client for the period of an interview.

———————— a.

———————— b.

CULTURAL GROUP
AND STYLE

CONTRAST LABEL

3.10. Manipulation: Bringing the client to accept what the counselor perceives as being clearly in the client's interest.

_____ a.

_____ b.

4. Recovery skills for getting out of multicultural trouble

4.1. Changing the topic: Appropriately redirecting the interview following a controversial interaction.

_____ a.

_____ b.

4.2. Focusing: Refocusing the counseling interview on the basic problem instead of on the issue in controversy.

_____ a.

_____ b.

4.3. Challenging: Confronting the client with the counselor's perception of what is really happening.

_____ a.

_____ b.

4.4. Silence: Tolerating periods of silence in the interview that contribute to multicultural rapport.

_____ a.

_____ b.

CULTURAL GROUP AND STYLE	CONTRAST LABEL

4.5. Role reversal: Soliciting consultation from the client as a resource for generating solutions and alternatives.

_____ a.

_____ b.

4.6. Referral: Referring the client to another counselor in a culturally appropriate way.

_____ a.

_____ b.

4.7. Termination: Terminating the interview prematurely in a culturally appropriate way.

_____ a.

_____ b.

4.8. Arbitration: Bringing in a third person or ''culture broker'' to mediate the dispute in a culturally appropriate way.

_____ a.

_____ b.

4.9. Metaphorical analysis: Identifying and developing metaphors initiated by a client toward the explication of a client's perspective.

_____ a.

_____ b.

4.10. Positioning: Identifying an area of unmet need or opportunity not yet recognized by the client and building on it to the client's advantage.

_____ a.

_____ b.

REFERENCES

Abramowitz, W.I., & Murray, J. (1983). Race effects in psychotherapy. In J. Murray & P.R. Abramson, *Bias in psychotherapy* (pp. 215–255). New York: Praeger.

Acosta, F., & Sheehan, J. (1976). Preferences toward Mexican-American and Anglo-American psychotherapies. *Journal of Consulting and Clinical Psychology, 44*, 272–279.

Adler, P. (1975). The translational experience: An alternative view of culture shock. *Journal of Humanistic Psychology, 15*(3), 13–23.

Ambrowitz, D., & Dokecki, P. (1977). The politics of clinical judgment: Early empirical returns. *Psychological Bulletin, 84*, 460–476.

American Psychological Association (APA). (1979). Council of Representatives minutes from the meeting of January 19–20, 1979.

Amir, Y. (1969). Contact hypothesis in ethnic relations. *Psychological Bulletin, 71*, 319–342.

Aronson, H., & Overall, B. (1966). Treatment expectancies in patients in two social cases. *Social Work, 11*, 35–41.

Arredondo-Dowd, P., & Gonslaves, J. (1980). Preparing culturally effective counselors. *Personnel and Guidance Journal, 58*(10), 657–661.

Atkinson, D.R. (1983). Ethnic similarity in counseling: A review of research. *The Counseling Psychologist, 11*, 79–92.

Atkinson, D.R. (1985a). A beta-review of research on cross-cultural counseling and psychotherapy. *Journal of Multicultural Counseling and Development, 13*, 138–153.

Atkinson, D.R. (1985b). Research on cross-cultural counseling and psychotherapy: A review and update on reviews. In P. Pedersen (Ed.), *Handbook of cross-cultural counseling and therapy* (pp. 189–197). Westport, CT: Greenwood Press.

Atkinson, D.R., Maruyama, M., & Matsui, S. (1978). Effects of counselor race and counseling approach on Asian Americans' perception of counselor credibility and utility. *Journal of Counseling Psychology, 25*, 76–83.

Atkinson, D.R., Morten, G., & Sue, D.W. (1983). *Counseling American minorities: A cross-cultural perspective*. (2nd ed.). Dubuque, IA: Wm. C. Brown.

Atkinson, D.R., & Schein, S. (1986). Similarity in counseling. *The Counseling Psychologist, 14*, 319–354.

Atkinson, D.R., Staso, D., & Hosford, R. (1978). Selecting counselor trainees with multicultural strengths: A solution to the Bakke decision crisis. *Personnel and Guidance Journal, 56*, 546–549.

Atkinson, D.R., & Wampold, B. (1981). Affirmative action efforts of counselor education programs. *Counselor Education and Supervision, 6*, 262–272.

Aubrey, R.F. (1977). Historical development of guidance and counseling and implications for the future. *Personnel and Guidance Journal, 55*, 288–295.

Bailey, F.M. (1981). *Cross-cultural counselor education: The impact of microcounseling paradigms and traditional classroom methods on counselor trainee effectiveness.* Unpublished doctoral dissertation, University of Hawaii.

Banikiotes, P.G. (1977). The training of counseling psychologists. *The Counseling Psychologist, 7*, 226.

Barna, L.M. (1982). Stumbling blocks in intercultural communication. In L. Samovar & R. Porter, *Intercultural communication: A reader* (pp. 330–338). Belmont, CA: Wadsworth.

Berman, J. (1979). Individual versus societal focus in problem diagnosis of Black and White male and female counselors. *Journal of Cross-cultural Psychology, 10*, 497–507.

Berry, J. (1975). Ecology, cultural adaptation and psychological differentiation: Traditional patterning and acculturative stress. In R. Brislin, S. Bochner, & W. Lonner (Eds.), *Cross cultural perspectives on learning* (pp. 207–231). New York: Wiley.

Bloom, B., et al. (1956). *Taxonomy of educational objectives; Handbook I: Cognitive domain and Handbook II: Affective domain.* New York, David McKay.

Bloombaum, M., Yamamoto, J., & James, Q. (1968). Cultural stereotyping among psychotherapists. *Journal of Consulting and Clinical Psychology, 32*, 99.

Bohr, N. (1950). On the notion of causality and complementarity. *Science, 11*, 51–54.

Bolman, W. (1968). Cross-cultural psychotherapy. *American Journal of Psychiatry, 124*, 1237–1244.

Brislin, R.S., Cushner, K., Cherrie, C., & Young, M. (1986). *Intercultural interactions: A practical guide.* Beverly Hills, CA: Sage.

Brislin, R., Landis, D., & Brandt, M. (1983). Conceptualizations of intercultural behavior and training. In D. Landis & R. Brislin (Eds.), *Handbook of intercultural training, Volume 1: Issues in theory and design* (pp. 1–36). New York: Pergamon Press.

Brislin, R., Lonner, W., & Thorndike, R. (1973). *Cross-cultural research methods.* New York: Wiley.

Brislin, R., & Pedersen, P. (1976). *Cross-cultural orientation programs.* New York: Wiley/Halstead.

Bryne, R.H. (1977). *Guidance: A behavioral approach.* Englewood Cliffs, NJ: Prentice-Hall.

Bryson, L., & Cody, J. (1973). Relationship of race and level of understanding between counselor and client. *Journal of Counseling Psychology, 20*, 495–498.

Bryson, S., Renzaglia, G.A., & Danish, S. (1974). Training counselors through simulated racial encounters. *Journal of Non-white Concerns in Personnel and Guidance, 3*, 218–223.

Calneck, M. (1970). Racial factors in the countertransference: The Black therapist and the Black client. *American Journal of Orthopsychiatry. 40*, 39–46.

Caplan, G. (1976). The family as support system. In G. Caplan & M. Killilea (Eds.), *Support systems and mutual help: Multidisciplinary explorations.* New York: Grune & Stratton.

Caplow, T. (1968). *Two against one: Coalitions in triads.* Englewood Cliffs, NJ: Prentice-Hall.

Carkhuff, R.R., & Pierce, R. (1967). Differential effects of therapist race and social class upon patient depth of self-exploration in the initial clinical interview. *Journal of Consulting Psychology, 31*, 632–634.

Carney, C.G., & Kahn, K.B. (1984). Building competencies for effective cross-cultural counseling: A developmental view. *The Counseling Psychologist, 12*, 111–119.

Casas, J.J. (1984). Policy training and research in counseling psychology: The racial/ethnic minority perspective. In S. Brown & R. Lent (Eds.), *Handbook of counseling psychology* (pp. 785–831). New York: Wiley.

Cobb, S. (1976). Social support as a moderator of life stress. *Psychosomatic Medicine, 38*, 300–314.

Coffman, T.L., & Harris, M.C. (1978, May 18). *Transition shock and the de-institutionalization of the mentally retarded citizen.* Paper presented at the 102nd annual meeting of the American Association on Mental Deficiency, Denver.

Copeland, E.J. (1983). Cross-cultural counseling and psychotherapy: A historical perspective, implications for research and training. *The Personnel and Guidance Journal, 62*, 10–15.

Cross, W.E. (1971). The negro-to-Black conversion experience. *Black Worlds, 20*, 13–17.

Diaz-Guerrero, R. (1977). A Mexican psychology. *American Psychologist, 32*, 934–944.

Dillard, J.M. (1983). *Multicultural counseling.* Chicago: Nelson-Hall.

Doi, T. (1974). *The anatomy of dependence.* Tokyo: Kodansha.

Draguns, J.G. (1974). Values reflected in psychopathology: The case of the Protestant Ethic. *Ethos, 2*, 115–136.

Draguns, J.G. (1977). Mental health and culture. In P. Pedersen, D. Hoopes, & G. Renwick, *Overview of intercultural education, training and research, Volume I: Theory* (pp. 56–71). Chicago: Intercultural Network.

Draguns, J.G. (1980). Psychological disorders of clinical severity. In H.C. Triandis & J.G. Draguns (Eds.), *Handbook of cross-cultural psychology, Volume VI: Psychopathology* (pp. 99–174). Boston: Allyn & Bacon.

Draguns, J.G. (1981a). Counseling across cultures: Common themes and distinct approaches. In P. Pedersen, J. Draguns, W. Lonner, & J. Trimble (Eds.), *Counseling across cultures: Revised and expanded edition* (pp. 3–22). Honolulu: University of Hawaii Press.

Draguns, J.G. (1981b). Cross-cultural counseling and psychotherapy: History, issues, current status. In A.J. Marsella & P.B. Pedersen (Eds.), *Cross-cultural counseling and psychotherapy* (pp. 3–27). New York: Pergamon.

Dreikurs, R. (1972, August). Equality: The life style of tomorrow. *The Futurist*, pp. 153–155.

Erickson, F., & Schultz, J. (1982). *The counselor as gatekeeper: Social interaction in interviews*. New York: Academic Press.

Ewing, T.N. (1974). Racial similarity of client and counselor and client satisfaction with counseling. *Journal of Counseling Psychology, 21*, 446–449.

Favazza, A.F., & Oman, M. (1977). *Anthropological and cross-cultural themes in mental health: An annotated bibliography 1925–1974*. Columbia and London: University of Missouri Press.

Fields, S. (1979). Mental health and the melting pot. *Innovations, 6*(2), 2–3.

Fierman, T.B. (1965). Myths in the practice of psychotherapy. *Archives of General Psychiatry, 12*, 408–414.

Filla, T., & Clarke, D. (1973). *Human relations resource guide on in-service programs*. St. Paul, MN: Department of Education.

Frijda, N., & Jahoda, G. (1966). On the scope and methods of cross-cultural research. *International Journal of Psychology, 1*, 109–127.

Gamboa, A.M., Tosi, D.J., & Riccio, A.C. (1976). Race and counselor climate in the counselor preference of delinquent girls. *Journal of Counseling Psychology, 23*, 160–162.

Gardner, L.H. (1971). The therapeutic relationship under varying conditions of race. *Psychotherapy, Theory, Research and Practice, 8*(1), 78–87.

Geertz, C. (1973). *The interpretation of cultures*. New York: Basic Books.

Gomez-Schwartz, B.S., Hadley, S.W., & Strupp, H.H. (1978). Individual psychotherapy and behavior therapy. *Annual Review of Psychology, 29*, 435–472.

Gottlieb, B.H., & Hall, A. (1980). Social networks and the utilization of preventive mental health services. In R.H. Price, R.F. Ketterer, B.C. Bader, & J. Monahan (Eds.), *Prevention in mental health: Research policy and practice* (pp. 167–194). Beverly Hills: Sage.

Grier, W.H., & Cobbs, P.M. (1968). *Black rage*. New York: Bantam Books.

Gudykunst, W.B., & Hammer, M.R. (1983). Basic training design: Approaches to intercultural training. In D. Landis & R. Brislin (Eds.), *Handbook of intercultural training. Volume 1: Issues in theory and design* (pp. 118–154). New York: Pergamon Press.

Harrison, D.K. (1975). Race as a counselor-client variable in counseling and psychotherapy. A review of the research. *The Counseling Psychologist, 5*, 124–133.

Harrison, R., & Hopkins, R. (1967). The design of cross-cultural training: An alternative to the university model. *The Journal of Applied Behavioral Science, 3*, 431–460.

Helms, J.E. (1984). Toward a theatrical explanation of the effects of race on counseling: A Black and White model. *The Counseling Psychologist, 12*, 153–165.

Helms, J.E. (1985). Cultural identity in the treatment process. In P. Pedersen (Ed.), *Handbook of cross-cultural counseling and therapy* (pp. 239–245). Westport, CT: Greenwood Press.

Hernandez, A.G., & Kerr, B.A. (in press). Evaluating the Triad Model and traditional cross-cultural counselor training. *Journal of Counseling and Development*.

Herr, E. (1985). International approaches to career counseling and guidance. In P. Pedersen (Ed.), *Handbook of cross-cultural counseling and therapy* (pp. 3–10). Westport, CT: Greenwood Press.

Higginbotham, H. (1979a). Culture and mental health services. In A. Marsella, R. Tharp, & T. Ciborowski (Eds.), *Perspectives in cross-cultural psychology* (pp. 307–332). New York: Academic Press.

Higginbotham, H. (1979b). Cultural issues in providing psychological services for foreign students in the United States. *International Journal of Intercultural Relations, 3*, 49–85.

Hilliard, A. (1986). *Keynote address*. Presented at the first National Symposium on Multicultural Counseling, Atlanta, GA.

Hines, A., & Pedersen, P. (1980). The Cultural Grid: Matching social system variables and cultural perspectives. *Asian Pacific Training Development Journal. 1*(1), 5–11.

Hosford, R., & Mills, M. (1983). Video in social skills training. In P. Dowrick & S. Biggs (Eds.), *Using video: Psychological and social applications* (pp. 125–166). New York: Wiley.

Hsu, F.L.K. (Ed.). (1972). *Psychological anthropology*. Cambridge, MA: Schenkman.

Ibrahim, F.A., & Kahn, H. (1985, August). *Assessment of world views*. Paper presented at 93rd annual meeting of the American Psychological Association, Los Angeles, CA.

Inouye, K., & Pedersen, P. (1985). Cultural and ethnic content of the 1977 to 1982 American Psychological Association convention programs. *The Counseling Psychologist, 4*, 639–648.

Ivey, A. (1980a). *Counseling and psychotherapy: Skills, theories and practice*. Englewood Cliffs, NJ: Prentice-Hall.

Ivey, A. (1980b). Counseling 2000: Time to take charge! In J.M. Whiteley & B.R. Feetz (Eds.), *The present and future of counseling psychology* (pp. 113–123). Monterey, CA: Brooks/Cole.

Ivey, A. (1981). A person-environment view of counseling and psychotherapy: Implications for social policy. In A. Marsella & P. Pedersen (Eds.), *Cross-cultural counseling and psychotherapy* (pp. 279–311). New York: Pergamon Press.

Ivey, A.E. (1988). *Intentional interviewing and counseling: Facilitating client development*. Pacific Grove, CA: Brooks/Cole.

Ivey, A.E., & Authier, J. (1978). *Microcounseling: Innovations in interviewing training*. Springfield, IL: Charles C Thomas.

Jackson, A.M. (1973). Psychotherapy: Factors associated with the race of the therapist. *Psychotherapy: Theory, Research and Practice, 10*, 273–277.

Jaslow, C. (1978). Exemplary programs, practices and policies. In G. Waltz & L. Benjamin (Eds.), *Transcultural counseling: Needs, programs and techniques* (pp. 191–213). New York: Human Sciences Press.

Jones, E.E., & Korchin, S.J. (1982). *Minority mental health*. New York: Praeger.

Jordan, C., & Tharp, R. (1979). Culture and education. In A. Marsella, R. Tharp, & T. Cibrowski, *Perspectives on cross-cultural psychology* (pp. 265–286). New York: Academic Press.

Jourard, S.M. (1964). *The transparent self*. Princeton, NJ: Van Nostrand.

Kagan, N., Krathwohl, D., & Farquhar, W. (1965). *Interpersonal process recall*. East Lansing, MI: Michigan State University.

Kagan, N., & McQuellen, K. (1981). Interpersonal process recall. In R. Corsini (Ed.), *Innovative psychotherapies* (pp. 443–458). New York: Wiley.

Katz, M., & Sanborn, K. (1976). Multiethnic studies of psychopathology and normality in Hawaii. In J. Westermeyer (Ed.), *Anthropology and mental health* (pp. 49–56). The Hague: Mouton.

Kennedy, C.D., & Wagner, N.N. (1979). Psychology and affirmative action: 1977. *Professional Psychology, 10*, 234–243.

Khatib, S.M., & Nobles, W.W. (1977). Historical foundations of African psychology and their philosophical consequences. *Journal of Black Psychology, 4*, 91–101.

Kiev, A. (1972). *Transcultural psychiatry*. New York: Free Press.

King, L.M. (1978). Social and cultural influences on psychopathology. *Annual Review of Psychology, 29*, 405–433.

Kinloch, G. (1979). *The sociology of minority group relations*. Englewood Cliffs, NJ: Prentice-Hall.

Klineberg, O. (1985). The social psychology of cross-cultural counseling. In P. Pedersen (Ed.), *Handbook of cross-cultural counseling and therapy* (pp. 29–36). Westport, CT: Greenwood Press.

Kleinman, A. (1978). Clinical relevance of anthropological and cross-cultural research: Concepts and strategies. *American Journal of Psychiatry, 135*, 427–431.

Kleinman, A. (1980). *Patients and healers in the context of culture*. London: University of California Press.

Kluckhohn, F.R., & Strodtbeck, F.L. (1961). *Variations in value orientations*. Evanston, IL: Row, Patterson.

Kohls, L.R. (1979). *Survival kit for overseas living*. Chicago, IL: Intercultural Network SYSTRAN.

Korchin, S.J. (1980). Clinical psychology and minority problems. *American Psychologist, 35*, 262–269.

Korman, M. (1974). National conference on levels and patterns of professional training in psychology: Major themes. *American Psychologist, 29*, 441–449.

Kroeber A.L., & Kluckhohn, C. (1952). *Culture: A critical review of concepts and definitions*. New York: Vintage Books.

Lambert, M.J. (1981). The implications of psychotherapy outcome research on cross-cultural psychotherapy. In A. Marsella & P. Pedersen (Eds.), *Cross-cultural counseling and psychotherapy* (pp. 126–158). New York: Pergamon Press.

Lee, J.D., Trimble, J., Cvetkovich, G., & Lonner, W. (1981). *Exploring ethnic/cultural content of APA conventions*. APA MONITOR, *12*(2), 3.

Lefley, H., & Pedersen, P. (Eds.). (1986). *Cross-cultural training for mental health professionals*. Springfield, IL: Charles C Thomas.

LeVine, D. (1972). A cross-cultural study of attitudes toward mental illness. *Journal of Abnormal Psychology, 80*, 111–112.

LeVine, R., & Campbell, D. (1972). *Ethnocentrism: Theories of conflict, ethnic attitudes and group behavior.* New York: Wiley.

LeVine, R., & Padilla, A. (1980). *Crossing cultures in therapy: Pluralistic counseling for the Hispanic.* Monterey, CA: Brooks/Cole.

Lonner, W.J., & Sundberg, N.D. (1985). Assessment in cross-cultural counseling and therapy. In P. Pedersen (Ed.), *Handbook of cross-cultural counseling and therapy* (pp. 199–205). Westport, CT: Greenwood Press.

Lorion, R.P. (1974). Patient and therapist variables in the treatment of low-income patients. *Psychological Bulletin, 81,* 344–354.

Lorion, R.P., & Parron, D.L. (1985). Countering the countertransference: A strategy for treating the untreatable. In P. Pedersen (Ed.), *Handbook of cross-cultural counseling and therapy* (pp. 79–86). Westport, CT: Greenwood Press.

MacKinnon, R.A., & Michels, R. (1971). *The psychiatric interview in clinical practice.* Philadelphia: W.B. Saunders.

Marsella, A. (1979). Culture and mental disorders. In A.J. Marsella, R. Tharp, & T. Ciborowski (Eds.), *Perspectives on cross-cultural psychology.* New York: Academic Press.

Marsella, A., & Golden, C.J. (1980). The structure of cognitive abilities in Americans of Japanese and of European ancestry in Hawaii. *Journal of Social Psychology, 112,* 19–20.

Marsella, A., & Pedersen, P. (1981). *Cross-cultural counseling and psychotherapy.* New York: Pergamon Press.

Martinez, J.L., Jr. (1977). *Chicano psychology.* New York: Academic Press.

Maruyama, M. (1978). Psychotopology and its application to cross-disciplinary, cross-professional and cross-cultural communication. In R.E. Hollowman & S.A. Arutiunov (Eds.), *Perspectives on ethnicity* (pp. 23–75). The Hague: Mouton.

McCraw, W. (1969). Objectives: North Carolina Department of Public Instruction. In The Commission on Secondary Schools, Southern Association of Colleges and Schools, *Adventure on a Blue Marble: Approaches to teaching intercultural understanding* (pp. 11–12). 795 Peachtree Street, N.E., Atlanta, Georgia 30308.

McDavis, R.J., & Parker, M. (1977). A course on counseling ethnic minorities: A model. *Counselor Education and Supervision, 17,* 146–149.

McGoldrick, M., Pearce, J., & Giordano, J. (1982). *Ethnicity and family therapy.* New York: Guilford Press.

Meadows, P. (1968). The cure of souls and the winds of change. *Psychoanalytic Review, 55,* 491–504.

Meichanbaum, D. (1974). *Cognitive-behavior modification.* Morristown, NJ: General Learning Press.

Miles, R.H. (1976). Role requirements as sources of organizational stress. *Journal of Applied Psychology, 61,* 172–179.

Miller, N., & Brewer, M. (1984). *Groups in contact: The psychology of desegregation.* New York: Academic Press.

Millione, S.J. (1980). Construction of a black consciousness measure: Psychotherapeutic implications. *Psychotherapy, 17,* 175–182.

Mitchell, H. (1970). The Black experience in higher education. *The Counseling Psychologist, 2*, 30–36.

Morrow, D.W. (1972). Cultural addiction. *Journal of Rehabilitation, 38*(3), 30–32.

Muliozzi, A.D. (1972, March). *Inter-racial counseling: Does it work?* Paper presented at the American Personnel and Guidance Association meeting, Chicago.

Neimeyer, G.J., Fukuyama, M.A., Bingham, R.P., Hall, L.E., & Mussenden, M.E. (1986). Training cross-cultural counselors: A comparison of the pro-counselor and the anti-counselor Triad Models. *Journal of Counseling and Development, 64*, 347–439.

Neimeyer, G.J., & Gonzales, M. (1983). Duration, satisfaction, and perceived effectiveness of cross-cultural counseling. *Journal of Counseling Psychology, 30*, 91–95.

Opler, M.K. (1959). The cultural backgrounds of mental health. In M.K. Opler (Ed.), *Culture and mental health*. New York: Macmillan.

Parham, T.A., & Helms, J.E. (1981). The influence of Black students' racial identity attitudes on preference for counselors' race. *Journal of Counseling Psychology, 28*, 250–257.

Parham, T.A., & Helms, J.E. (1985a). Attitudes of racial identity and self-esteem of Black students: An exploratory investigation. *Journal of College Student Personnel, 26*, 143–147.

Parham, T.A., & Helms, J.E. (1985b). Relation of racial identity attitudes to self-actualization and affective states of Black students. *Journal of Counseling Psychology, 32*, 431–440.

Parloff, M.B., Waskow, I.E., & Wolfe, B.E. (1978). Research on therapist variables in relation to process and outcome. In S. Garfield & A. Bergin (Eds.), *Handbook of psychotherapy and behavior change* (pp. 233–282). New York: Wiley.

Patterson, C.H. (1974). *Relationship of counseling and psychotherapy*. New York: Harper & Row.

Patterson, C.H. (1978). Cross-cultural or intercultural psychotherapy. *International Journal for the Advancement of Counseling, 1*, 231–248.

Pearce, W.B. (1983, Summer). *International Communication Association Newsletter, 11*(3).

Pearson, R.E. (1982). Support: Exploration of a basic dimension of informal help and counseling. *The Personnel and Guidance Journal, 61*(2), 83–87.

Pearson, R.E. (1985). The recognition and use of natural support systems in cross-cultural counseling. In P. Pedersen (Ed.), *Handbook of cross-cultural counseling and therapy* (pp. 299–306). Westport, CT: Greenwood Press.

Pedersen, A., & Pedersen, P. (1985). The Cultural Grid: A personal cultural orientation. In L. Samovar & R. Porter (Eds.), *Intercultural communication: A reader* (pp. 50–62). Belmont, CA: Wadsworth.

Pedersen, P. (1968, September). A proposal: That counseling be viewed as an instance of coalition. *Journal of Pastoral Care*.

Pedersen, P. (1976). *Triad model: Four simulated interviews on a one-hour videotape with training manual*. Minneapolis: University of Minnesota International Student Advisor's Office.

Pedersen, P. (1979). Non-Western psychologies: The search for alternatives. In A. Marsella, R. Tharpe, & T. Cibrowski (Eds.), *Perspectives on cross-cultural psychology* (pp. 77–98). New York: Academic Press.

Pedersen, P. (1981). The cultural inclusiveness of counseling. In P. Pedersen, J. Draguns, W. Lonner, & J. Trimble (Eds.), *Counseling across cultures: Revised and expanded edition* (pp. 22–58). Honolulu: University of Hawaii Press.

Pedersen, P. (1982). The intercultural context of counseling and therapy. In A. Marsella & G. White (Eds.), *Cultural conceptions of mental health and therapy* (pp. 333–358). Dordrecht. Holland: D. Reidel.

Pedersen, P. (1983a). Asian theories of personality. In R. Corsini & A. Marsella (Eds.), *Contemporary theories of personality* (rev. ed.) (pp. 537–582). Itasca, IL: Peacock.

Pedersen, P. (1983b). The cultural complexity of counseling. *International Journal for the Advancement of Counseling, 6*, 177–192.

Pedersen, P. (1985). *Handbook of cross-cultural counseling and therapy*. Westport, CT: Greenwood Press.

Pedersen, P. (1986a). The cultural role of conceptual and contextual support systems in counseling. *Journal of the American Mental Health Counselor Association, 8*(1), 35–42.

Pedersen, P. (1986b) Developing interculturally skilled counselors: A training program. In H. Lefley & P. Pedersen (Eds.), *Cross-cultural training of mental health professionals*. Springfield, IL: Charles C Thomas.

Pedersen, P., Draguns, J., Lonner, W., & Trimble, J. (1981). *Counseling across cultures: Revised and expanded edition*. Honolulu: University Press of Hawaii.

Pedersen, P., Holwill, C.F., & Shapiro, J.L. (1978). A cross-cultural training procedure for classes in counselor education. *Journal of Counselor Education and Supervision, 17*, 233–237.

Pedersen, P., & Marsella, A. (1982). The ethical crisis for cross-cultural counseling and therapy. *Professional Psychology, 13*, 492–500.

Pedersen, P.B. (1977). The Triad Model of cross-cultural counselor training. *Personnel and Guidance Journal, 56*, 94–100.

Pedersen, P.B. (1978). Four dimensions of cross-cultural skill in counselor training. *Personnel and Guidance Journal, 56*(8), 480–484.

Peoples, V.Y., & Dell, D.M. (1975). Black and white student preferences for counselor roles. *Journal of Counseling Psychology, 22*, 529–534.

Pepinsky, H.B., & Karst, T.C. (1964). Convergency: A phenomenon in counseling and therapy. *American Psychologist, 19*, 333–338.

Prince, R. (1976). Psychotherapy as the manipulation of endogenous healing mechanism: A transcultural survey. *Transcultural Psychiatric Research Review, 13*, 155–233.

Prince, R.H. (1980). Variations in psychotherapeutic experience. In H.C. Triandis & J.G. Draguns (Eds.), *Handbook of cross-cultural psychology, Vol. 6: Psychopathology*. Boston: Allyn & Bacon.

Revich, R., & Geertsma, R. (1969). Observations media and psychotherapy training. *Journal of Nervous and Mental Disorders, 148*, 310–327.

Reynolds, D.K. (1980). *The quiet therapies: Japanese pathways to personal growth.* Honolulu: The University of Hawaii Press.

Rosch, E. (1975). Universals and cultural specifics in human categorization. In R. Brislin, S. Bochner, & W. Lonner (Eds.), *Cross-cultural perspectives on learning* (pp. 177–206). New York: Wiley.

Rotenberg, M. (1974). The Protestant Ethic versus Western people-changing sciences. In J.L.M. Dawson & W. Lonner (Eds.), *Readings in cross-cultural psychology* (pp. 277–291). Hong Kong: University of Hong Kong Press.

Rothenberg, A. (1979). Einstein's creative thinking and the general theory of relativity: A documented report. *American Journal of Psychiatry, 136*, 38–43.

Rothenberg, A. (1983). Psychopathology and creative cognition. In the *Archives of General Psychiatry, 40*, 937–942.

Ruben, B.D., & Kealey, D.J. (1970). Behavioral assessment of communication competency and the prediction of cross-cultural adaptation. *International Journal of Intercultural Relations, 3*(1), 15–47.

Ruiz, R., & Casas, M.M. (1981). Culturally relevant and behavioristic counseling for Chicano college students. In P. Pedersen, J. Draguns, W. Lonner, & J. Trimble (Eds.), *Counseling across cultures: Revised and expanded edition* (pp. 203–226). Honolulu: University of Hawaii Press.

Russo, N.F., Olmedo, E.L., Stapp, J., & Fulcher, R. (1981). Women and minorities in psychology. *American Psychologist, 36*, 1315–1363.

Sampson, E. (1977). Psychology and the American ideal. *Journal of Personality and Social Psychology, 11*, 767–782.

Sanchez, A.R., & Atkinson, D.R. (1983). Mexican American cultural commitment preference for counselor ethnicity and willingness to use counseling. *Journal of Counseling Psychology, 30*, 215–220.

Satir, V. (1964). *Conjoint family therapy.* Palo Alto, CA: Science & Behavior Books.

Sattler, J.M. (1970). Racial "Experimenter Effects" in experimentation, testing, interviewing and psychotherapy. *Psychological Bulletin, 73*, 137–160.

Sattler, J.M. (1977). The effects of therapist client racial similarity. In A.S. Gurman & A.M. Razin (Eds.), *Effective psychotherapy: A Handbook of research* (pp. 252–290). New York: Pergamon.

Slack, C.W., & Slack, E.N. (1976, February). It takes three to break a habit. *Psychology Today*, pp. 46–50.

Smith, E.J. (1982). Counseling psychology in the market place: The status of ethnic minorities. *The Counseling Psychologist, 10*, 61–68.

Solomon, G., & McDonald, F.J. (1970). Pretest and posttest reactions to self-viewing one's teaching performance on videotape. *Journal of Educational Psychology, 61*, 280–286.

Soo-Hoo, T. (1979). The development of culturally relevant psychologies. *Journal of the Asian American Psychological Association, 5*(1), 13–19.

Stanges, B., & Riccio, A. (1970). A counselee preference for counselors: Some implications for counselor education. *Counselor Education and Supervision, 10,* 39–46.

Stapp, J., Tucker, A.N., & VanderBos, G.R. (1985). Census of psychological personnel: 1983. *American Psychologist 40,* 1317–1351.

Stonequist, F.V. (1937). *The marginal man: A study in personality and culture conflict.* New York: Russel & Russell.

Strauss, J.S. (1979). Social and cultural influences on psychopathology. *Annual Review of Psychology, 30,* 397–416.

Strong, S.R. (1978). Social psychological approach to psychotherapy research. In S. Garfield & A. Bergin (Eds.), *Handbook of psychotherapy and behavior change: An empirical analysis.* New York: Wiley.

Sue, D.W. (1973). Ethnic identity: The impact of two cultures on the psychological development of Asians in America. In S. Sue & N.N. Wagner (Eds.), *Asian-Americans: Psychological perspectives.* Palo Alto, CA: Science & Behavior Books.

Sue, D.W. (1977). Barriers to effective cross-cultural counseling. *Journal of Counseling Psychology, 24,* 420–429.

Sue, D.W. (1978). Eliminating cultural oppression in counseling: Toward a general theory. *Journal of Counseling Psychology, 25,* 419–428.

Sue, D.W. (1980). *Evaluation report from DISC 1978–1979.* Honolulu: East-West Center.

Sue, D.W. (1981). *Counseling the culturally different.* New York: Wiley Interscience.

Sue, D.W., Bernier, J.E., Durran, A., Feinberg, L., Pedersen, P., Smith, C.J., & Vasquez-Nuttall, G. (1982). Cross-cultural counseling competencies. *The Counseling Psychologist, 19*(2), 45–52.

Sue, D.W., & Sue, S. (1972). Counseling Chinese Americans. *Personnel and Guidance Journal, 50,* 637–645.

Sundberg, N.D. (1981a). Cross-cultural counseling and psychotherapy: A research overview. In A. Marsella & P. Pedersen (Eds.), *Cross-cultural counseling and psychotherapy* (pp. 28–62). New York: Pergamon Press.

Sundberg, N.D. (1981b). Research and research hypotheses about effectiveness in intercultural counseling. In P. Pedersen, J. Draguns, W. Lonner, & J. Trimble (Eds.), *Counseling across cultures* (2nd ed.) (pp. 304–342). Honolulu, University of Hawaii Press.

Super, C. (1977, January). Minority graduate enrollments—looking up or peaking out? *APA Monitor, 16.*

Szapocznik, J., & Kurtines, W. (1980). Acculturation, biculturalism and adjustment among Cuban Americans. In A. Padilla (Ed.), *Acculturation: Theory, models and some new findings.* Boulder, CO: Westwood Press.

Szapocznik, J., Kurtines, W.M., & Fernandez, T. (1980). Bicultural involvement and adjustment in Hispanic-American youths. *International Journal of Intercultural Relations, 4,* 353–365.

Szapocznik, J., Rio, A., Perez-Vidal, A., Kurtines, W., & Sanisteban, D. (1986). Family effectiveness training for Hispanic families. In H. Lefley & P. Pedersen, *Cross-cultural training for mental health professionals.* Springfield, IL: Charles C Thomas.

Tapp, J.L. (1980). Studying personality development. In H.C. Triandis & A. Heron (Eds.), *Handbook of cross-cultural psychology, Vol. IV* (pp. 343–424). Boston, MA: Allyn & Bacon.

Tong, B. (1971). The ghetto of the mind: Notes on the historical psychology of Chinese Americans. *Amerasia Journal, 1*, 28.

Torrey, E.F. (1972). The mind game: *Witchdoctors and psychiatrists*. New York: Emmerson Hall.

Torrey, E.F. (1986). *Witchdoctors and psychiatrists: The common roots of psychotherapy and its future*. New York: Harper & Row.

Triandis, H. (1985). Some major dimensions of cultural variation in client populations. In P. Pedersen (Ed.), *Handbook of cross-cultural counseling and therapy* (pp. 21–28). Westport, CT: Greenwood Press.

Triandis, H.C. (1975). Cultural training, cognitive complexity and interpersonal attitudes. In R. Brislin, S. Bochner, & W. Lonner (Eds.), *Cross-cultural perspectives on learning* (pp. 39–78). New York: Wiley.

Triandis, H.C. (1980). Values, attitudes and interpersonal behavior. In H. Howe & M. Page (Eds.), *Nebraska Symposium on Motivation, 1979, Vol. 27* (pp. 195–260). Lincoln: University of Nebraska Press.

Triandis, H.C., Vassiliou, V., Vassiliou, G., Tanaka, Y., & Shanmugam, A.V. (1972). *The analysis of subjective culture*. New York: Wiley.

Trimble, J. (1981). Value differentials and their importance in counseling American Indians. In P. Pedersen, J. Draguns, W. Lonner, & J. Trimble (Eds.), *Counseling across cultures: Revised and expanded edition* (pp. 203–226). Honolulu: University of Hawaii Press.

Tseng, W.S., & Hsu, J. (1980). Minor psychological disturbances of everyday life. In H. Triandis & J. Draguns (Eds.), *Handbook of cross-cultural psychology, Volume VI: Psychopathology* (pp. 61–98). Boston: Allyn & Bacon.

Vontress, C.E. (1971). The black male personality. *The Black Scholar, 2*, 10–16.

Vontress, C.E. (1981). Racial and ethnic barriers in counseling. In P. Pedersen, J. Draguns, W. Lonner, & J. Trimble (Eds.), *Counseling across cultures: Revised and expanded edition* (pp. 87–107). Honolulu: University of Hawaii Press.

Walz, G.R., & Johnson, J.A. (1963). Counselors look at themselves on videotape. *Journal of Counseling Psychology, 10*, 232–236.

Wampold, B.E., Casas, J.M., & Atkinson, D.R. (1981). Ethnic bias in counseling: An information processing approach. *Journal of Counseling Psychology, 28*, 498–503.

Warheit, G.J., Holzer, C.E., & Areye, S.A. (1975). Race and mental illness: An epidemiological update. *Journal of Health and Social Behavior, 16*, 243–256.

Watts, A. (1963) *The two hands of God: The myths of polarity*. New York: Braziller.

Watts, A.G., & Herr, E.L. (1976). Career education in Britain and the USA. *British Journal of Guidance and Counseling, 4*(2), 129–142.

Watts, A.W. (1961). *Psychotherapy East and West*. New York: Mentor Press.

Weidman, H. (1975). Concepts as strategies for change. *Psychiatric Annals, 5*, 312–314.

White, J.L. (1984). *The psychology of Blacks: An Afro-American perspective*. Englewood Cliffs, NJ: Prentice-Hall.

Whitely, J.M., & Jakubowski, P.A. (1969). The coached clients as a research and training resource in counseling. *Counselor Education and Supervision, 2*, 19–29.

Wilson, W., & Calhoon, J.F. (1974). Behavior therapy and the minority client. *Psychotherapy: Theory, Research and Practice, 11*, 317–325.

Wintrob, R.M., & Harvey, Y.K. (1981). The self-awareness factor in intercultural psychotherapy: Some personal reflections. In P. Pedersen, J. Draguns, W. Lonner, & J. Trimble (Eds.), *Counseling across cultures: Revised and expanded edition* (pp. 87–107). Honolulu: University of Hawaii Press.

Wohl, J. (1981). Intercultural psychotherapy issues, questions and reflections. In P. Pedersen, W. Draguns, W. Lonner, & J. Trimble (Eds.), *Counseling across cultures: Revised and expanded edition* (pp. 133–159). Honolulu: University of Hawaii Press.

World Health Organization (WHO) (1979). *Schizophrenia: An international follow-up study*. New York: Wiley.

Wrenn, C.G. (1962). The culturally encapsulated counselor. *Harvard Educational Review, 32*, 444–449.

Wrenn, C.G. (1985). Afterward: The culturally encapsulated counselor revisited. In P. Pedersen (Ed.), *Handbook of cross-cultural counseling and therapy* (pp. 323–329). Westport, CT: Greenwood Press.

Zuk, G. (1971). *Family therapy: A triadic-based approach*. New York: Behavioral Publications.

INDEX